What Others Are Saying About **StoryJacking**

"A refreshingly creative debut that focuses on taking control of one's life. Life coach deHart lays out a contemporary method for achieving "self-awareness and self-mastery"; she calls it "StoryJacking," a clever term that might suggest elevating one's own life story or, potentially, "hijacking" one's thinking to shift "internal dialogue.".... Throughout, deHart gently prods and at times exhorts readers to take control of their stories, noting that "the hardest thing that you will ever do is get out of your own way." This is typical of her candid, perceptive counsel; the best advice is neatly enclosed in her self-proclaimed "super-secrets of the universe"; for example, "The longest and most intimate relationship you will have in your entire life is the one you will have with yourself." deHart's breezy style and natural storytelling skills keep things moving along. Heady, insightful content packaged in a nonthreatening, engaging manner; includes ample opportunity for the dedicated reader to consider life-altering directions."

— *Kirkus Review*

"Five Stars! The vast majority of people are discontented in their life in some way. This isn't some statistic I can quote; it's just a part of the human condition. The author laid out her idea, *StoryJacking*, in plain, simple language and her friendly, conversational style kept me engaged throughout. The basic idea is that viewing our life as a story gives us more power over it than if we view it as a series of random events. We need to see ourselves as the authors of our tales rather than as passive, powerless bystanders."

— *Manhattan Book Review*

"Five Stars! It is not every day that I can say a book affected my life in a way that was profound, impactful, and inspirational the way Lyssa Danehy deHart's did. But the truth of the matter is everyone needs to get storyjacked. While maintaining sensitivity, Lyssa is brutally honest and raw. She does not sugarcoat things in a complex labyrinth of words but instead tells you the way it is. Think of her as your personal life coach, screaming, telling, and talking to you in a way to help you understand that we all have a purpose, a story to be told. *Storyjacking* is a cornucopia of raw, brutal honesty, wisdom, humor, and life lessons. *Storyjacking* is a book that doesn't end. It is a book that continues to gift readers like myself wisdom, integrity, and strength. So, are you ready to get storyjacked?"

— *San Francisco Book Review*

"With *StoryJacking*, life coach Lyssa Danehy deHart provides tools for changing your life stories, for digging out inculcated limiting beliefs and replacing them with empowering narratives. She has chosen to call her method of working with these life stories "StoryJacking," with all the implications inherent in the use of the verb 'to jack.' The information on neuroplasticity was fascinating to me. I already knew about the concept, of course, but still I find it interesting to read about. In fact, reading about it here prompted me to resume my language studies. If you find yourself wanting to change your inner narratives, to weave a new story for yourself, *StoryJacking* offers a brilliant manner of doing so."

— ***Seattle Book Review***

"Inspired pragmatism weaves throughout this delightful book of gems for anyone seeking to realize and maximize personal potential. Lyssa's easy vulnerability and naked revelations about how every person's life unfolds is shared through her unique story that is at once our universal story of being human. It is a book to savor over time, to rest into on a rainy day by the fire while you allow your imagination to soar. It is also a book to turn to in a moment of anxiety or despair. *StoryJacking* is a spark to the banked fire in your heart that's waiting to roar."

— **Janet M. Harvey, MA, MCC, founder and CEO of inviteCHANGE**

"Lyssa Danehy deHart, a transformational coach and self-professed storyjacker, reveals in her new book, *StoryJacking*, how our lives are determined by the stories we tell ourselves. While the concept isn't new, the term storyjacking is and it's about time we had a term for this concept. I've always found that when a problem exists and we find a way to label it, we become empowered to overcome it. If you're ready to tell yourself a new story, I recommend learning the life-transforming art of storyjacking."

— **Tyler R. Tichelaar, Ph.D. and Award-Winning Author of *Narrow Lives* and *The Best Place***

"*StoryJacking* by Lyssa Danehy deHart is that best friend we all wish we had, the one who calls us on our crap and shows us the way to a better life. Unsing the magic of story, this book demonstrates how to recapture the creativity and joy that is every person's birthright. Lyssa includes accessible exercises that build self-awareness and self-compassion and she provides the tools we need to change our stories and create our best future."

— **Jessica Lourey, MA, MS and Author of *Rewrite Your Life: Discover Your Truth Through the Healing Power of Fiction***

"Very simply, Lyssa Danehy deHart has written a helpful book that supports getting curious and changing your relationship to your stories. If you are ready to make important transformations in your personal narrative, then *StoryJacking* is a method through the madness!"

— Jeff A. Barnes, Ph.D., Author of *The Wisdom of Walt:*
Leadership Lessons from the Happiest Place on Earth

"*StoryJacking* is filled with wisdom, humor and practical tips for creating the life you want. It goes far beyond the empty platitudes or simplistic ideals that many books offer, but instead offers a constructive approach to making change, through countless examples, stories and exercises that will help you see how to get out of your own way and harness your inner spirit to take you where you want to go. This book is one gift I'm giving everyone this year—the secret to success."

— Wendy Hinman, Adventurer, Speaker and
Author of *Tightwads on the Loose* and *Sea Trials*

"Do you ever feel stuck, your mind swirling with negative stories? Then *StoryJacking* is the book for you. This book gave me several new tools to change my own internal narratives and supported the belief that I can create new stories that take me where I want to go, while rewriting the stories that limit me."

— Patrick Snow, Publishing Coach and International
Best-Selling Author of *Creating Your Own Destiny*

"Who doesn't have parts of their life story they'd like to change? Lyssa Danehy deHart's book *StoryJacking* makes it easy and do-able to tap into the power of the reader, who Lyssa emphasizes is whole, capable, resourceful, creative and the owner of his or her own story. I found a wealth of tools and exercises to play with as I focused on generating that new, updated version of my life story. Reading the book is like having a personal coach and a friend in my corner.

— Maureen Purcell, MS, PCC, Career/Life Coach at SoLwork.com

"I thoroughly enjoyed *StoryJacking*. With humor, insight and a remarkably understandable synthesis of our psychological processes, Lyssa provides her knowledge and experience as a therapist, coach and human to inspire readers to look at their own stories through a new lens so they can rewrite or tweak their stories to write the life story *they choose*."

— BJ Levy, JD, MA, PCC, Coach and
Author of *Roadmap to Success*

"*StoryJacking* is inspiring, energizing and insightful! This book helped me be more aware of how I create my life story moment by moment. It helped me think consciously about: What is my life story? What am I telling myself? How do I want my story to go? I can change it! I can affect it! Lyssa's book *StoryJacking* will help you write your story about who you are and who you want to be in the world. She will shift your thinking so you can have the life you want!"

— **Penny Rempfer, Ed.D., ACC, Coach at PennyRempfer.com**

"For many of us, our most often-told and most deeply held, intimate, internal stories are keeping us from being the people we aspire to be. They keep us from living the life we desire. Too often our oldest, most familiar internal stories keep us stuck, feeling sad, mad and downtrodden. Enough! If you're ready to dive deep into why you keep telling yourself these stories and what you can do about it, then look no further. Here's to *StoryJacking*!"

— **Margie Beiswanger, Business Coach at TransformYourBrilliance.com**

"Reading *StoryJacking* is like sitting in Lyssa's office engaging in the most profound and enlightening conversations where the subject matter is my inner world. "Get curious" now means the opportunity for exploration into stories I have told myself for years, but that do not serve me well in the present. *StoryJacking* and the therapist/coach that bore its creation, have invited me to confront those stories that I unknowingly absorbed and lived with as if they were truth. By "getting curious" about our emotions, thoughts and reactions, we put a spotlight on stories that need "jacking" so we have a choice in the next chapter of our life and the next and the next."

— **Pamela Moore, MA, LMHC**

StoryJacking

StoryJacking

Change Your Inner Dialogue
Transform Your Life

Lyssa Danehy deHart

MSW, LICSW, PCC

AVIVA
PUBLISHING
New York

StoryJacking®

Change Your Inner Dialogue, Transform Your Life

Published by:
Aviva Publishing
Lake Placid, NY
518-523-1320
www.avivapubs.com

All Sales Inquiries to:
Barn Swallow Publishing
support@barnswallowpub.com

Address all inquiries to:
Barn Swallow Publishing

The author of this book is not dispensing medical advice or prescribing the use of any technique as a form of treatment for mental, emotional, physical or medical problem. The reader is responsible to seek appropriate medical care with their Doctor or Therapist. The intent of the author is only to offer information to support getting curious about your life and add some tools to your toolbox. The information is for you, the author and the publisher assume no responsibility for your choices or actions.

Library of Congress Control Number: 2016919079
ISBN 978-1-944335-31-1 (hard cover)
ISBN 978-1-944335-32-8 (soft cover)
ISBN 978-1-944335-33-5 (ebook)

Editor: Tyler Tichelaar
Cover Designer: Lyssa Danehy deHart
Interior Book Layout: Nicole Gabriel/AngelDog Productions
Author Photo: Nora Emily Photograpy
Old Typewriter Images: JGroup/BigStockPhoto.com

Every attempt has been made to source properly all quotes.
Printed in the United States of America
First Edition: April 2017

10 9 8 7 6 5 4 3 2 1

CONTENTS

Acknowledgments .... *xvii*

Introduction .... *xix*

SECTION I - YOU ARE WHOLE

Chapter 1   Coaching to the Story 29

Chapter 2   Becoming Wired for Stories 37

Chapter 3   Story-Making Machines 43

Chapter 4   Let's Meet Your Psyche 47

Chapter 5   The Magic of Your Mind 53

Chapter 6   Magical Baby Brains 57

Chapter 7   StoryJacking 67

Chapter 8   What Is Your Why? 75

Chapter 9   Discover Your Strengths 81

Chapter 10   Your Life as a Pie 87

Chapter 11   Your Authentic Core Self 91

SECTION II - YOU ARE CAPABLE

Chapter 12   Your Mind Doesn't Know the Difference 105

Chapter 13   A Case for Visualization 111

Chapter 14   Conscious Choices 115

Chapter 15   Curiouser and Curiouser 119

Chapter 16   The Best Kind of Curious 125

Chapter 17   Expanding Awareness 133

Chapter 18   JoHari's Window 141

Chapter 19   Catch and Release 147

Chapter 20   Nothing Is Personal 153

Chapter 21   Archetypes 159

Chapter 22   Your Voices and Your Parts 163

Chapter 23   Recognizing Your Stories 169

Chapter 24   Snapshot Stories 175

SECTION III - YOU ARE RESOURCEFUL

Chapter 25 How We Make Sense of the World 183
Chapter 26 Locus of Control 189
Chapter 27 If You Have a Brain, You're Biased 197
Chapter 28 Threats and Other Traumas 205
Chapter 29 Emotions Are Like Road Signs 209
Chapter 30 Clarifying Values 217
Chapter 31 Defense and Safety 223
Chapter 32 Judging Your Insides by Other People's Outsides 235
Chapter 33 Letting Go of Judgment 239
Chapter 34 The Drama Triangle 247
Chapter 35 Courage in the Face of Our Choices 259
Chapter 36 Developing Courage 265
Chapter 37 Reincarnating Patterns 271
Chapter 38 Vulnerability 275
Chapter 39 Visualizing the Goal 283
Chapter 40 You Are Always at Choice 287
Chapter 41 Habits Are Hard-Wired Stories 293
Chapter 42 Creating Boundaries 299
Chapter 43 Fairy Tales and Growing Up 307

SECTION IV - YOU ARE CREATIVE

Chapter 44 Exploring Your Creativity 315
Chapter 45 Plot Twist 321
Chapter 46 Getting Out of Your Own Way 327
Chapter 47 Rewriting the Story 331
A Final Note: You Can Do This! 335

References 339
Let's Build a Fire & You Tell Me a Story 345
Book Lyssa Danehy deHart to Speak at Your Next Event 347
About the Author 349

You have brains in your head.
You have feet in your shoes.

You can steer yourself
Any direction you choose.
And will you succeed?

Yes! You will, indeed!
(98 and ¾ percent guaranteed.)

— Dr. Seuss, excerpted from *Oh, the Places You'll Go*

To L181
In the vastness of the universe,
playing upon this human stage,
I am glad I met you. xoxo

ACKNOWLEDGMENTS

I don't care who you are; no one writes a book alone. There are so many contributions from so many places, and it is through the generous sharing of conversation and time that any author completes a book. I am honored and blessed for the richness of experiences that each person has brought into the sandbox for me to explore.

I am deeply grateful to my mother, Elsa LaFlamme, Ph.D. Mom, you set the stage for my creativity, curiosity and questioning. Your willingness to talk things through, explore self-reflection was pivotal. While at times it was difficult to muddle through for both of us, you demonstrated what it looked like to follow your dreams, leap into the unexplored life and explore it.

I am also deeply grateful to my father, Edward Danehy. Dad, you pushed me to do more when I would have wanted to have it a bit easier. By doing so, you helped instill in me a mindset that I could push through difficulties. By not giving up, I could figure things out.

Into each of our lives, if we are lucky, comes the family that we choose entirely with our eyes and heart wide open. For me, that family is my soul sister, Michele Logan. I love you for every deep conversation, each kerfuffle we have had to work through and for every night of laughter that hurt my face and sides. You have been the best friend I could ever have. You are my John Wayne friend.

Jody McCrain, you were instrumental in my sorting through ideas and concepts as I muddled through thinking about StoryJacking. I love our talks, and I appreciate all your support. Thank you for being such a good friend.

I also owe a debt of gratitude to the many people who have helped and influenced me, including Dale Albers, Kayla Black, John Bradshaw, Joseph Campbell, Carii Clawson, Stephen Covey, Maureen Cooke, Norman Doidge, Albert Einstein, David Emerald, Lamia Faruki, Joseph and Annette Fourbears, B.J. Fogg, John Gottman, Jonathan Haidt, Janet Harvey and everyone at inviteCHANGE, Wendy Hinman, Mindy Jones, Carl Jung, Jack Kornfield, Jane Lancaster, Brad Lohrding, Anna Masterson, Pamela Moore, Daniel Peebles, George and Alice Pryor, Nanny Rawlings, Michelle Rios, Don Miguel Ruiz, Rumi, Nina Serpiello, Michael Singer, Dr. Seuss, Jocelyn Tate, The Buy Nothing Project and Marianne Williamson.

Thank you to my publishing coach, Patrick Snow, for supporting me and helping me get past the first few paragraphs. You have been immeasurably valuable to my completing this book.

Thank you to my editor, Tyler Tichelaar. I don't know how editors do what they do, but I appreciate your help in sorting through my verbosity, my love affair with the comma and my confounding grammar.

Thank you to Susan Friedmann, Aviva Publishing. Your enthusiasm for my book gave me a lift at just the right time—at that final push when I needed a bit of breeze to get across the finish line.

I have extrapolated from many people and many stories that have passed through my life along the way. All client stories are fictionalized versions coming from multiple sources and experiences and filtered through my lens. That said, I want to thank, with a deep bow, every client I have had the privilege to work with through the past twenty-five years. I cannot express the depth of my gratitude for the trust you have given me, your willingness to explore, get curious, challenge me, challenge yourselves and teach me to be a better therapist, coach and human being. Thank you.

INTRODUCTION

"Anyone who has never made a mistake has never tried anything new."
— Albert Einstein

In the words of Stephen Covey, I want to start this book with the end in mind. StoryJacking® is a play on words, about changing our relationship to our stories. This might mean to "jack" and elevate a story. For example, moving from seeing yourself as a waitress who wants to ask more interesting questions, who becomes a counselor and then a coach, as in my case. Another StoryJacking experience could be about challenging and shifting your internal dialogue, thus "hijacking" your thinking. And lastly "jacking into" an existing story that aligns with your purpose.

In these pages, you will explore:

- the manner you consciously determine what self-mastery will look like
- what impact you would like to have on your life and the lives around you
- the pathway that will help you as you move through the world toward your goal

As human beings, we often live our lives focused on the things we want.

Often not thinking as deeply about what we need, or even more importantly, how we want to be with ourselves in the world. An anger management technique I use and recommend to my clients is to distract yourself when you are intensely angry or upset. When you are angry about something, it hijacks your brain, releasing a chemical cocktail of upset, increasing your reactivity and decreasing your ability to process information in a useful way. One distraction you might try is thinking about winning the Lotto. I am sure you can distract yourself for a few hours with what you would do with your bounty of money, the car you would buy, the house you would build, the gifts you would give and causes you would support. To be sure, this distraction can help your brain to calm down so you can get it back online.

Distraction is a great technique for the short term from your original annoyance, giving you the space to relax, breathe and get your brain calmed down, but constant distraction is no way to live your life. In a state of permanent distraction, you are living asleep, missing the moments of brilliance, of learning, of actualizing as a human being. When your primary focus is on superficial stuff, on numbing your pain or avoiding reality, you can't focus on what is truly important.

- Learning to spend your time and attention on who you are at your core.
- Deciding which parts of yourself you would like to encourage.
- Developing insights into what your purpose and your passions are.
- Discovering what you want to bring into the world.
- And determining how you want to manifest your life in a way that is in alignment with your core essence, purpose and values.

Throughout this book, I have sprinkled concepts that I call the super-secrets of the universe. These super-secrets give weight to ideas that I think are important. Here is the first super-secret that you need to know: You are not living your life for today. Your yesterday self already made all the decisions that got you where you find yourself now and your today self will be making all the decisions for your tomorrow self. If you're happy and content with your life, then yea you! If you are a bit less than content, then your today self has the opportunity to make some small or big changes and your tomorrow self might be extremely grateful for the work.

There are many aspects of your life to consider as you muddle through where you want your life story to go and how you might rewrite certain chapters. You may not always think through the consequences of your "in the moment" actions, but that doesn't mean your future self isn't going to be dealing with those consequences down the road. Hopefully, your life is a long game. No matter what your life is like at this moment, you can impact the last chapter significantly. As you discover what you want the rest of your story to be like, look at all the tools you can develop, shift your mindset and attitudes, and then commit yourself to your personal evolution. For me, there is empowerment in the idea that. While you may fail at times, when you have a deep connection to knowing yourself, trusting yourself and having a vision for yourself, and when those aspects align with your end goal, you can steer your course directly toward your goal line. You have heard many metaphors for this: "They lost the battle, but won the war," or Scarlett O'Hara's "Tomorrow is another day." I expect you can reflect on times when you made a fast and unconscious decision, only to have to live with a longer-term consequence shortly after. For example, the teenager who breaks curfew, only to lose his privileges for a month. Or the one nanosecond misstep on an adventure that leads to six months of rehab after you break your leg. And while having a big audacious goal to work toward is important, it's just as important that your goal resonates and aligns with your core essence. It's a balancing act to be mindful in the moment. Learning to appreciate and be grateful for the life you are in the middle of living. This process can be challenging, so I honor you for taking steps to explore yourself.

My purpose for StoryJacking is that I want my today self to develop self-awareness and self-mastery so my tomorrow self can live as open to the opportunities that present themselves to me as I possibly can. I would like to share with you the ideas and tools that will allow you to develop your self-awareness and self-mastery. You don't have control over the world, bad things will happen, but you have power over how you will interpret those bad things. Even when times are hard or painful, you will be able to watch your life's experiences with curiosity and an open-minded perspective. You will find the pathways to joy, gratitude for the life you are living. And hopefully, you will find a way to make changes that improve not only your life but the lives of those around you.

I imagine there are people who feel they have never suffered, but I have not met any of them. Most people on this planet have experienced trials and tribulations. Bad things have happened, beyond personal control, that have created drama or chaos for them. Life is not a competition to the bottom based on who's suffered the most. Rather, it's about the stories you choose to align yourself with despite the suffering. When the Dalai Lama was forced to flee his country, lose his home and was set adrift on the seas of change, he had all the same choices as any human being—to be bitter and angry, or to choose another path. He has chosen the path of compassion, gratitude and generosity. Ask yourself, "Which paths are set before me? How will I embrace my opportunities to be a hero and leader in my life? What impact do I want to have on others, my family, my community and the world? And, of the paths before me, which will bring me more joy and less suffering?" It's your choice, so choose wisely.

In this book, I am going to share ideas about how to StoryJack your life, by doing what I have done with my clients for years. I am going to share my understanding of how we, you and me, create stories. I am going to use examples and share with you the tools I have used with myself and my clients over the past twenty-five years. I will do my utmost to illustrate the concepts we will explore. Along the way, I will also use myself as an example of how stories show up for people, not always in pretty ways. My stories may not be your stories, but I think we have enough commonality that you may recognize yourself in some of my experiences. I am not sharing my stories because they are so unique or fascinating. Instead, I am intimately familiar with my stories and the inner workings of my mind. I don't have to assume anything or guess how someone else might think, feel, or react because I'm drawing upon my personal experiences and perspectives. My stories will allow me to share with you what I have learned, what I have had to explore in my inner world and how I muddled through, or at the very least, got clarity about just what stories I was telling myself. Then I could consciously choose which stories I wanted to encourage and which I needed to let go of so I could move forward in the direction of my dreams.

I hope this helps you to see that:
- You are not alone.
- This journey into self-awareness is the path to self-mastery.
- Grappling with yourself, your perceptions, attitude and mindset will free you in ways you have yet to imagine.
- Self-mastery leads to becoming a better leader, parent, partner, friend and human being.

Throughout my life, I have kept journals, recordings, poems and notes. These became tools to help me remember more clearly how I felt at different times. I recommend looking at the tools you already have and then building a bigger toolbox. If you have kept journals, pull them out and see where you have been and where you are so you can chart a course toward where you want to go. When you keep a journal, you can step back from the inside perspective of the events and then look at your life from an outside perspective. You might call this the bird's eye or 30,000-foot view. Realize that you are the expert in your own life. You will have your longest and most intimate relationship with yourself. You have been with yourself since the moment of your creation, and you will be with yourself until your last breath. Spending time getting to know yourself, understanding your motivations, questioning your beliefs, exploring what has meaning, and why, is always a worthy endeavor. So, again, a powerful tool is to journal. Seeing your stories in the safety of your personal notebook can lead you to some illuminating insights. And that is, of course, what I hope for you—that through the process of getting curious and thinking about how to do your own StoryJacking, you will develop insights into the stories you can challenge and change.

In reflecting upon one's life or any event, each of us is always coming from our own voice and looking through our own lens. The lenses and filters that we see the world through are so firmly attached to our faces that it requires great awareness and then the courage to pull the lenses off and look at ourselves and the world around us from any other viewpoint. You may find that you don't always like what you have been telling yourself, or that you have been your own worst problem so placing blame on others is wasting time and stopping you from moving forward. Blame and anger are backward-looking emotions. They are most useful when you decide to look at why you're feeling them. In this book, you will explore who you are, what gets in your way, your filters and your emotions. You will have many tools to choose from to support you in changing habits of behavior and thinking. I will give you some new ways to explore the inner landscape of your mind and look at the stories you are telling yourself. I have used stories from my work with clients, just like you, but I have changed names and mixed up the situations a bit, so in reading this, if you recognize yourself, it's confirmation that you are not the only wanderer on the road. The path is filled with people muddling through, just like you.

I often talk to my clients about calming themselves I love to say, "Rub your tummy and repeat, 'I'm okay, I'm okay, I'm okay.'" I still say this, and it still is helpful. But these days, I am much more likely to say, "Plot twist! How do you want to change your relationship to the story?"

A plot twist is a set of circumstances. It could be a big and life-changing event, such as losing your vision, your home, a job, or getting divorced. Your plot twist could be any of the small daily interruptions that toss you off your game, like getting stuck in traffic, stuck in line at the post office when you are running late, or being pulled into unexpected meetings. These are the events you weren't expecting, but they showed up. Now you need to recognize them, pivot and adjust the plan forward. Plot twists can also be lovely things like an unexpected introduction that leads to a great friendship or a business opportunity. In each plot twist, you have a choice. And your choice hinges on how you decide to shift your relationship to the situation and the story. Now it's time to StoryJack.

This book is my way to help you understand your internal processes, the ways you interact with the world and how you make stories and meaning. I invite you to become more curious, deepen your self-awareness, learn from your insights and become your best version of you. This book won't change the world outside of you into the perfect place for you to live happily ever after. However, it will open your eyes to look at the ways you have created the box you now live in and then determine whether that box is the one you wish to stick with. If it isn't, then let's Story-Jack the heck out of it. By the end of this book, I hope you can create new narratives and write a new ending to the story you call your life.

Lyssa M. Danehy deHart, MSW, LICSW, PCC
Bainbridge Island, WA * Spring 2017

SECTION I
You Are Whole

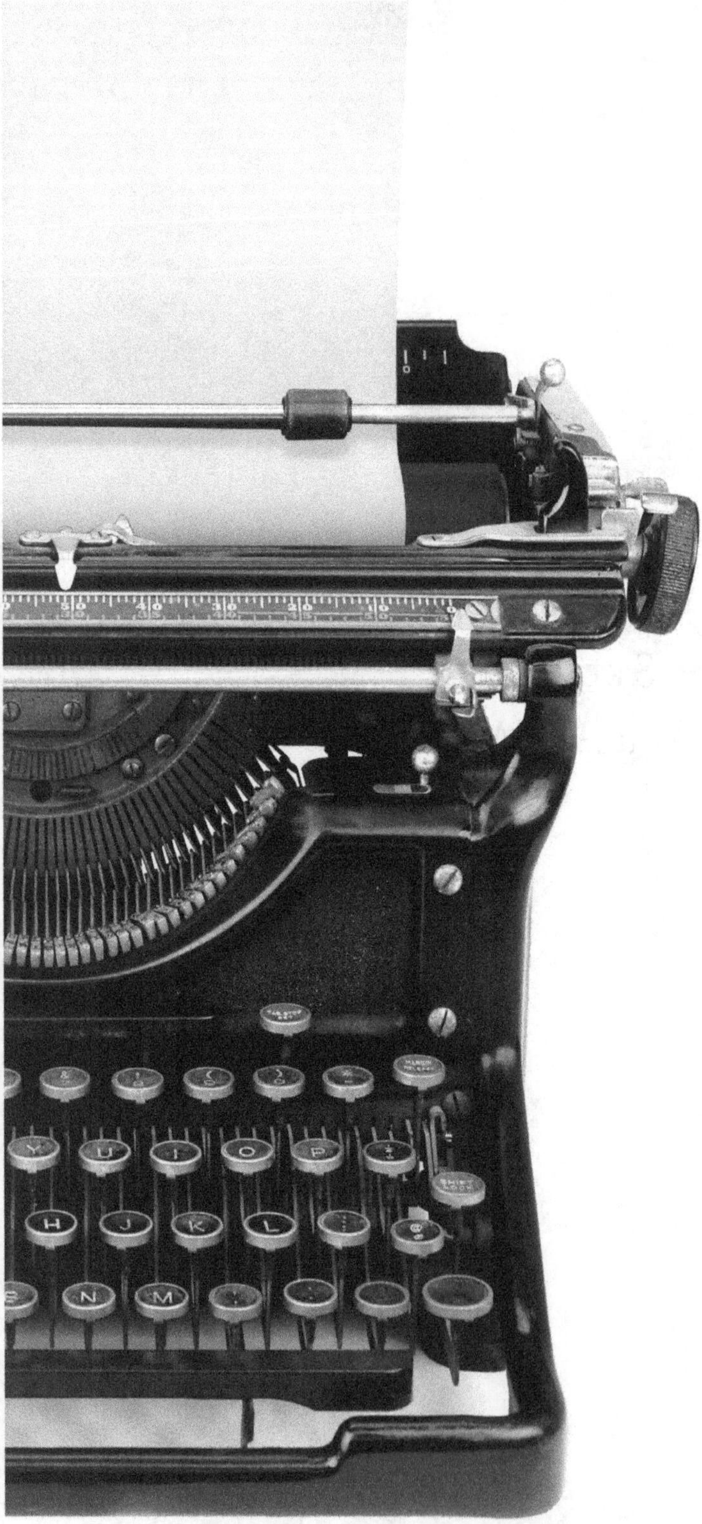

I

COACHING TO THE STORY

"The only thing standing between you and your goal is the bullshit story
you keep telling yourself as to why you can't achieve it."

— *Jordan Belfort*

Let's begin by looking at StoryJacking from a coaching perspective. This
process asks you to consider the core competencies and best practices of
coaching. While there are many similarities, real differences exist between coaching and counseling. StoryJacking is used in both counseling
and coaching to build insights and skills to help you shift. In this book,
I am writing from a coaching perspective. I think that is important for
you to understand, so let me explain.

Most therapists are comfortable listening to the stories their clients bring,
while coaches often want to "bottom line" or "nutshell" the story. "Let's
get to the point and not get lost in the weeds." What I find interesting
about this perspective is that all your beliefs, identified limitations, pos-

sibilities and ideas of meaning are wrapped up in the stories you share with others. I think it is vital that coaches challenge their mindsets and recognize the opportunity that exists to explore their clients' meaning through the stories they create and share about themselves. There is a big difference between listening to an interesting story and recognizing an important one. For example, I once watched a coach working with a client around the idea of buying a home. The conversation got mired in the interesting but unimportant details around the cost of housing, real estate markets and neighborhoods. The coaching never delved into what was important about the idea of "home." By not inviting the client to explore the meaning below the story's surface, "What does home look and feel like?" the client missed the opportunity to explore at a deeper level what was important to him about owning a home. For instance, when the client stated, "My home is my safe place," the coach might have asked, "Would it be of use to explore what you mean by safe place?" "What is the difference between the safe places inside and outside of you?" Given that home ownership is not the only way to address the need for safety, getting curious about what is meant by safety or where that need comes from could open a conversation that helps someone learn more about himself. And that's what it's all about—self-aware-ness—to be able to choose consciously what you need.

So, let's agree that listening and coaching to the story doesn't mean that either you, the individual receiving coaching, or I, the coach, are listening to the surface, superficial, or repetitive story until both of us are tired of telling and hearing it. Instead, let's get curious about the underlying meaning the story's narrative illuminates. Let's use the story as the platform to jump into deeper waters, where you can know yourself better.

Since much of my career has been as a therapist, let me share some differ-ences between counseling and credentialed coaching that I have noticed:

Counseling	Coaching
A long history, beginning as a science in the 1800s.	Thomas Leonard started the International Coaching Federation (ICF) in 1995.
Historical use of labels like crazy, insane, lunatic, or mentally ill.	Sees clients as whole, resourceful, capable and creative.
Stigma of patient as broken and needs to be fixed.	Client is leader in co-creative process.
Medical Model – insurance and diagnosis.	Non-medical Model – Client in full ownership.
Many different therapeutic theories.	Eleven Core Competencies that support client growth.
Masters level degree or higher and State Licensure	Training through an ICF Credentialed program
Therapist as expert.	Client as expert.

I would hazard to guess that most therapists don't see themselves as the expert in their clients' lives, but there is a larger perception that the therapist is an expert. And, there is a large group of people who call themselves coaches, but have minimal to no training as a coach, they may act more as consultants. Both therapists and coaches use many similar tools to help support insight awareness and personal growth. Coaching owes much of its foundation to the work of many different psychological theories. Yet the idea of you, the client, as expert, and these eleven core competencies that a practicing International Coach Federation (ICF) coach uses, set the foundation that you are the person in the driver's seat.

You can read more about these core competencies at the ICF website, coachfederation.org. Here are the Core Competencies in a nutshell:

- Ethical Guidelines and Professional Standards
- Establishing a Coaching Agreement
- Establishing Trust and Intimacy with the Client
- Coaching Presence
- Active Listening
- Powerful Questioning
- Direct Communication
- Creating Awareness
- Designing Actions
- Planning and Goal Setting
- Managing Progress and Accountability

What is so special and pivotal about these competencies is that all coaches who are following the ICF coaching model and not consulting or doing counseling, are working to integrate these competencies into their work with their clients. There is a mental shift, where both you and your coach see you as the expert. You are a powerful human being, capable of your own insights, competent to determine what tools work best for you, able to be self-knowing and able to rewrite your stories. I ask you now, which would you prefer to be—the expert or the patient?

I bring this up because I believe that if you start with the idea that you are whole, capable, resourceful and creative, then you are empowered to shift any ideas, beliefs, or behaviors that keep you stuck or feeling powerless. You can change your world. If I believe you are broken and that I, or any outside person, has either the responsibility or the power to "fix" you in some way, you are already working at a deficit. To be clear, good therapists do not try to fix their clients. But insurance requires diagnoses, so to get paid, therapists must give you a diagnosis. The medical model requires this, and frankly, the medical model implies implicitly and explicitly that you are ill. Some people are mentally or emotionally ill to the degree that the medical model does apply and can be quite useful. Yet, when I think back over the twenty-plus years I have been working with people, maybe 10 percent of my clients were severely mentally ill. Most of my clients were stuck—they came to therapy because they were struggling with relationship issues or situational anxiety and depression that was directly linked to things in their lives, like their finances, their relationships, their kids, their careers, or a crisis. Most wanted to figure out their place in the world and discover how to create a life they resonated with. I would hazard a guess that most of my therapy clients would have been just as well served by coaching as by counseling. I believe that the world is filled with people who could benefit from the growth opportunities that psychological insights and tools offer without needing the medical model.

It's important to acknowledge that a power differential shows up when one person is in a higher position, like a doctor, counselor, or expert and you are a patient coming to him or her with a problem. You might consider abdicating your power to these professional people, because, well, they're supposed to know everything and wouldn't it be nice if there was a pill, fairy dust, or a magic wand they could just wave around your head to "fix" you and your situation?

In coaching, the responsibility and work are focused on you, the client, and it comes from you, your situation, your insights, your desires and your expert knowledge of yourself. It's an internal generative process where you own your sovereignty. As the expert in knowing yourself, you get to decide what you want to explore in your internal landscape. Coaching trusts that you are able to determine your life and that you are capable of uncovering your deeper needs. The coach holds the space for you to be heard, facilitates the agreement and clarity around what you want to explore, asks powerful questions to help you get curious and helps you develop insights and deepen your current insights and awareness. The coach also supports you in creating the map and steps that will keep you moving in the direction of your stated goals, helping you to hold yourself accountable to the actions that you decide you need to take.

Coaching is a co-creative process where you are encouraged to design your life, set powerful goals and visions about your future. You are invited to take actions that will support your growth toward your goals and ultimately learn to manage your own progress. The coach provides some accountability in this process, but as you grow, you are supported to take more ownership for yourself. In a nutshell, coaching gives you, the client, permission to be a full grown up. With all the choices, responsibilities and consequences of overseeing yourself, and being grown up entails. StoryJacking fits seamlessly with coaching because StoryJacking is all about you evolving into the person you want to become and having the support that challenges you to live for more.

Each of us accomplishes more with support. What matters is having a supportive environment so you can do more than you might do alone. Let's look at an example. You have a beautiful draft horse, and this horse can pull 1,500 pounds. But you need to pull more weight than that, so you gather up a second draft horse that can also pull 1,500 pounds. You might assume that between the two horses, they could now pull 3,000 pounds, right? Well, yes, they can, but here is where Psychology shows up. The two horses can pull something closer to 4,500 pounds. Because something fascinating happens when the animals work together, they are empowered and benefit from the teamwork. And, even more interestingly, if the horses have trained together and developed their relationship, they can pull more and faster than they could have pulled alone. In my life, I have multiple examples of this relational empowerment. When I clean my house alone, it takes longer than if my husband helps. If we add music and dancing, we have more fun and get more done. Just think about the growth of "coworking" spaces—because humans enjoy being around other humans. When we have company, we are more productive, generate new ideas and are emboldened to stretch ourselves. Imagine working alone all day at home with no interactions. After the novelty wears off, it's a lonely slough. This is what you do for yourself when you get a coach or a counselor. You give yourself the support to go farther than you believe you could go if you were alone. If you are in a co-creative process, developing your personal team, I am guessing you can move four times as much of your baggage as you could if you tried to muscle through it alone. Similarly, having support from someone else is an excellent way to change your stories faster and with more fun than if you did it by yourself.

I love the co-creative process. I have a coach, and I continue to have a support network. I will staunchly say that I owe all my StoryJacking to the people in this circle. The ability to gain perspective from the observations and questions that my circle brings to me has supported me in my personal life and my career. I also like the shift from the medical model to the coaching model. It hasn't been easy; it's taken a concentrated effort. The transformation from counselor to coach has asked me to stretch and let go of some ideas about my insights for others and be open to their insights for themselves. It is one way I have been StoryJacking my own paradigm, changing how I see myself in relation to the work I do. Challenging my ideas about how I want to be with people, as a human being and as a coach. I am sharing many of the tools I use, and I hope these tools will support you to move forward on a clear and direct path. I love starting with the perspective that you are whole, capable, resourceful and creative. I have worked in the helping field for a long time, and I believe that each one of us can change. I believe wholeheartedly in your ability to heal your wounds, determine your dreams and then work like the dickens to make those dreams a reality.

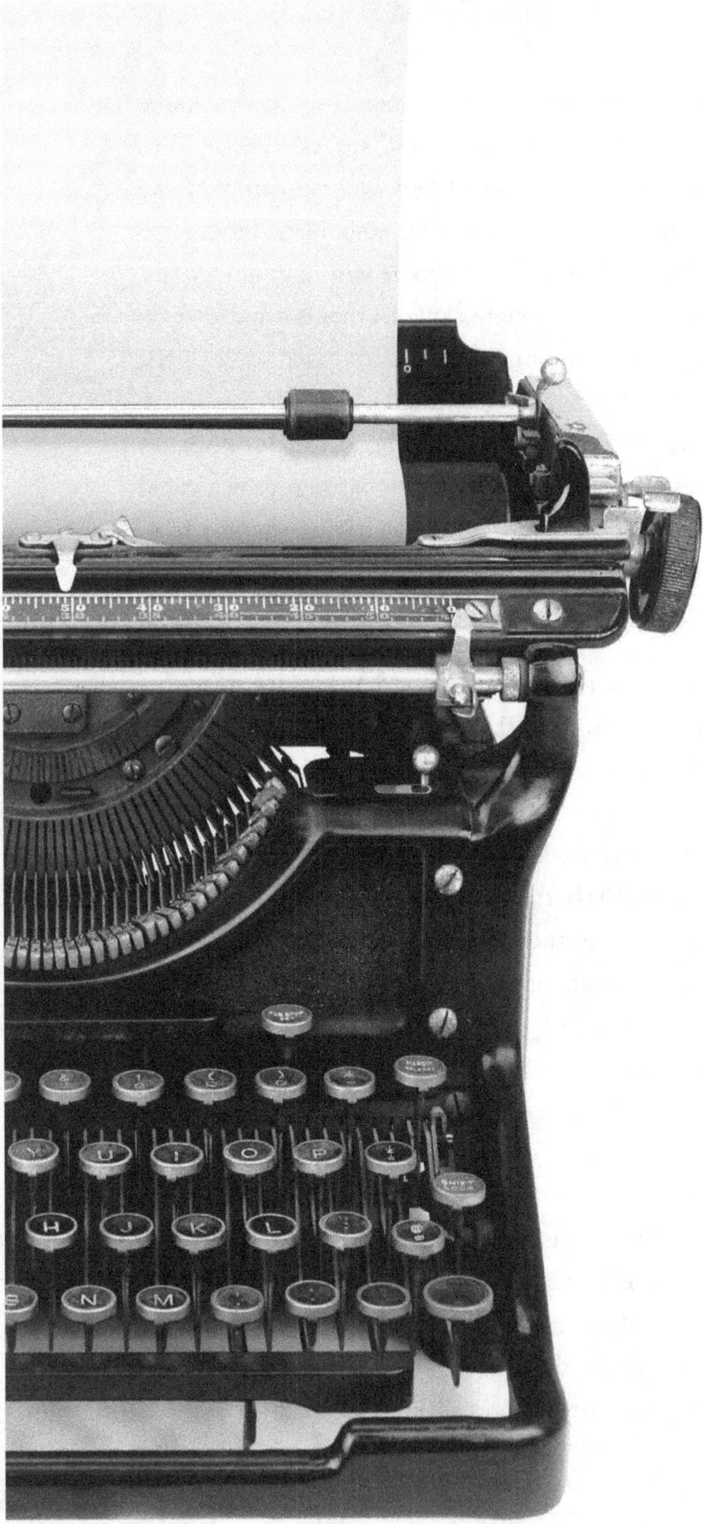

2

BECOMING WIRED FOR STORIES

"The world isn't just the way it is. It is how we understand it, no?
And in understanding something, we bring something to it, no?
Doesn't that make life a story?"

— *Yann Martel*

Let's go back in time, about 5,000 years. You are a traveler, crossing a vast and dark forest as you explore an unknown world and look to find your place in it. You are on a quest to find a vision for your future. It takes courage to show the world that you are here and to make your shout out into the darkness. You are not alone. You are following the footsteps of those before you, and you are laying the groundwork for those who follow you. You've come to a good spot to stop for the night, so you start to prepare for the long night ahead. The night slowly creeps over the sky, and the last pale strands of light are slowly eaten by the dark. You are sitting alone in this dark and alive forest. You hear night creatures as they hunt, the long wing beats of an owl and then a short time later, a screech and then the quick cry of a rabbit meeting its end. As you sit in the dark forest, your sight is limited, but your body is alive with intense awareness. Your ears prick up at every small sound—each slight rustling of leaves or branches in the spaces around you. Your world and vision have gone black and gray in the night. When you look up through the dark outlines of trees, you see a sky filled with the bright pinpoints of 100 billion stars. You are struck by the enormity of the universe around you, and you feel small. As you place yourself in this scene, allow your mind and body to feel what that smallness in the bigness of the universe feels like. What do you notice in your body right now? Are you feeling comfortable, or feeling dread? Excited or anxious? Name the feeling(s) you notice.

_____

_____

_____

As you sit in this darkness, you decide that enough is enough and pull your belongings close. You feel around in your camp bundle and find your flints. You have gathered some wood together and set some dried moss in the middle of the pile. You strike your flints together, creating small sparks of light and as you strike, a small ember hits your dry kindling and you softly blow. In a few moments, you see the hot red outline of the moss catching fire. You gently breathe life into this new fire until the flames start dancing. The darkness around you begins receding. Soft yellows, oranges and blues light up your surroundings and warmth begins to fill the air. How do you feel now? What are you noticing in your body? Are you feeling safer? Are you relaxing?

_____

_____

_____

Fire and our ability to harness it changed the course of human history. Fire offered us warmth in the cold and light in the dark. Fire protected us from the dangers of predators who wished to snatch us up as dinner. Fire allowed us to cook food, expand our diet and smoke meat. It gave our bodies the opportunity to suck more nutrients from our food and to keep our food lasting longer, so we didn't have to forage the whole day. That gave us the most precious commodity in life: time. I would argue that fire created stronger communities. That all art, music, and innovations are directly linked to our harnessing of this powerful tool. The emergence of stone tool designs and manufacturing and the control of fire are the first two significant technological advancements in the human experience.

Not needing to forage constantly gave us time to become creative and innovative. You, yes you, come from the most creative and innovative species on this planet. You are the dream of those early people—that they would still exist in you in some faraway future. And along with creativity and innovation, this spaciousness of time gave us the opportunity to share our stories around a fire. We shared stories to share the adventure of the hunt. We shared stories to build bonds between us. We shared family stories that strengthened our familial and tribal bonds. And ultimately, as we sat around the fire looking up into those 100 billion pinpoints of light, we shared stories to create meaning and develop understanding about a world that was mostly unknown and wildly beyond our control. The fire danced and cavorted in our rings of stone. Fire helped us to feel safe, warm and full. The stories helped us make sense of the world around us and feel a little bit more in control. They allowed us to learn from others and think new thoughts of our own. As we decided what things meant, we labeled, named and defined each thing we saw. By doing this, we felt powerful and set about deciding that we were the masters of all we saw.

As we moved forward in time, through thousands of years, our minds developed networks for transporting understanding about what we saw, what we dreamed, our emotions and how we felt both physically and psychologically. All these senses then connected to stories we used to explain what our senses were telling us. Stories became how we communicated, traded information, explored ideas and shared our explanations and understanding of the world.

Paul Zak, author of *The Moral Molecule: The Source of Love and Prosperity*, describes his research about how we connect to the emotion in stories. The brain releases chemicals in response to stories. Chemicals like cortisol, adrenaline, or oxytocin. These chemicals help your neurons to express responses, such as sadness, excitement, or love. Let's say you are watching a sad movie like *The Notebook*. You find yourself sad, possibly even crying, maybe to the point that your husband shakes his head at you and your sobbing best friend and asks, "Why do you two watch that stuff?" Your sobbing brain is being triggered to release cortisol for your distress and oxytocin for your connection to and empathy for the characters in the story. The more powerfully this reaction is triggered, the more connected you feel to the characters and in the case of *The Notebook*, the more tightness you might feel in your throat, the redder your nose would become and the more you might cry. Zak's research explores the connection between the evolution of oxytocin and our ability to create attachment. When these chemicals are released together, it makes it more likely that we will have empathy and caring for another person in the story. Over hundreds of thousands of years, our storytelling brain developed these chemical connections and storytelling networks. As neurons fired, chemicals were released, and as we responded, we became hardwired for stories.

Our brain lights up with stories. When we listen to a slow and lackluster lecture, our brain processes the words into meaning, but little else happens. Only when the information is shared in a compelling way that gets us to think and feel simultaneously do we experience the story from an inside perspective. Then we begin to feel and not just know what the meaning is. Stories have the power to help our brains sync up with others—be they humans or animals—so we can share their feelings and perspectives. If you have been moved by the story of an animal who is suffering, you are not suffering with the animal because what you have heard goes against your moral code. You suffer because you have felt the power of empathy and on some deep level, you have internalized that suffering. The funny thing is that our brains don't know the difference between being immersed in a powerful story and physically being in the situation. When we internalize the story, it becomes a part of our experience and shapes how we see the world.

In his book *The Storytelling Animal: How Stories Make Us Human*, Jonathan Gottschall writes that "most of the stories told the world over are almost always about people with problems. The people want something badly—to survive, to win the girl or boy, to find a lost child. But big obstacles loom between the protagonists and what they want. Just about any story is about the protagonist's efforts to secure, usually at some cost, what he or she desires. Story = Character + Predicament + Attempted Extrication." This pattern is great so long as we don't stop at Character + Predicament…. When we apply this storytelling pattern to our personal lives, we realize that most of the stories we tell ourselves inside our heads are also about problems—our problems. They include what's wrong with our lives, what's wrong with other people and ultimately, what is wrong with us. What our stories don't often include is how we will succeed at getting out of our particular predicament.

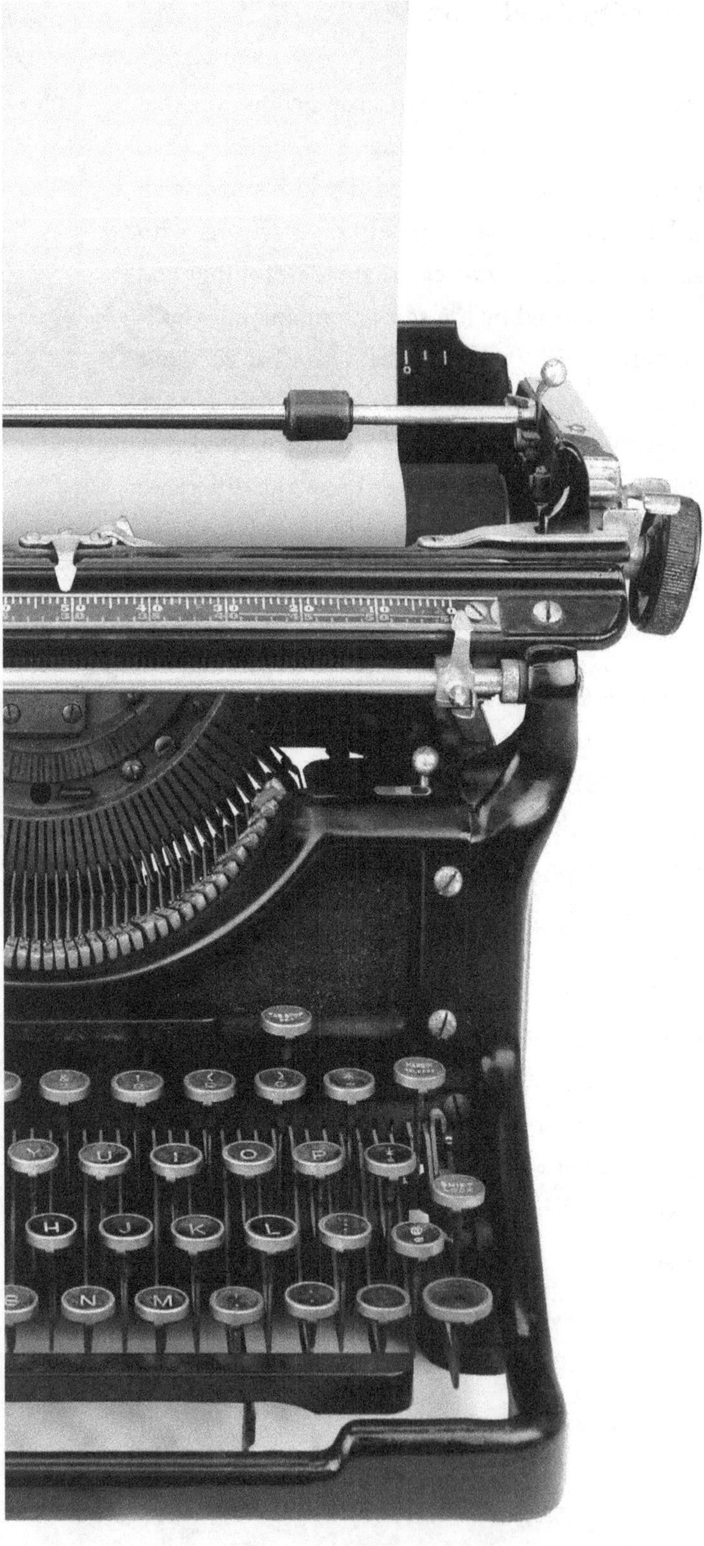
Y
U
I
O
P
H
J
K
L
N
M

3

STORY-MAKING MACHINES

*"Who are we but the stories we tell ourselves,
about ourselves and believe?"*

— *Scott Turow*

If you are human, then you are a story-making machine. You know stories. You invent and create them about everything that you see, think and do. You create them about each thing that you see others say, think, or do. You know a good story when you hear one. You most likely love to tell stories, and you will stop and listen with great intensity to someone else's story if it captures your head and your heart. I am sure that you have heard and maybe even told, a wild fish story—you know, about the one that got away. Your brain is designed to recognize that you are hearing stories or telling stories when you share something that happened to you, like "I've met 'the one.'" You might want to shout this news out to the world, or at least tell it to your best friends. Maybe you are sharing an adventure that you had, where you were chased into a bathroom with an English couple by a slowly ambling bear (true story). There is an agreement and understanding that when you talk about something that just happened, you are sharing a story. You probably also have strong ideas about the truthfulness of stories. In the wise words of Marcus Aurelius, "Everything we hear is an opinion, not a fact. Everything we see is a perspective, not the truth." When the pieces of a story don't fit, you might quickly realize that you are being told a tall tale. Perhaps you call these lies.

You may love funny stories. Funny stories tend to help you find your tribe of fellow funny folk. You can be mesmerized by a good dramatic story or a passionate one, especially if the passion and excitement are yours. You may even enjoy the occasional scary story, especially if you aren't in the middle of living it yourself and no chainsaw-wielding psycho killers are at the door. And I hope you recognize that all these stories are the way we communicate with others.

Where we get shagged up is the stories we tell ourselves that we rarely share. The stories about how we can't do something because we aren't good enough, or smart enough, or capable enough. These stories cause us problems because we often keep them secret, hidden away in some dark closet in our mind, sometimes even from ourselves. And this, my friend, is a problem.

These negative and often unconscious narratives are so powerful that they can derail you from completing goals, changing jobs, creating boundaries, or showing up authentically in your life. I am fascinated by how our stories affect us, so I have been working to develop my curiosity, gain clarity and begin to challenge the stories that have been limiting me. I hope to share what I am learning so that if it resonates with you, you might have some tools to challenge and change the stories you are telling yourself and that are keeping you stuck and playing small in your life.

We can get tangled in our stories. It's the "I can't see the forest for the trees" metaphor. We are so "up close and personal" in our lives and our relationships that we can't see our lives from any other angle. My clients often come to me wanting forward motion in their lives around issues they have been wrangling with, often for a long time. Depending on what the client and I decide to get curious about, we may find ourselves trundling down any number of rabbit holes of stories. I continually notice how many different stories we tell: stories that focus on what isn't working, on how we are stuck or trapped, that tangle us up in details, or that are so wrapped up in a lot of emotions that they don't lead anywhere useful. Yet if everything is a story, as I believe, which are the stories to explore? Are there stories that are helpful to you, or would the story about the story be an interesting place to look? Where are you ready to get curious? What do you focus on so the stories will be useful and help you shift your life in meaningful ways? And what do you need to support yourself to gain perspective, expanding the willingness to show up differently and generally get out of your habits of thinking, reacting and avoiding so you can show up differently in the world? If you want a different life experience, you must become different yourself. Otherwise, it's an easy slip right back into your old habits and old stories.

I ask that you have compassion and empathy for yourself on this journey. That you are even reading this book shows that you are courageous and ready to take a good look at what you are saying to yourself. To Story-Jack your life means you are willing to get out of your stories and get curious about what they are about—to discover what is going on below the surface. Are you willing to practice getting into your own shoes and then out of them again—to try on some new shoes and even play with all the shoes in the store? Trying on different ones so you can tromp through your stories and see and understand them in some new ways? Being willing to gain perspective is an act of courage. As your perspective shifts so does your world.

There is the empathy you will develop for yourself and others as you explore all the possible stories. Empathy gives you a window into the struggles of other people. To see the world from another person's viewpoint opens your mind, especially if you don't agree with that perspective, allowing room for forgiveness and understanding. You didn't live the life that got another person to the place he is, yet you can develop an appreciation for that person and make an effort to hear his unique perspective.

What I hope you gain is the willingness to look at all of us from a position of compassion, empathy and kindness—to look at what you think might be going on in someone else's story.

Ultimately, I hope to share the thoughts, ideas, understandings, new thinking and tools I have used in changing some painful and problematic stories that I have held onto myself and which are not serving me in my present life situation. This is not about navel-gazing or "The Great American experiment of me," as in the words of Walt Whitman. Story-Jacking is about learning to grow yourself as a person of self-mastery by exploring your relationship to the stories that you tell yourself. It's about developing insights, courageously holding yourself accountable for your life and owning your baggage so you can change your story. It is about getting out of your own way so you can be successful. If this process is helpful to you, I will be glad. If it doesn't work for you, I encourage you to take care of yourself in ways that do resonate for you. But either way, stay curious and find the pathway you need to change your stories and create a successful life in whatever way you determine success.

4
MEET YOUR PSYCHE

"Stories are psycho-diagnostic—they diagnose the condition of our psyches. When we watch, read or hear a story, whatever detail jumps out reflects an issue in our psyche that requires our attention."

— *Thea Euryphaessa*

You have most likely heard of Sigmund Freud, the Austrian neurologist at the turn of the twentieth century who founded a psychological process called psychoanalysis, which he used to treat psychopathology. Psychology attached itself to the medical model of seeing any mental disorder as psychopathology so it would be considered a "real" science and not a bunch of hocus pocus. And, in all fairness, it is a real science, in part thanks to people like Freud. Through his work with his patients in Vienna, Freud developed many psychological theories. I am not going into all of them, but the one I want to explain quickly is that of the id, ego and superego.

The id, ego and superego are the three parts that make up your psyche. And your psyche is defined as your soul, mind and spirit. Understanding these three parts will give us a common language when we talk about ideas throughout the rest of this book.

Your id is your instinctual self. You have some simple impulses to eat, breathe, procreate and survive. If you're alive and you want to stay that way, your id is the part of your psyche that drives these aspects of your life. It is also the aspect of your psyche that operates most obviously on the "pleasure principle," which, in a nutshell, means that you seek to move away from pain toward pleasure. Would you prefer to be burned or have a cupcake? Well, regardless of what your mouth is saying, trust me, your id wants the cupcake. And your id will take the cupcake by force if it must because it wants what it wants. Most likely, you are in alignment with your id on this cupcake dilemma. Your id wants your satisfaction with no insight or thought to consequences. Let's make this choice a little harder. Would you prefer an apple to a cupcake? You know what your head is telling you right now: "Apples are good for you and cupcakes are filled with sugar and butter." But your id is that impulsive part of you that doesn't give a flip and would gobble down that cupcake in the blink of an eye, lick its lips and smile.

Now, if you ran around acting only on your impulses, you wouldn't get much done past eating, breathing, shitting and screwing. Which might sound fun for an evening, but it limits a lot of possibilities for your life. So as our minds developed, we also developed the ego. Your ego is the moderator between your superego and your id. It works hard to please your id in ways that will get you what you want within the limits of the reality you are living in and within the reflections of the superego, which is the internalization of your societal, cultural and familial rules.

Let's say you are living in a sugar-free household. Your family thinks sugar is bad for you. That is your reality and on some level, to avoid grief at home, you have to operate under the principle that sugar is bad for you. When you bring a snack to school on share day, your mom sends you with beautiful apple slices. They are delicious and your mom has gone to great effort to slice them and arrange them like swans. Seriously, the presentation is amazing. When you get to school, everyone exclaims that your apples are the most beautiful they have ever seen. I mean, they're swans! Right next to your swan apples, on the snack table, is an old blue Tupperware box filled with cupcakes—just normal cupcakes, some chocolate, some vanilla, simple. Which snack do you think is going to be gone first? The swan apples? No? That's right, those sweet, fat-filled cups of sugar with sugar frosting; blink, blink, gone. Your ego will make this id desire okay. It will tell a story to make you entirely happy. "Well, you don't eat cupcakes every day, do you? In fact, you have been so good at eating fruits and veggies that you deserve a cupcake. And after the morning you had running around making sure those swan apples didn't fall apart on the ride to school, you've done your part to offer a beautiful, healthy option, plus, you don't get cupcakes at home, soooo...." You get the point. Your id wants the cupcakes, your ego is going to make it happen and your superego, in this case, is just fine this once with a little sugar snack.

Now, let's look at a situation that's more concerning than a cupcake. Let's say someone is hindering your ability to be successful or feel okay about your life. Maybe he is messing with your opinions, your beliefs, or questioning your values. All these things feel like threats to your brain. They make your id want to scream, call names, poke the person in the eye and basically destroy him. But your superego believes that, in your world, screaming at someone because he disagrees is rude, and you are not allowed to do that. Therefore, your ego must find a way to navigate between your id and your superego.

Your ego must find a way to navigate between your id, which wants what it wants and your superego, which judges and punishes with guilt, shame, worry and inferiority. So, your ego creates a story to survive in the middle between these two powerful systems. The ego tries to balance what your id is demanding with a) the reality you are in the middle of experiencing and b) the cultural and social rules that have been indoctrinated into your values and ideas of appropriate ways to think and act. To that end, your ego employs a vast array of tools, safety strategies, or defense mechanisms to make the story work or to justify poking the person in the eye. Your ego is always working to please these two demanding tyrants, the id and the superego.

Your ego is the part of your psyche that most people see when they interact with you. It's also, from a conceptual angle, the part that makes up stories to survive the other parts. Obviously, there are brain regions and structures that are incorporated into the process, but it's still important to understand that your ego gets hooked by events, creates stories, tries to make sense of the information and then navigates between your survival instincts and your social norms. This process can be exhausting for your ego, and you're probably exhausted just reading about it. You deserve a cupcake. It's okay. I'll wait.

YOUR EGO IN YOUR EVERY DAY LIFE

It's good to understand how your ego runs interference between your id and your superego. Yet, your ego also has another hat to wear. Its job isn't only to run interference in your psyche between your wants, needs and rules. It has also taken on the task of protecting your psyche from the big bad world.

Let's say you're an art student as I was. You've put your soul into your object d'art, and you have brought your prized baby into your class for the weekly critique. Now, you are in love with what you created, passionately in love, so you walk into class with pride. Your psyche is ready to receive all measure of adulation from your professor and your class.

Only, wait—what's that? Someone says, "This art object seems immature. It lacks depth, needs more color, or less, it's missing something, it's sloppy, or doesn't communicate anything important." "What?" As the critique continues, your heart shuts down and your ego engages. Then your internal "What the hell?" might become the external version. Your ego is not going to take this sitting down, oh no. You might swing fiercely between denial, "I'm not here. This isn't happening," to projection, "You idiots don't know what you're talking about!" to exaggeration, "This is the worst thing that has ever happened to me! I am giving up art," and even to fantasies of revenge, "I'll make you all sorry when I am super-famous!"

Your ego developed these strategies to protect you in childhood and has continued to evolve them through the years. Let's say when you were five, you wanted to do something, but your parents said, "No!" Then your sister started calling you names, chanting how weird you were. Well, your ego didn't want your psyche to be "weird," so it had to defend you, right? So you responded with something truly awesome, "You're a doo-doo head! I'm gonna tell Mom that you're mean!" Under just the right circumstances, your sister backed off. And you learned something important—you could protect yourself from two things in this situation:

1. From feeling weird for wanting to do something you got judged about.
2. From your sister's big mouth.

Fast forward twenty years. You may still be using these strategies, albeit more adult versions. You used a strategy, and it worked. Then you decided that it was a powerful tool that you could use to stay safe from situations worse than your sister, in a world wildly beyond your control. So to be clear, there is nothing wrong with defense mechanisms or safety strategies. You do them, and I do them. I do, however, see them all on a spectrum and if we are using one or two for every situation, what is the outcome of that? If all you have is a hammer, then everything might look like a nail—capisce?

If I were to leave you with one key point, a super-secret of the universe, about your ego and defense mechanisms, it would be this: *Everything that we human beings do is on a spectrum,* and the same is true for these defenses. There is withdrawal where we ask for a time out all the way to the other end of the spectrum where we just refuse to speak to the other person. Or in the case of anger, the spectrum might slide from self-harm all the way to rage and throwing things.

If it's any comfort, we all fall on the spectrum with most psychological things. Not to digress too much, but in my work, I have found that we like to define what is wrong with other people. We label people with all kinds of things: "That person is a narcissist," or "That person is passive-aggressive." We tell people our labels for them when we say things like, "You're withdrawing from the conversation or the relationship," "You're in denial," "You're crazy," or...insert label here. This is all just projection. What matters is what is going on with us, what we say, think and do. If I am finding myself at the unhealthy end of the spectrum, if I'm exaggerating how terrible, awful, or horrible something or someone is, I can challenge myself and get curious about my own extremes. Then I can engage in some mental jujitsu and look at ways to get back into emotional and psychological balance in my story.

5
THE MAGIC OF YOUR MIND

"The human mind is a story processor, not a logic processor."

— *Jonathan Haidt*

In his book *The Brain That Changes Itself,* Dr. Norman Doidge explores the amazing capacity of the brain to heal itself, to change and to develop new neural networks. He discusses a prevalent idea in science, the "machine brain" fixed and unchanging, or, as he calls it, the doctrine of the unchanging brain. Dr. Doidge questions the truth of this idea and makes a very important point: What if this is a spectacularly wrong belief? What if we have a lot to learn about how the brain works and just what it is capable of? What if you can change your brain whenever you decide you're ready to do the work to make those changes happen?

Research supports that our brains are in a state of constant change. When I was in college in the '90s, a shift was occurring from the idea that once you reached a certain age, twenty-four give or take, your brain became fixed and wouldn't grow or change. Once your brain became fixed, you would never be able to recover from a brain injury, like a stroke. You were stuck with whatever damage your childhood did to you, and you were on a set course for the remainder of your life. In hindsight, this is a very limiting belief and, frankly, a depressing one. Who wants to be stuck with the life you had no control over as a child? What if your parents were toxic, or you had a terrible accident, or what if your learning disability stopped you from learning in a traditional manner? Sorry, I guess you're stuck with that…. That sucks, right?

Thankfully, some curious and great minds have challenged these ideas of limits and fixedness. Science is now exploring and expanding knowledge around the idea of neuroplasticity—that our brains can and, in fact, do change, with every thought we have, with our every experience and this change occurs from birth until death. While it may be easier for a child's brain to learn and develop, it's because a child's brain is in a full-on "input open welcome mode." The older brain can also change. The only difference is in our mindset. If, as an adult, we put out the open welcome mat for learning and growth, our brains can continue to develop and change in powerful ways, right up to our final breath. At the University of Wisconsin-Madison, researchers have been pioneering the field of neuroplasticity, originally founded by Dr. Paul Bach-y-Rita. Their curiosity has led to many new insights into how the brain works.

Dr. Bach-y-Rita found ways to rewire the brain. He built devices to help develop new neuropathways. He stated, "The brain is able to use information coming from the skin and use it as if it were coming from the eyes." One of his devices worked by sending signals to the tongue. As people used the device, they created new neural pathways. Individuals who had lost their sight were then able to see. This ability to create new pathways for the brain to read information is epically important to understand. Super-secret of the universe: *You are not stuck with any neuropathway you may currently have.* The development of new pathways is possible. It's demonstrable as far back as 1976. Now, that doesn't mean that you can keep doing the same thing and expect a new result, but if you begin the process of catching yourself in an old pattern/neuropathway, you do have the capacity to change the way your brain reacts and responds to the trigger.

Everything that you think, believe and experience changes your brain. If you grew up in a family with a lot of violence, anger and fear, the correlating area of your brain, the amygdala, might grow larger. It grows bigger as it adapts to your life experience in order to give you the tools to survive in the scary world you were born into. This larger amygdala might make you super-sensitive to danger and more reactive, with a heightened anger response. I want you to know you aren't stuck with that, kind of cool huh? By the same token, if you are born into a safe and loving family, your brain would develop a normal amygdala because you tended to feel safe and secure. Your brain didn't need to overdevelop in that area to keep you safe. As your brain develops, it adapts, through plasticity, to mold itself in ways to help you survive in the world you have found yourself in.

Neuroplasticity isn't a good or bad thing. It's just a thing the brain does. Dr. Doidge explains that while all brains have plasticity, as some of us grow and develop, we continue the process of expanding our mind's flexibility. Some of us do not. In the above examples are very different life experiences, which represent extremes. It might seem that one brain is stuck with fear, but that is a fixed way of thinking about this. If someone has suffered terrible abuse for most of her childhood, she can still change her brain. It just may take more time, support, practice and compassion through the process. Others with similar backgrounds may become rigid and inflexible. Fear and survival are powerful motivators to become rigid in thinking because they help you stay alive. The important takeaway is that no matter what has happened to you, your brain can change, you can develop new ways of thinking, create new neural networks and completely shift how you think and act. You can always develop a more flexible and open mindset.

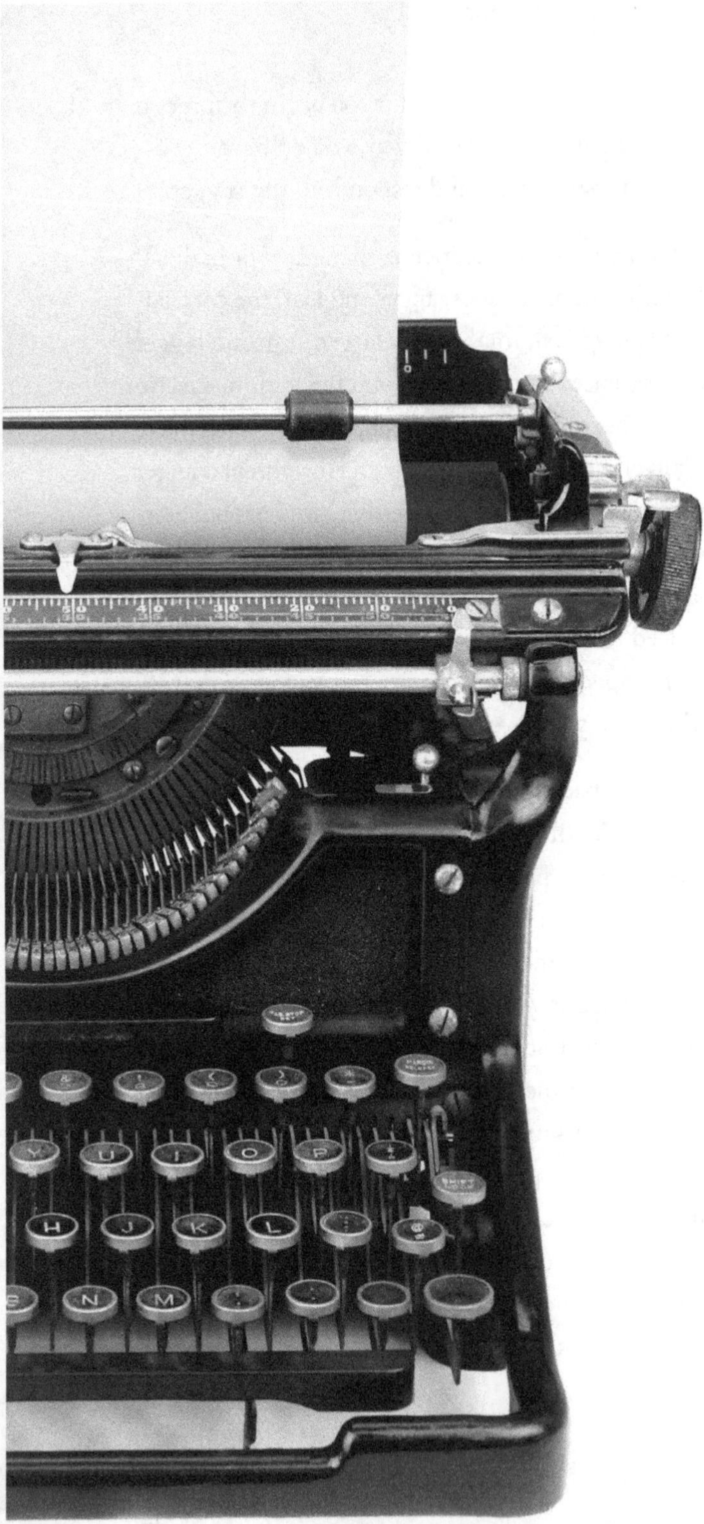

6
MAGICAL BABY BRAINS

"Children see magic because they look for it."

— *Christopher Moore*

Do you remember when you were a kid, how you made meaning by making up stories to explain everything that you touched, saw, heard, or experienced? I still do this, as do you. As a child, you had a much more limited view of the world. Your world was mostly made up of the experiences you were having with your immediate family. As you got older, you began to use your imagination to make meaning and to invent stories about who you were. You began the process of determining what you were good at and where you thought you sucked. You took the words of the adults around you, the advertising you saw and maybe a few mean comments from another kid at school and you internalized them. Over time, these internalizations melded to create your sense of yourself. You could say harsh or sweet things, and you could be more judgmental about yourself than anyone else because you had intimate access to your own mind. You might tell yourself things that made you feel smart and powerful, counting off all the good things you had done, or were planning to do and then you could do a 180 and say some pretty ugly things to and about yourself. You could explore, build and be curious about yourself, only to turn around and tear yourself down again. You might spin on a dime: "I am smart. No, I am not. Yes, I am. Nonsense! I'm not smart, pretty, or good enough. Oh, shut up! You're absolutely fine."

These stories aren't created in a vacuum. Your stories are mirrors of what is in the world around you and your interpretation of what the world is telling you about yourself. For example, let's look at our cultural ideas of beauty. Advertising has played one massive role in defining what beauty is or isn't, for both men and women. We have been sold an idea of beauty that requires us to have a perfectly symmetrical face and flawless skin and to be in top physical shape. If all you see are thin, willowy, buff, pouty-lipped, wide-eyed, wrinkleless, thick-haired, six-packed beauties, you might be forgiven for forgetting that the pretty that you see on the outside might not reflect anything on the inside. Just because you might be physically beautiful on the outside doesn't mean you're beautiful or, even more important, interesting on the inside. Wouldn't you rather take a curious, funny, interesting, passionate person to a desert island over one who is only pretty? It would benefit you to be very mindful of the standards you are going to judge yourself by. What do you have control over anyway?

My DNA expressed itself with every recessive gene in my family, that was set at conception. That hasn't stopped me from developing my mind, expanding my willingness to laugh and being joyful. Ask yourself, "Can I become a bright light? Can I be creative, funny, wise and insightful?" The only answer I can hear is "Absolutely," regardless of what you just said. You can, absolutely, develop yourself as a human being. You can become interesting, insightful, funny and passionate. We've all heard beautiful models and actresses talk about how they don't even look like they look in photographs without the makeup, their hair stylist and great clothes. They typically look like, well, normal people. Yes, like normal people who are tall, willowy, with symmetrical faces, but still people. If all the above applies to your standards of intelligence as well, frankly, you've been sold a bill of goods there too. As if only those people with 140 IQs and perfect recall, who got all A's in school, are the only smart ones. And when you look at any of these ideas of perfection and judge yourself by saying, "I am clearly not attractive or intelligent enough," you are creating a ridiculous standard for yourself, and it's a story. If you relegate your ideas of beauty to only those people who look great naked, then you are creating a very tight box to stick yourself in.

Pushing direct advertising to the side, you also get ideas of what you should be from all the comments made by your peers, parents, coaches, teachers and the occasional stranger. All these folks have their own interpretations about what is or isn't wrong with you, based on what they think smart, pretty and/or athletic means. All these outside perspectives, which bombarded you your entire childhood, still bombard you if you internalize them, let them determine what you are capable of and allow them to define your place in the world. For what it's worth, I have some physically beautiful friends. They can check all the boxes—beautiful, smart, funny, look great naked—I mean all the boxes, but what's interesting is that they are dealing with all the same internal issues as everyone else. Apparently, beauty doesn't save you from yourself and your internal narratives.

A client of mine was adopted. When she came to work with me, we were looking at helping her feel more empowered. She was plagued with self-doubts, and her insecurities were affecting her relationships and her career. As we worked together, an interesting story showed up. When she was about nine, a little girl in her class said, "My mom told me that I am like homemade bread and you're like store-bought bread," implying that my client wasn't as good. This message colored my client's internal view of herself for years. She had a story of being less than. We worked on this message and rewrote it because it was a) not true and b) not helpful. Once she confronted the story, she began the work of rewriting it. Only then could she see what a beautiful, smart, funny and wonderful a person she was.

MAGICAL THINKING

Children, between the ages of birth and about ten, lack the frontal lobe development that gives us what we think of as reasoning. All kids make sense and form beliefs based on these perceptions, attributions and relationships between events and actions. This is a classic stimulus response. But what makes children's brains unique is that they often form magical connections.

Let me give you a personal example of such magical connections. When I was two, we had a fish tank with many little fish in it. I don't remember what kind of fish, probably goldfish and guppies, but I have a distinct memory of coming down the stairs after I woke up and going straight to that fish tank each morning. I would stand there, my face pressed up against the glass and look at all the fish. I loved them. They mesmerized me as they flitted and sparkled, bright pops of color and liveliness. Where this memory gets odd is how I remember the fish disappearing. I don't have a day-by-day recollection, just a vague but real memory of disappearing fish. For a long time, I didn't think about it because my baby brain didn't know whether disappearing was just what fish did, so I decided that maybe it was okay. Maybe all fish stay for a while and then disappear. Maybe that's normal.

Then when I was fifteen, my reasoning brain came online and this memory struck me as completely odd. While magically beautiful, I knew fish could not magically disappear. So I asked my mom, "Do you remember those fish we had in Virginia Beach at the bottom of the stairs?" She replied, "Oh, yes. I am surprised you remember them. You were so young." "Well," I said, "I have this memory of them vanishing. Do you remember that?" "Ha, yes I remember that. Except the fish were not just disappearing. The fish tank had a heater on it, and you were always tampering with the heater." And, bingo, it all made sense. She had removed the "cooked" ones—move along, no magic here.

Obviously, the reasoning of a teen or an adult is very different from the way young children make meaning. Remember that young children don't have the depth of experience adults have. Their brains are not fully developed, and they still believe that what they know or how their family is, is how everyone is.

Do you remember the first time you went to a friend's house and the family had different food, or requested different manners at the table? Maybe they said or didn't say a dinner prayer. It was one of those "aha" moments when you find out that people, families and cultures are different in some unique ways. So here we are, at one, two, or three years old, trying to make sense of the world around us. What we are is sponges, with that input welcome mat soaking up all the learning we can, but what we know is based on the stories we make up in our heads to make meaning from the events around us. If you add to that any stress or fear, that little three-year-old baby brain may just get scared and shut down for a long time. Or start telling stories about being bad, "Maybe if I am super-good, my mom or dad will stop fighting," or "It's my job to make my sad/angry parent happy." The magical can be summed up as the non-linear way that children make sense of the world and create the stories that become unconscious motivators as we age. Those neural networks we develop may go through a process called synaptic pruning where we prune off the links we don't use, like an English-speaking baby letting go of the network that will help it speak Chinese. But synaptic pruning only happens to the networks we don't have activated on a regular basis. If your parents are fighting a lot, the neural network to "be good" or to "help" them, might not get pruned. In fact, it might just get so hardwired that you don't even notice when it pops up in every adult relationship you have down the road.

So why does this even matter? Well, how we help children understand the world is how they form their interpretation of what is possible. It's what happened to us, and it tends to be what we pass forward. We most certainly are capable of passing on possibility, but we often pass on our ideas about limits. Is it any wonder that most children's second or third word is "No"? Instead of finding ways to say "Yes," we begin creating limits around everything. Often, these limiting stories come directly from our attempts to share our wisdom with kids. They take all the wisdom you're sharing and hear, "Blah, blah, blah; you can't do that," or, "Blah, blah, blah; you're bad." And what started off as our sharing "great wisdom" with our children becomes setting limits on what they are capable of, what they should or shouldn't do and what is or isn't possible. Without noticing what we are doing when we perpetuate these limits, it's very easy to ignore our impact. But our impact is impacting the neural networks they are developing.

To be fair, in the years that I worked with Child Protective Services, I found that about 95 percent of the parents loved their kids and wanted to help their children to be better people. They wanted to impart the rules on how to be good or successful. They had hopes and desires that their child would grow up into their idea of a "good person." Yet how adults impart wisdom to children can generate some powerful "less than" or "not good" stories in kids. While some sound bite of advice may sound good and even come from a good place, how we interpret the learning can sometimes lead us down a bumpy road.

I remember one of my earliest stories was about being quiet. Honestly, I don't have just one memory of this "be quiet" story because I heard it often until I was about fifty—wait I am fifty as I am writing this.... Yep, I hear this story, sometimes from another person, but more often I hear it in my own head even when no one else is saying anything at all.

Here's my "Kid, be quiet" story: I am super-excited about something. If I know me, I was probably excitedly and loudly exclaiming about whatever had captured my imagination, and I wanted to share with my mom or dad, maybe my grandparents, basically any warm body that happened to be near. As I was excitedly exclaiming, in would come a voice, interrupting my mojo, to tell me to "Be quiet!" The message came through in multiple ways, "Be quiet," "Shut up," "Speak with your inside voice," "You flood me with your words," "Are you deaf? Because I am sitting right here," "Can you please stop talking?" You name it; I've heard them all. And, I did what any kid would do. I internalized this message into my story.

I could have chosen a myriad of stories: "People who won't listen to me are mean," "Nobody loves me," "I'm bad." But the one I chose for myself was, "No one wants to hear what you have to say...." As I grew up, I unconsciously integrated my chosen story into my sense of self. The message was so deeply ingrained in my thinking that I didn't even realize I had integrated it. It just rode quiet shotgun in my life. In hindsight, I can see the ways it showed up for me. If anyone seemed to be annoyed by me or my opinion, my heart would race and I would shut down. I would shut down if I didn't feel safe to share, or my feelings would get hurt if people didn't appear interested in what I was saying. I could feel my heart or stomach clench if I heard a certain tone that said to me, "Shut up." Even writing this book can be a drudge some days because I can sometimes hear the "No one will care" monster before I even finish a sentence.

Because I am so good at creating a negative narrative, I didn't just leave the story as "No one wants to hear what I have to say." Oh no, I added to it through the other experiences I had in my life. I basically expanded the story into a novella of negativity. And who the heck wants to tangle with a novella of negativity? Really, that is some scary crap right there. Because what if I find out that, in all reality, people don't want to hear anything I have to say? I mean, I logically know that not everyone who reads this book is going to love it, or me, or even get where I am coming from. Yet some deep part of me might have the desire for everyone in the world to love me, think that I am wonderful and believe I have something impressively important to share.

As I grew up, I had to create other stories to help me handle the first story. You may know some of these stories. They often sound like: "I'll never share my stories because nobody cares," or "I don't care if you hear me or not, so there," or "Maybe I am just so brilliant it's hard for normal people to understand me." My favorite as a kid was "Whatever," the implication being "You're not worthy of my words." Or I could always just put my fingers in my ears and sing loudly, "La, la, la. I can't hear you." And all of these responses are stories too. These stories are defense mechanisms I used to protect my ego from the trigger of not feeling good enough or worthy enough, stemming from the first story. It gets complicated quickly, if you see what I mean. And sometimes it feels like turtles all the way down, only the turtles are stories, and there are a million of them. And I rapidly think, *Crap this might take some time,* and in that moment, I have a choice to make: Do I want to get curious, or do I want to pretend it's fine and just shut up and go back to being quiet?

In a nutshell, I wish I was the only person on the planet who had this issue. No, really I do, because then I would be special. But, alas, I am not so special. And the world is filled with people making up stories that keep them small and then quietly living their lives in fear. Fear that someone, someday, will discover that the stories they have been playing in their heads are true and that they aren't good enough, that they do suck, aren't smart, are scared and have no talents or strengths to share with the world. I hope it's becoming clear to you. You might need to challenge your stories.

EXERCISE:

Is there a story theme that you need to challenge?

_____

_____

_____

_____

_____

_____

What triggers your "go to" story?

_____

_____

_____

_____

_____

_____

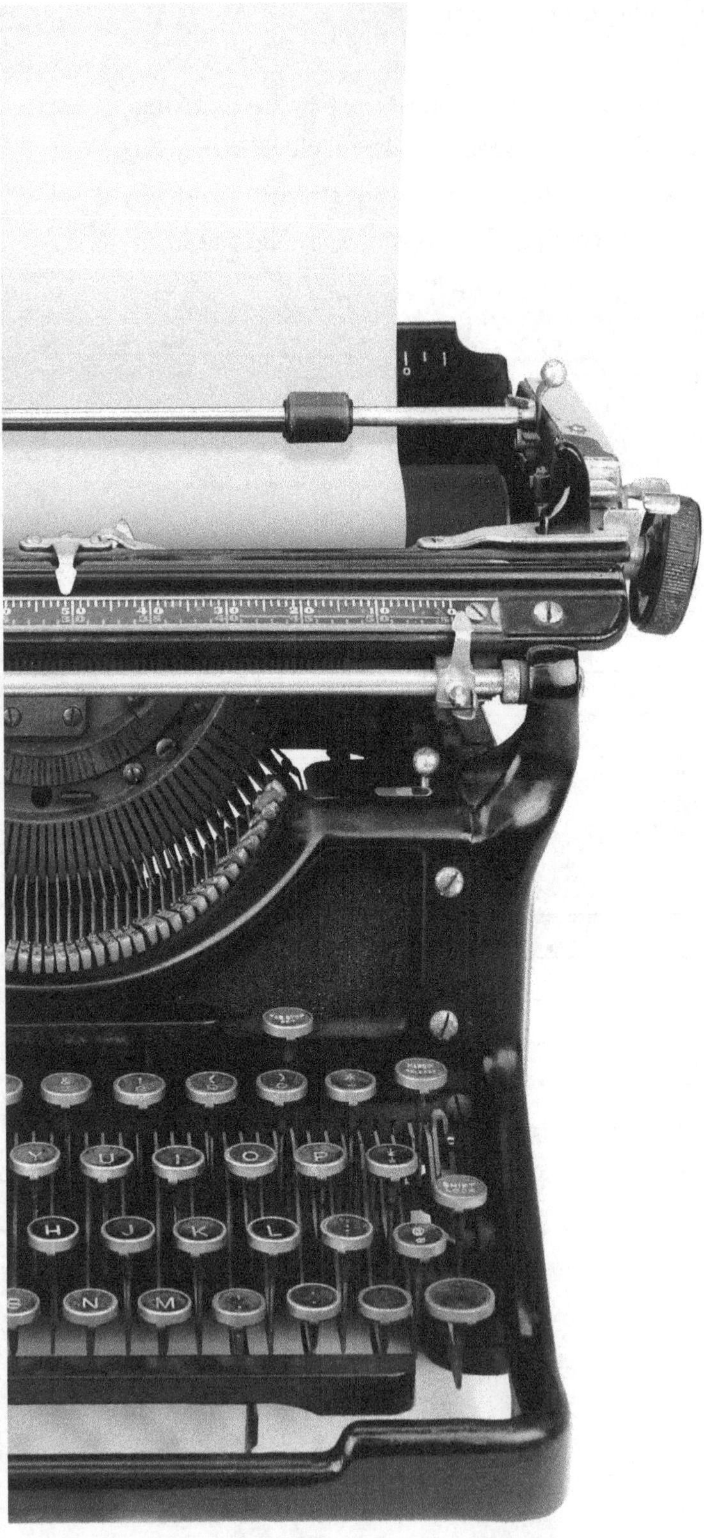
Y U I O P
H J K L
N M

7
STORYJACKING

"It's like everyone tells a story about themselves inside their own head. Always. All the time. That story makes you what you are. We build ourselves out of that story."

— *Patrick Rothfuss*

Let's go back to neuroplasticity. The brain may be hardwired to create meaning, but it is not hardwired to specific meaning. Luckily, you can StoryJack, transforming and shifting stories anytime you decide you are ready. If you are reading this, I suspect it's because you have come to the place in your life where you are ready to grow and change the stories that keep you stuck.

StoryJacking is a process that at its core is about getting curious, developing awareness about your internal narrative and then consciously choosing to rewrite your stories in ways that point you toward a life that resonates and is in alignment with your goals. It's about looking at who you are, where you are in your life, seeing where you're stuck and deciding whether you are ready for an adventure into the exploration of what your stories mean to you. It's about exploring which stories keep you stuck, how to use your mind to challenge its limits and how to show up in powerful new ways in the world. It is all about rewriting your story and rewiring your brain along the way.

Neuroplasticity is proof that a) it is possible to change long-standing neurological habits of thinking, behavior and the synopsis of neurons firing in a specific pattern and b) that what it takes to make these changes is a willingness to be curious, try new ways of doing things to create new networks so we can get out of emotional and psychological ruts. And then do what works in a wash, rinse, repeat method until the new networks get developed. You so have this, if you want it.

I came up with the term StoryJacking after years of developing my understanding of how people's minds work, including my own mind, through my work as a therapist and coach. As with most ideas I have, I was having a lively conversation with my husband, Michael, around our favorite topic: Why are people the way they are? And how do we capture what it takes to develop as leaders, parents, partners and friends? And, as with most things, this exploration was self-centered since we were also exploring why we are the way we are. The conversation centered on something I have been noticing for a very long time in my practice and with my clients, namely that people weave all their experiences, their focus, powerful beliefs, wishes, desires and fears into the stories they tell themselves and others. My clients, my friends and I were all telling stories at every turn and, in fact, we were so wired for stories that we created them about everything, sometimes out of thin air. My sense was that if we could learn to shift our stories to empower ourselves and support our being healthy people, it would help us navigate our dreams and that would be a wonderful thing.

What I found was that with many of the people I coached or met through the years, including myself and Michael, there was a theme. Most people have internal stories that are problematic for their long-term success. This isn't to say that they don't also have empowering stories, but those stories are not the ones derailing them from living boldly or feeling empowered. The negative stories were the ones stopping people from feeling joy, loving their lives, making friends, being great leaders, finding romantic partners and creating purpose. These negative stories were keeping people feeling anxious, unhappy and stuck in their life experiences. And someplace in this conversation, I said, "What people need are ways to change or jack their stories," and StoryJacking was born.

I began by asking myself a lot of questions. In fact, I am the first guinea pig for all the ideas I share. I started by asking myself, "What would be helpful in changing the deep, often unconscious stories that we tell ourselves? What tools would it take? How could StoryJacking support people in sticking to the changes and not defaulting back into the old story as soon as their attention drifted or some new stress showed up?" Because that is exactly what I was struggling with in my own life. I had some very good insights around some stories I was telling myself that weren't helping me. I was struggling and wrangling with the reality that despite all my knowing, my insights and my desire to change the story I was telling myself, it was amazingly easy to fall back into the old story. Seemingly at the drop of the proverbial hat. As soon as I got angry or fear showed up, I found myself right back in the old story. It could be hard to stick to changes I had decided on.

This process illuminated the idea that for me to be successful at changing my stories, I was going to have to get curious about what it takes to make deep, long-lasting changes.

These are the Seven Steps to StoryJacking®:

1. Develop Awareness
2. Get Curious about Your Relationship to Your Stories
3. Create a New Vision or Goal
4. Gather Your Tools
5. Be Courageous
6. Navigate the Plot Twists
7. Write a New Story

Practice, Practice, Practice: Wash, Rinse, Repeat, Ta-da! That's all there is to it!

StoryJacking is the recognition that your stories are important to who you are and how you operate in the world. You tell yourself stories of success and stories of failure all the time. You tell yourself stories about what you can and cannot do. You tell yourself stories about who other people are and what they can and cannot do. Some of these stories are painful, while others lift our spirits. In each story, we are playing out different parts and which part we are playing makes all the difference in how we move forward in our lives.

Stories are of epic importance to how you view and interact in the world around you. You define yourself, your abilities and even your goals by the stories you tell yourself, believe and then share with the world. These stories become part of your personal view of your world. Your stories have attracted the friends you have, your partners, your relationships and all the people in your tribe. Stories fill out your memories, impact your feelings and adjust how you perceive the world.

Now and again when you notice something in your life that isn't working or isn't feeling right, you might get curious and begin looking for what's not working. Have you ever noticed that when things are not working well, or you feel stuck, you begin looking for the problem in the world around you? Maybe it's your girlfriend or job that's the problem. When you look for the problem externally, you may find things that need to change, but all those external changes have an internal genesis. Unfortunately, if you fail to notice the stories going on internally, you may not be able to affect long-term changes. For StoryJacking, you are going to have to get curious about your relationship to your situation and to the stories you are telling yourself about your situation. If your story isn't serving you, if it negatively impacts your family, your community, or your organization, then you might just have to find a way to StoryJack the story, transforming it and creating a new story that will resonate with what you want in your life so you can change your story for a better version, or experience the story—and your life—in a new way.

Is there a story you've heard about yourself or a story you tell yourself that you're ready to rewrite? Are you ready to change a negative message into something that works better for you? Maybe you have a story about not being good enough or smart enough. Maybe you heard, "People like you can't write a book or change careers." All these would be good stories to StoryJack. You might be StoryJacking already. Anytime you create a vision of a future that is different than the moment you find yourself in, you have started.

When you feel an energetic and emotional connection to your new story, you have, in effect, "jacked" into it. Jacking our story takes more than words. It's a decision to commit to change. There is also an emotional piece that must be expressed, connecting your head, your heart and your body to your new path. Ultimately, for long-term changes to happen and for the new story to stick, you need your head, heart and body in alignment with the requirements to complete the shift. We have all had that experience when you hear something that creates a powerful and positive emotion or excites you. You feel it tingling in your stomach. Your excitement is energizing, and you may even find yourself dancing a little jiggy dance of delight. This feeling of exuberance is the energetic connection that you need so you can envision yourself in your new story. You absolutely need to feel yourself having the new experience. Then a resonance occurs that deepens your connection to your storyline. It's in these moments that the story and you connect. "Jacking" into a new story can be exciting and even scary. It may be moving from the story of being a student to becoming a fully-fledged adult. Maybe it's shifting from being an employee to becoming an entrepreneur. In business, it may be shaking up the story of the dysfunctional team and evolving into a leader who can support and develop the new story of "the Team that Rocks It!" In your intimate relationships, it might be the move from being "unlovable" to seeing yourself as "lovable." These story shifts sound minor and yet they are epic. I can't express this enough; these story shifts happen in your head. And you must get your head, heart, and body vibrating at the same level to cement the new pathway.

You are in charge, so it's your choice. You get to decide when you are tired of the old stuck storyline. Once you commit yourself to a new path, start getting curious and let go of your limiting stories, then you free yourself to create a story that matters to you. This takes courage, and you may want to stop along the journey. What I promise you that if you continue the adventure, work like the dickens and muscle through the rough patches, you can make the new story a solid part of who you are. These changes are enormous, they are epic, they are the most important thing you will ever do in your life, and I mean that. Because when you change your story, you teach your children how to change their limiting stories too. You model what is possible to your friends, your family and your coworkers. It is important to create a rich and full-bodied story, to create an excitement that propels you into your next story and you can change your personal world and then influence the entire world around you.

And, trust me, you need to get ready to develop a big audacious vision because you won't truly commit to stories that feel lukewarm to you. No one wants the cold oatmeal story! We want the exciting, passionate and empowering story. You may want your story to be a force for good, even a force for change. You may want to share your gifts with your family, with your community and even with the whole wide world. All change is possible with passion. In the words of W.H. Murray:

> Concerning all acts of initiative (and creation), there is one elementary truth, the ignorance of which kills countless ideas and splendid plans: that the moment one definitely commits oneself, then providence moves, too. All sorts of things occur to help one that would never otherwise have occurred. A whole stream of events issues from the decision, raising in one's favor all manner of unforeseen incidents and meetings and material assistance, which no man could have dreamt would have come his way.

I have learned a deep respect for one of Goethe's couplets:

> *Whatever you can do, or dream you can, begin it.*
> *Boldness has genius, power and magic in it.*

StoryJacking is a path to help you envision, challenge, create and manage the narrative you have about who you are and how you want to be in the world.

EXERCISE:

Is there a situation in your life that, when you get curious about it, you notice a negative story attached?

_____

_____

_____

_____

_____

_____

_____

What is the story you are telling yourself?

_____

_____

_____

_____

_____

From your gut, what do you think your relationship to the story might be?

_____

_____

_____

_____

_____

8
WHAT IS YOUR WHY?

"Tell me, what is it you plan to do with your one wild and precious life?"

— *Mary Oliver*

Neuroscience and understanding your mind is only part of the process. Our sense of self and our identification with our energetic or spiritual nature is just as important. The two aspects work together. For a long time, I believed we were just the explosion of neurons and chemicals alone. But this take doesn't honor the reality that there is a life force inside each of us. It arrives with the first growth of our cells and ends at our last breath. So, for me, there is more than just a scientific experience happening. There is also a spiritual experience happening. In the words of Pierre Teilhard de Chardin, "You are not a human being having a spiritual experience. You are all spiritual beings having a human experience."

Adapting this powerful and true perspective will help you muddle through the ups and down of the folly we call life. We take the outside experiences far too seriously, fighting with external realities, trying to make people or situations different, banging our heads against the pro-verbial wall. All the while, we are ignoring the internal process—how our beliefs, perspectives, judgments and preferences impact our experiences. You may not recognize that you have the power to change these, but when you change your mindset, you change the very trajectory of your life.

There are few things I am absolutely certain of, but this I know for sure: there's a super-secret of the universe that is vital for understanding StoryJacking. Hold onto your hat—here it is: *The longest and most intimate relationship you will have in your entire life is the one you will have with yourself.*

You were there the day you were born and took that first breath, and you will be there for that last breath of your life. You are the only person who has the profound ability to read your mind. You know what you like and what you don't. You can read the shifts of emotion and energy in your body. You have the ability to choose your attitudes and beliefs. And you have the capacity to change those same attitudes and beliefs. This relationship with yourself is the foundation for every other relationship you will have with all the other people you will meet throughout your life. Your ability to develop insights and grow awareness about who you are, what you need and then to learn to take care of yourself is a cornerstone of the way you will move through the "one wild and precious life" you have been given.

By taking a deep dive into a greater understanding of yourself, you are seeking the pathway toward the divine inside of you. You are, after all, stardust and spirit playing upon this human stage. I hope we can agree that you are the expert on yourself and the more you understand yourself, the more access you have to your brilliance. You are the key, you are the map and you are also the compass. So understanding yourself, owning your baggage, learning to take personal responsibility for your actions and your feelings, learning to be brave enough to love yourself and also calling yourself out on your nonsense is what it's all about.

In my fifty-plus years, I have yet to meet a person who on his deathbed took anything other than his core essence or life force with him. Your core essence is that spirit, soul, electricity, or universal energy that is far bigger and more profound than our human experience. Your core essence is the part of you that you were born with and that is reabsorbed into the universe when we leave this life. I honestly believe that at the end of the day, the only thing you will be taking with you is the energy you have attuned yourself with, such as love and compassion or anger and greed. These different emotional states have different energetic signatures. By deciding which aspects of your life you are going to focus on, you will help to develop your sense of your true essence.

Personally, I want my essence to reflect the love I give and am willing to accept. I resonate with compassion, curiosity, love and joy. My truth is that the love we see is based entirely on where we focus our attention and how we decide to show up and grow up in our lives. It is your choice; you can decide to focus on anger, drama and hatred. However, you need to understand that those ideas and emotions will shift your energy as you connect to the world. You will send out your unique signature of energy and intention into the world and attract similar people to you. So, if your energy, life force, or core essence is all you have in the end, it begs the question: What energy or core essence do you want to take with you when you leave this world? I promise you that your body feels an energetic difference between the word love and the word hate. If you sit with both words, notice how they play out as feelings in your body. When you sit and focus on how your heart feels, what does each of those words do to your heart? Which word opens your heart and which one tightens it up? Where you focus will impact who you are. The words and attitudes you choose, either consciously or unconsciously, will impact who you become and the story you will tell at the end of your life.

Self-mastery is about awareness, curiosity, choice and bravery. It's about realizing that if you don't love yourself or the life you're experiencing, you have the option to change your relationship to yourself and your experiences. These are not just some platitudes from a white chick who has never had a hard day in her life. This comes from the work I have done with myself and the traumas I have muddled through personally. And the over 20,000 hours of work I have done with brave men and women of every color, culture, religious belief system. It comes from the insights and learning that came from the exploration of their courage as they changed their minds and focus, discovering their "whys." Self-awareness is about understanding ourselves and our motives. To discover and bring your true purpose into the world, into your family and into your community, you will need to explore what is important enough for you to do this work.

Exercise:

What is your why?

_____

_____

_____

_____

_____

_____

_____

_____

_____

_____

What is important enough to you, to do the work of StoryJacking?

_____

_____

_____

_____

_____

_____

_____

What is at risk if you don't shift some of your stories?

_____

_____

_____

_____

_____

_____

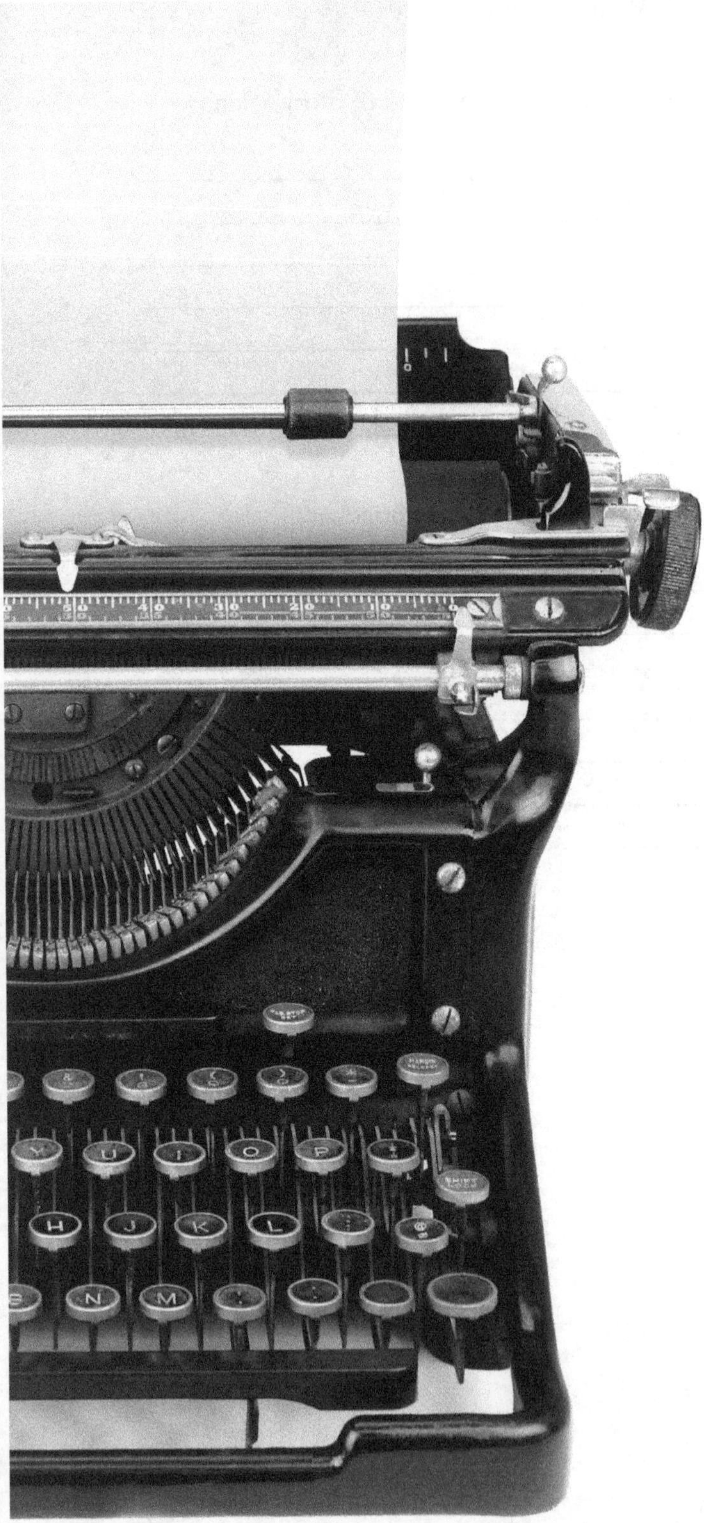

9
DISCOVER YOUR STRENGTHS

"Accept yourself, your strengths, your weaknesses, your truths and know what tools you have to fulfill your purpose."

— *Steve Maraboli*

You are stronger than you could ever imagine. Through every experience that you have had in your life, you have developed different strengths of knowledge, intuition and character. Intuitively most of us understand that we have strengths, yet we often focus on what we perceive to be our weaknesses. From a Solutions Focused and Positive Psychology mindset, what I have learned is, it's important to understand our growth opportunities. Having an honest sense of ourselves helps us discover what does or doesn't work. Our strengths are what help us to find our pathway to workable solutions. Being able to name your strengths is helpful in developing your sense of yourself. Knowing your strengths will support you with any difficulties you may encounter and ultimately drawing on your strengths will help you as you choose the stories you want to explore. Your strengths are like the lights in the dark. They are more than simple tools. Your strengths give you the fortitude to continue moving forward.

There are many assessment tools available online. One great resource for assessing your strengths is the University of Pennsylvania's (UofP) website on Authentic Happiness. You can access it quickly from my website, on the resources page at StoryJacking.com. The UofP website has multiple questionnaires, on everything from happiness to strengths, so look for the VIA Survey of Character Strengths to give you insights into your strengths. The VIA Survey measures twenty-four character strengths and will put them into order based on your answers.

The twenty-four character strengths run the gamut from Curiosity and Interest in the World, Bravery, Leadership, Self-Control, or Perspective Wisdom all the way to Kindness and Generosity, Diligence, Optimism or Caution. All strengths are important, and by taking the test, you can find your top five as well as the order of all twenty-four of the strengths. We each have within us all the strengths. Only we may draw on some strengths more than others.

Let's say your top five strengths are Curiosity, Gratitude, Humor, Love of Learning and Teamwork. When you consider these strengths, what does it say about the kind of person you imagine you are? Let's say you find yourself in an awkward situation with your coworker. How might these strengths support you in developing a healthy plan for healing the situation? Or, what if you were worried about your finances? How might you use these strengths to lessen your worry and make a plan to help yourself move forward?

Your resilience connects to your strengths by supporting your ability to bounce back from the plot twists that you will find yourself tangling with on occasion. Your strengths are not only what you are good at, but from an energetic perspective, these are the qualities that you exhibit with less effort. In fact, you often access them unconsciously. You may find that your strengths energize you. Have you ever gotten lost in a task and the time flew by. You looked up and the day was gone? From your strength of curiosity, you get into research mode. You're trying to understand something or heck, maybe you're trying to find the best deal on a new computer. You sit down, start your research and the next time you look up, you have been happily working for hours. You've researched multiple options, been looking at RAM, HD capacity, you are checking off the pro's and con's, price comparisons and honing in on a choice. You are in your element—effortlessly in the flow.

Another avenue to discover your strengths is to read Tom Rath's book *StrengthsFinder 2.0*. He states that your strengths are composed of your skills, knowledge and talents. Skills are the abilities that you have developed, usually through formal or informal education. Knowledge is what you know; it isn't intuitive, it's learned. Lastly, your talents are the ways that you naturally think, feel and behave in the world. An example might be that competitive edge you might have or your introversion or extroversion at an event. What is cool about the *StrengthFinders 2.0* model is that it allows that you can develop your strengths with attention and awareness. You also have three levels to your talents. You have dominant talents which you use effortlessly and that often show up naturally. You probably use them all the time without much thought. You have supporting talents that typically surface when they are needed to support your primary talents. And then there are your lesser talents. These rarely show up because your brain will most likely have pruned these neural networks almost entirely away.

DeAnna Murphy, a colleague of mine, is an expert on *StrengthsFinder 2.0* and is writing a book called *Strengths Strategies*. She can excitedly talk for hours about finding and using your strengths to become more empowered. One point she makes is that we all have strengths and no strength is better than another. The point of recognizing our strengths is so we can consciously know ourselves. Our strengths give us energy and increase our performance, but because our strengths are so intuitive to us, we may not recognize them.

Your strengths can be broken into four categories or types of people:

- Strategic Thinking: These are the 30,000-foot view people. They have vision.

- Executing: These are the follow-through people, the worker bees, and they get things done.
- Influencing: These people are verbal processors, so they talk a bunch and are all about getting other people to join with their vision.
- Relationship Building: These folks want to have a connection. They like harmony, and they can be adaptable.

Each of these four quadrants fits under the matrix of Task-Oriented and Relationship-Oriented. Each strength has traits and each strength has needs. I created a quick diagram to help look at this.

Task Oriented	Relationship Oriented
Strategic **Contributes:** - Creating Possibilities - Direction - Information - Ideas **Needs:** - Room to imagine - High level why/why not - Give/share of information - Exploration of meaning	**Influencing** **Contributes:** - Convincing - Igniting - Enrolling - Energizing **Needs:** - Verbal Processing - Connection to a Cause - Validation - Energy
Executing **Contributes:** - Concrete Reality - Details - Goals - Processes **Needs:** - Practical Application - Step by Step Guide - Clear Goal - System/procedures/rules	**Relation Building** **Contributes:** - Connecting - Inviting - Listening - Accepting **Needs:** - Authentic Relationships - Encouragement - Deep Listening - Non-Judgment

DeAnna discussed two concepts with me that I believe are important for how you understand yourself and your strengths. First, she stated that when you are working within your area of strength, your energy level increases. The more in alignment with your strengths you are, the higher your energy and the higher your level of performance. It goes hand in hand. So, for instance, if you are a relator person like me, you get energy from connecting with another person at a deep level, often one on one. Yet in order to operate a business, you may need to do other, possibly draining activities, like respond to emails, write business plans, or do your bookkeeping. All these office tasks may suck the life out of us relator types. Because these tasks are not in alignment with my primary strengths, my energy goes down and my performance slows down too. I must expend a lot of energy to make myself do the things I don't enjoy doing. Understanding your strengths might mean that when you look at your calendar, you need to fit the energy-sucking activities between the energy-expanding activities to carry yourself through your day. For example, I may write a blog (energy up), read emails and respond to them (energy down), have a client session (energy up), send out invoices (energy down), then go to the gym (energy up). Overall, understanding my strengths gives me the ability to leverage my time and energy so I can be at my peak performance.

Secondly, we need to be aware of the outcomes from our overuse of our strengths. Let's say that your top StrengthsFinder strength is Connectedness. You tend to look for similarities between people, seeing the links between all things. You listen deeply, and you enjoy assisting people. You look for opportunities to cooperate and find ways to be inclusive in all your relationships. These are all excellent qualities, but what happens if you, unconsciously, overuse this strength? You might not hold people accountable. You might sacrifice the team's needs for the needs of an individual. You could be more supportive to the whole if you were a bit firmer. When you look closely at your strengths, pay attention to the times when your overuse of a strength may derail your goals. At some point, you may need to explore and develop other strengths to stretch and become more successful.

All these assessments give you insights into yourself, so you can see yourself with greater clarity and know yourself more fully. Gallup research has shown that if you are using your strengths daily, you are six times more likely to be engaged in your work, your relationships and your life. Explore and discover your strengths because they will help to support and guide you as you grow!

EXERCISE:

Take the VIA Survey of Character Strengths Assessment

What are your top 5 Strengths?

1.

2.

3.

4.

5.

What is a situation that you are wrestling with and which of your strengths could most support you in handling the situation?

_____

_____

_____

_____

_____

In what ways can you use your strengths to StoryJack your limiting stories and support your growth?

_____

_____

_____

_____

I O

YOUR LIFE AS A PIE

"I realized how truly hard it was, really, to see someone you love change right before your eyes. Not only is it scary, it throws your balance off as well."

— *Sarah Dessen*

Let's look at a snapshot of your whole life using the balance wheel as pictured below. When you start to rewrite your stories, you can begin by filling out where you feel you currently are in the different aspects of your life. It will give you a starting point to help you decide what aspects of your life you want to focus on. You don't need to change everything to StoryJack yourself, but you do need clarity and a place to begin the adventure.

Looking at the wheel on the next page, take some colored pens and fill in the rings for the areas where you feel you are doing well. The more you fill in the wheel, the better you feel you are doing. The less you fill in the wheel, the more opportunity for exploration you have in those areas. It is possible for someone not to have something in one of the spokes and still be perfectly happy with the absence. Let's say at this moment in time that your work may be more important than an intimate relationship. Understanding your focus can help you make clear choices. When I was in graduate school, I didn't want a boyfriend. I didn't have the time, and that spoke of my wheel was full, even without an intimate relationship. In noting where I was on the wheel, I could focus on what was important to me at the time: school, friends and personal development. Later, when I moved back home, I wanted an intimate relationship, so when I worked the wheel again, that spoke was empty, aha a place to work!

Your awareness of where you are and what you need each step along the way can support you in having the life you want. Keep your focus on the

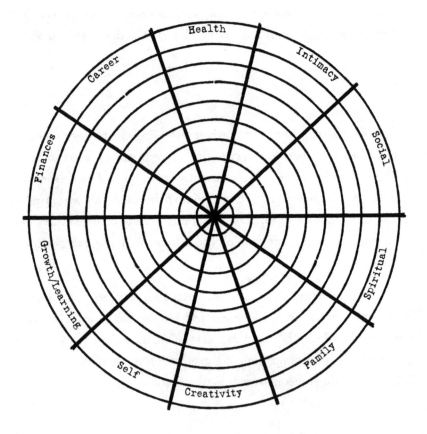

areas of your life that are important to you. If for instance, your health is important to you yet you fill in only the two most inner rings in that category, maybe you're not honoring your value about your health.

Take a bit of time to color in your slices of pie. Notice where you feel right about the different parts of your life and where you aren't paying attention to certain areas of your life. If you are a loner or introverted, you might not go out with people and party, but that pie may still have a full, satisfied feeling because that's what healthy interaction feels like to you. On the other hand, if you're an introvert and you have isolated yourself to the point that even you are lonely, that slice of your pie might need some attention.

EXERCISE:

When you look at the completed pie, what do you notice?

_____

_____

_____

_____

_____

_____

What areas need your attention?

_____

_____

_____

_____

_____

What sections are your priority?

_____

_____

_____

_____

_____

What goals do you have for yourself in different sections?

_____

_____

_____

_____

_____

When you think about your goals for each of these sections, what is between you and your goal?

_____

_____

_____

_____

These questions become helpful in focusing on what is important to you and what you want specific aspects of your life to look like. All good information for moving forward.

I I
YOUR AUTHENTIC CORE SELF

"Your hand opens and closes, opens and closes. If it were always a fist or always stretched open, you would be paralyzed. Your deepest presence is in every small contracting and expanding, the two as beautifully balanced and coordinated as birds' wings."

— *Jalaluddin Rumi*

I am ending this section with an exploration into your essence. Core Essence is the wholeness of who you truly are. It is not the façade of yourself that you may present to the world. This is the part of you that is your truest substance and your essential inward nature. Multiple philosophies and religions consider the possibility of a life force or spirit. Maslow's hierarchy of needs states that at the top of the pyramid, once you get past your need for food, safety, belonging and self-esteem, your most important need is to self-actualize—to have a sense of purpose, meaning and inner potential. If all ideas are stories, then the story I would share with you is that your life force, spirit, or essence, if you will, is that part of you that is your inner vitality and holds all your potential.

When you were born, you had a direct connection to your essence. You didn't question it. You just moved forward, learning and growing. Then, alas, through the years, the experiences you have had affected you. You may have needed to survive by tucking down and hiding that essential part of yourself. Maybe it wasn't safe to share ideas that seemed odd, or to say no, or to be different, so your mind helped you to conform to your environment. Never fear. If you are alive, the "you" deep within the core energetic life force of your aliveness is with you. Your essence is the part of you that you came into the world with and it is the spark you will take with you when you leave your body. In the words of Sri Ramanasramam, "But with the death of this body, am I dead? Is the body I? It is silent and inert, but I feel the full force of my personality and even the voice of the 'I' within me, apart from it. I am Spirit transcending the body. The body dies but the Spirit that transcends it cannot be touched by death. That means I am the deathless Spirit." This is not some random thought, some simple question that you might explore. This is the point at which your sense of self can be expanded. This is a question that only you can answer. You are, in fact, the only person who has direct experience and knowledge of the spirit within you. If somewhere along the journey you have disconnected yourself from this truth, you have lost nothing. You have the right to your soul, and you can meet it at the crossroads where you stand, in this moment.

When I began the work of connecting to my essence or spirit, many of my fears drained away. If—and I believe this is one of the super-secrets of the universe—*I am an aspect of the divine spirit having a human experience, then why am I afraid?* This is not a simple question. In fact, the recognition of your connection to the divine, the universal oneness, or God—whatever you wish to call it—is not simple at all. It is the underpinning of every major religion that has ever been. It is the seed of all spirituality and the foundation of our recognition that we are part of something far larger and more complex than we can see. The "I" inside you is a very real thing. It is the divine part of you, having a human experience. You may be taking the human experience very seriously right now. It feels concrete; you can taste, touch and feel the world around you. Remember, the only real thing about your present life is that it is just a small moment in your soul's vast experience. Ponder for a moment what might shift in your life if you changed this one idea about your sense of self and attunement to your core energetic self? What if your "I" is eternal and has a bright and beautiful song that your soul needs to sing? If you learn that song and honor it, you will begin to live the life you are meant to live in alignment with the unique gifts you offer. This perspective can give you the spaciousness to explore the world with less anxiety, anger and fear.

There is a freedom that comes from recognizing that we are all more than our bodies, our personality and our circumstances. Freedom is letting go of the story we attach to all the little things that cause us anxiety or depression and hold us hostage, causing our lives to lack connection and sovereignty. Michael Singer is a pivotal voice in this exploration. His book *The Untethered Soul* offers many perspectives on the question of "Who am I?" What I am finding is that this old question is still relevant in our modern, fast-paced world. While writing this book I took a class on Authentic Presence through inviteCHANGE, a coaching school here in the Seattle area. In the class, we are exploring what it means to be authentic. Knowing our essential essence is important to the process of discovering ourselves.

For many of us, authentic is a loaded word. It's overused in marketing. It's overused just about everywhere. We want the real thing, the authentic experience and not some knock off that has no value. Yet getting to one's authentic core essence is an inside-out job. You are the only one it matters to and the only one who can access yourself at the level you need to so you can introduce yourself to yourself. I am going to make a promise to you, and I don't do this lightly: *No one on this planet or in this universe is more qualified to answer for you what makes up your essence. You are the expert.* You may have forgotten it, or hidden it, or gotten busy and left your essence in the coat closet in your head, but you can never lose your core self because it's the part of you that transcends time and space. So, let's begin with "Who am I?"

For myself, I know that we are more than just a set of labels—labels being the words we use to describe ourselves, state our values, our identity, our culture affiliation, or education. Repeat: We are more than our labels. We are all a complex and paradoxical combination of multiple elements. We are each unique expressions of divine energy. Words and labels aside, as we develop a language for our essence, it can open the door to the idea of our essential self. Doing so gives us the power to decide, actualize and develop our authentic selves. What would it even mean to you if you developed the language of your soul's song? We use words to describe everything, so what if you begin to use words that resonate on an energetic level to whom you want to be, to describe your essence? Just by thinking about doing this, you create a connection to the part of yourself that will guide you to show up authentically in the world.

I believe you were born with a loving and kind heart. I have not yet met a baby who was born with the desire to harm others, or judge them, or destroy them. Many research studies show how babies and toddlers have great compassion and empathy. When they hear another baby cry, they often start crying themselves and try to comfort the other baby. Certainly, some babies are born with neural structures and chemistry that lead to less compassion or empathy, but those attributes can be developed by parenting, training and positive experiences. What I will say, emphatically, is that you were born curious, growth-oriented, wanting to form connections and to be a part of something bigger than yourself. You were born wanting to have fun, laugh, be joyous and be a conduit for bringing your light into the world. Our life job is to reconnect to our child's knowing state that we all started off within ourselves. Christ said, "Anyone who will not receive the kingdom of God like a little child will never enter it" (Mark 10:15). In that case, isn't your essential, curious, silly and loving self the part of you that you must rediscover and embrace? I know these beautiful qualities may have been manipulated and used against you, when you were taught to fear, to hate, to shut down your love and to disrespect others and yourself. I do not believe that these aspects of your fearful self are your true self. I could be wrong, but if I am going to commit myself to a belief, I am consciously going to choose to believe in our all having a better nature. That our truest essence is about being an aspect of the divine, an energetic conduit of love, connection, compassion, joyful bliss and curiosity.

What if, for all of us, our essence is the deepest, truest part of our connection to the universe, to God, to others, to nature, to everything? The labels are meaningless if we are unconscious of what they mean to us. Since we know we give meaning to everything, we are talking about giving conscious meaning to the words we use to describe our essence. This is not about giving lip service to these words. It is about sitting with, reflecting on and resonating to the energetic meanings of the word you use to describe your essence. If you are ready to be more than a set of behaviors, opinions and attitudes, then you must be willing to explore the nature of your truest self. Instead of becoming attached to the set of labels we like, let's find ourselves by going with the flow, in the space of becoming and evolving in the moment. Think of this activity as: "I am the experiencing being who is exploring how I wish to show up in the world and express myself. Opening myself to the exploration helps me to honor and hold myself accountable to what I say is true for me. I show up in the world with the willingness and courage to unearth myself. And, in this place, at this time, I breathe into the adventure."

EXERCISE:

What is your core essence? Brainstorm a list of qualities that resonate in your head, heart and body as aspects of your true core essence. Allow the list to be as big and comprehensive as you can make it. Below is some of the list that shows up for many people, but please do not feel limited or directed by it. Only use it as a jumping off place for your own exploration.

Essence Qualities and Traits:

Creative	Connector	Passionate
Joyful	Loving	Dreamer
Courageous	Evolving	Thoughtful
Borderless	Allowing	Open
Inquisitive	Intuitive	Challenger
Adventurer	Whimsical	Free-Spirited
Flexible	Conscious	Curious
Kinetic	Whole	Unique
Bold	Transformative	Tribe of Funny
Limitless	Boundless	Explorer
Provocateur	Willing to Leap	Brave
Add your own words:		

This exercise sheet came out of the inviteCHANGE class I was in. It simplified capturing the words and exploring the idea of essence. As you develop your list with your own words, notice which words most resonate for you. When you say different words, what do you notice in your core? How does your heart open or close to each word you've chosen?

Janet Harvey, whom I have great respect for, said to me, "Essence is also a vibration we recognize without words, a physical and emotional felt experience for which words come later. The journey of self-actualization is a process of stripping away the learned personality descriptors in favor of what you describe as the heart's knowing that is beyond time and space."

Sometimes clients ask me, "Am I, at all times, the embodiment of these essences?" I say, "Yes, but sometimes our ego gets in the way, trying to please our superego, which is judging us with our, 'I am not enough' stories." The judgments and fears stir up all manner of nonsense that can lead you to forget that you are a spiritual being having a human experience. If you decide to acknowledge your truest self, it will ground you in what is authentic about your inner knowing, supporting you to remember your truth regardless of the situations and dramas you might find yourself lost within. We are, each of us, ships upon a very turbulent sea and our insight into our essence gives us the tool to hang onto so we can continue moving forward, letting go of fear and deciding what course we wish to follow.

In what ways will you explore these essences and claim them? How will you hold onto them inside of yourself so that you can ride upon the swells and waves that life brings to you? And how will you change your intrinsic responses to the external expression that we call reality?

EXERCISE:

Choose 10 to 20 of your essence words and sit with them. How do these words feel inside of you? Give yourself permission to play with the words and find the expression that resonates in your body. Remember this is your soul or spirit song.

Fill in the blank: *I am:*

_____

_____

_____

_____

Example: I am transcendent conscious bliss. I am laughing spirit energy. I am creative, fluid and free. I am the moment and the observer of the moment. I am a courageous explorer. I am star dust. I am the star. I am love. I am boundless energy flowing into and throughout all things, connected and whole. I am a unique spirit. I am a human being.

Your essence is your soul's song. Be as creative as you want. Allow the words to sing to you. What is the song of your deep spiritual essence? Who are you below the façade of your body, your beliefs and your experiences? Who is the you that exists for all time?

It's important to remember that different words carry different energy. Tones of voice are energetic also. So how we say what we say and what we actually say, all touches us on an energetic level. We are energetic beings who can't help but react and respond to the energy around us. Have you ever had someone yell at you? Have you ever yelled at someone? How does your body feel afterward? If we use words like bad, angry, blaming, or hate, they carry certain meanings, but more importantly, they carry energy. If we use words like loving, curious, or compassionate, those words also carry energy. Take a moment to say these words. Play with your tone. When you say the different words, what do you notice in your body? Do you notice certain words tighten your body, maybe in your chest or throat? Which words calm or relax you, or make you notice your heart expanding and opening up?

One day, I sent a client home with this exercise as a way for her to explore her essence since her goal in our work was to reconnect to herself. When we met a few weeks later, I asked, "What came up as you played with this exercise?" "I didn't try," she replied. "Really?" I said. "Would it be useful to get curious about why?" She said, "Sure, but when I looked at those words, none of them fit how I think about myself." I asked her whether she would be willing to do a guided visualization to find words that did resonate for her. She agreed, so we did a Spiral Technique visualization and worked on opening, then closing, then again opening and closing her heart. With her heart in the open mode, I asked her to allow her heart to speak the words it felt were true about her essence. Words started bursting to the surface—words like tenacious, loving, passionate, connected to God, humble, caring, funny, generous, etc. Once the words slowed down, I read them back to her, asking her what she had noticed. Her first response was, "My head is not sure about this, but my heart feels amazing." I laughed and said, "Your head is not invited yet, but I'd be curious what your heart would say about this list." Her response was, "I have a pretty awesome essence." In her words, it was easy to see that how she thought about herself had shifted.

So, finding the words that express your soul, spirit, or energy is important. Just as in this example, the words give you a starting place, like a foundation on a life you're building. They will help guide you into finding the pathway to express these deeper aspects of your authentic self with the world. The expressions of gratitude, compassion and joy can be authentically expressed by each one of us. The more clarity you have about your essence, the easier it will be for you to find ways you can bring that energy forward and manifest it in the world. Being clear about your essence is one of the paths to conscious awakening, and after all, that's what the world needs more of—people who have come alive and woken up.

EXERCISE:

What resonated for you in this section? It could be a positive or negative feeling. What are you noticing?

_____

_____

_____

_____

_____

_____

_____

Is there even a small part of the section that you could relate to?

_____

_____

_____

_____

_____

_____

Looking inside yourself, what is a story you need to unwrap?

_____

_____

_____

_____

_____

Going back to your strengths, how might you use your strengths to live in alignment with your core essence?

_____

_____

_____

_____

_____

_____

SECTION II
You Are Capable

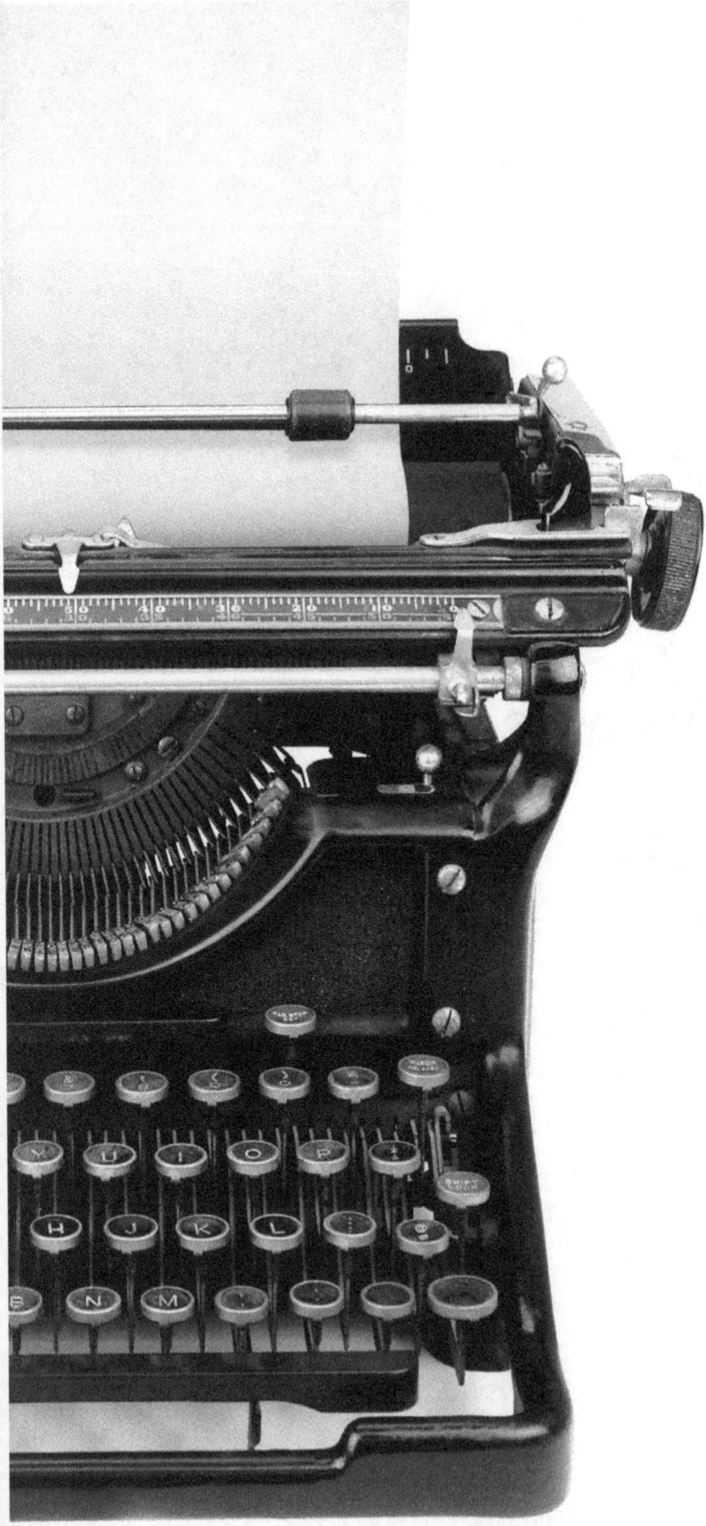

I 2

YOUR MIND DOESN'T KNOW THE DIFFERENCE

"Recent brain scans have shed light on how the brain simulates the future."

— *Michio Kaku*

How you think about your own ability will define what you can do. In this section, I want to explore ideas that can illuminate just how capable you are. You are your very best opportunity to change the story of your life—to gain the understanding and insights that will give you the tools to manifest a rewrite on the ending. One way you can rewrite that ending is by visualizing how you want your life to be. Visualization is a powerful tool—athletes use it to improve their games, and the military uses it to train soldiers. Is it possible, then, that there are some powerful tools available to you by using only your mind? Is it possible that the brain doesn't know the difference between doing an activity and visualizing an activity? Could you get the same benefits, or close to the same benefits, only using your mind to make significant changes?

I love to watch the Olympics. While watching the 2010 Winter Olympics, I made a fascinating connection about visualization. I was watching a lot of downhill skiing. Color me a fan of American Lindsey Vonn. I was struck by what she did before she made her runs. She would stand at the top of the course going through the motions of the event. She wasn't alone. I saw many of the athletes standing at the top of their courses, moving their arms around, eyes closed, leaning into, bending knees, shifting their balance, as they visualized what they were about to do. I was so mesmerized that I started talking to all my clients about the power of visualization.

I began seeking more information on visualization. A lot of research showed that visualization could help with gaining skills. But there wasn't much research on whether visualization alone could make a difference. The first "evidence" I found was a study from Bishop's University. Erin M. Shackell and Lionel G. Standing conducted a study, the results of which they published as an article titled "Mind Over Matter: Mental Training Increases Physical Strength" in the 2007 edition of *The North American Journal of Psychology*. In the study, they explored whether mental training alone could produce any gain in physical strength. They were trying to find out whether there was any merit to the idea that solely using mental practice could enhance actual performance.

They took thirty male undergraduate students, who were in sports at Bishop's University and asked them to participate in a two-week study. These men were broken into three groups: the control group, the mental training group and the physical training group. All three groups were tested for strength at the beginning and the end of the study, using a hip flexor task.

The control group was initially tested for strength, then asked not to return for two weeks to be tested again.

The mental training group trained for two weeks, with five training sessions of fifteen minutes each week. During the training session, the participant was instructed to visualize himself using the hip flexor machine for four sets of eight reps. Each set was followed by a one-minute rest period. Each day the participant came to do the training, he was asked to imagine that he had increased the lifted weight by five pounds. Each participant was not only visualizing the exercise, but also imagining increasing the weight lifted.

The physical training group trained the same as the mental training group, except that the participants used the hip flexor machine for two weeks, doing the same number of reps and sets and increasing the weight each day.

The results? The control group didn't realize any gains, of course. The physical training group saw a gain of 28.3 percent in strength, which wasn't a surprise. But what blew minds was that the mental training group had a 23.7 percent increase in strength! In other words, they had almost the same increase in strength as the group that physically exercised and they did it with their minds.

THINKING IT CAN MAKE IT SO

In a Harvard study that same year, 2007, researchers Ellen Langer and Alia Crum studied eighty-four female housekeepers from seven hotels in the Boston area. The study explored mindset. To begin, the researchers assessed each of the women's health. The underlying premise was based on the surgeon general's recommendation that you need thirty minutes of daily exercise to maintain a healthy lifestyle. The researchers were curious what would happen if you changed the person's perception of what she was doing from work to exercise.

On average, each of the women in the study cleaned fifteen rooms per day, taking about twenty to thirty minutes per room. The study surmised that the housekeepers might not perceive their jobs as exercise, but if that perception were shifted, they might experience health improvements.

Very simply, women in four hotels were told that their regular work was enough exercise to meet the requirements for a healthy, active lifestyle. Women from the other three hotels were told nothing. Four weeks later, the researchers returned and reassessed the women's health. What they found was that the women who had been in the informed group had lost an average of two pounds, lowered their blood pressure by almost 10 percent and were significantly healthier as measured by body-fat percentage, body mass index and waist-to-hip ratio. These changes were significantly higher than those reported in the control group and were especially remarkable given the time period of only four weeks. Mindset matters.

AND ONE MORE THING...

If the two studies above aren't interesting or compelling enough, let me just toss this one in your lap. In a 1996 Harvard study, neuroscientist Dr. Alvaro Pascual-Leone and his band of merry helpers created a simple little experiment using volunteers and a little five-finger piano exercise. The volunteers were divided into two groups. Each group began with having the cortex region of his or her brain mapped using a transcranial magnetic stimulator (TMS). One group was instructed to play the simple five-finger piano keys as fluidly as possible. They practiced for two hours every day for five days and at the end of each day, they took a test. The test consisted of twenty repetitions of the five-finger exercise. It was notable but expected that after practicing so much, the students improved. They became more fluid, faster, more accurate, etc. Then after the final day and the final test, the good doctor, using TMS, sent a brief magnetic pulse to the motor cortex of the participants' brains and measured and mapped the motor cortex region responsible for managing the finger controls to see whether any changes had occurred. A significant increase was found in the size of the cortical representation devoted to the finger movements. Their brain region was growing with the practice. As the brain did the new activity, it increased the area devoted to the skill. Okay, that's cool, right?

But here is where it gets even cooler. The second group of volunteers only *imagined* practicing the piano exercise. They imagined the practice and they imagined the test and guess what? When Dr. Alvaro took out the TMS and measured the same region of the motor cortex, that region also expanded for these volunteers. The region of the motor cortex that controlled those prancing fingers playing the ivories grew, regardless of whether the person was doing the action or just imagining it. In fact, it was noted that "mental practice alone may be sufficient to promote the plastic modulation of neural circuits placing the subjects at an advantage for faster skill learning with minimal physical practice, presumably by making the reinforcement of existing connections easier and perhaps speeding up the process." Now that is a mind blower. What does this mean for you? Well, I think it means that you can truly change your brain, change structures, create new neural networks and StoryJack your stories, moving past your past. It happens in your mind, to your mind and thinking makes it so.

Here is a picture of the changes over five days:

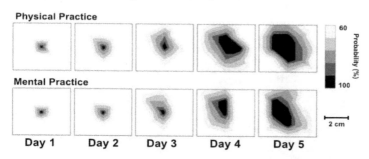

Pascual-Leone, A. et al. (2005). "The Plastic Human Brain Cortex." *Annual Review of Neuroscience.* p. 381.

All of these studies represent fascinating documentations of change. Each of them has important points to make. And each requires something to help with the change. The two main points we might take away here are that if we employ a) mental practice and b) mindset, we can create significant changes. I am going to make an educated guess here. What if you did both, employed mental practice and shifted mindset? I believe how you think—the very structures of your brain and body—could change.

When you think about your situation, what might you start to practice that would help you shift your mindset? Perhaps you could practice meditation, journaling about your true essence, writing your goals daily, or creating a gratitude list, where you notice three things that you are grateful for each day. Look for gratitude in things you didn't create yourself. For example: I am grateful for the beautiful sunrise. I am grateful for the hummingbirds in my window. I am grateful that my mom shared a funny story with me. Each of these activities can change your brain. It's up to you, but it's clear that you can choose a different path. You can develop new habits to practice and challenge your mindset and you can jack your stories. Doing the work and visualizing yourself doing the work will support your long-term goals for change.

I 3
A CASE FOR VISUALIZATION

"You must give everything to make your life as beautiful as the dreams that dance in your imagination."

— *Roman Payne*

I was working with a young man in the Air Force whom I will call John. Like many of my anger management clients, John was required to come to my class. He had gotten into a verbal argument with his first sergeant over a duty issue, then compounded that act of genius by screaming at another military member on the road, who happened to work for the base commander. You could almost say John was screaming for help. Yet, he didn't come willingly into my class, either by choice or attitude.

One tool we used in class was relaxation visualizations. As you now know, visualization gives people the opportunity to practice new behaviors, but a calming visualization can also give you access to a space in your head that you can use to calm down. John made his entrance to the class on a visualization day. He was quite critical from the beginning, basically saying, "This is stupid. Do I have to do this?" Fortunately, John wasn't my first critic. I smiled, laughing on the inside and said, "Yep, you're screwed, let's visualize."

The visualization began with a simple 4/8 beat breathing exercise. On the in breath, you breathe in at a count of four, then slow your exhale breath and exhale at a count of eight. We shifted our breathing to a relaxed breath, one where you bring your attention to your body. You notice your feet and calves, tighten the muscles, then relax, then tighten, then relax. You notice your thighs and repeat the tightening and relaxing. Then you continue through your other muscle groups—your stomach, shoulders, neck, arms and fists. This is a very relaxing technique and tends to help you be in the right mindset for the calm place visualization.

I then walked us through the calm place visualization. It begins by visualizing a space, room, or environment, in which you feel completely safe. I asked the men to, "Breathe into this space for about ten breaths. What do you notice when you look around the space in your head? Explore and develop your vision of the space. Is it by a stream, on a beach, in the kitchen at the house your grandma lived in? What else do you notice? Is there a breeze? What sounds do you hear? What colors do you notice? Do you smell anything? Continue breathing slowly, developing the details of the space and allow your body to be completely relaxed." At about the twenty-minute mark, I asked the men to imagine anger as an object. "Let yourself give it a shape and color," Then I asked, "Does it have a texture? What size is your anger? When you have a good strong image of what your anger looks like, let it expand, then shrink it back down, then grow it larger again, letting it grow bigger than it was when you first visualized it. Then shrink your anger back down to the size of a marble. Then grow it again and then shrink it down, ending with you holding your anger in the palm of your hand. Then set your anger in a container, knowing that it's available when you need it and appreciating it for being there to keep you safe. After your anger is safely tucked in, bring your attention back to your breathing and when you are ready, allow yourself to come back into the classroom, doing a body scan. Notice any place in your body that is tight and if you notice any discomfort, breathe into the discomfort and allow yourself to release it. Continue doing this until your body is calm." We sat silently breathing for a while and then I asked them slowly to bring themselves back to our shared room.

There was a lot of yawning and stretching, people were relaxed. We went around the room and everyone shared what he had created. When I turned to John, he smiled and then described his calm space. He saw himself in his truck as he drove down a dirt country road. He had his dirt bike strapped down in the bed of the truck and the sky was blue with big white clouds. He could feel the wind on his face and his arm was resting in the open window. A cloud of dust was rising behind him. When I asked about his anger, he said it started off as a giant grizzly bear, but as we shrank and grew and shrank the anger during the exercise, it ended up being a small palm-sized bear. "So I hung it on my rearview mirror where I can keep an eye on it." We all laughed. It was one of those delightful moments when someone takes a tool and makes it his own.

John stayed with my class for about a year, of his own accord. He practiced the tools, getting curious and being courageous in facing his triggers. Then he moved on. A few years later he sent me an email telling me that he was still using his tools and especially his calm place. He used it every time he felt himself getting mad and it was helping him with his wife and kids. He wrote, "I haven't gotten into any trouble with my anger since I left the class." My heart expanded just a bit more.

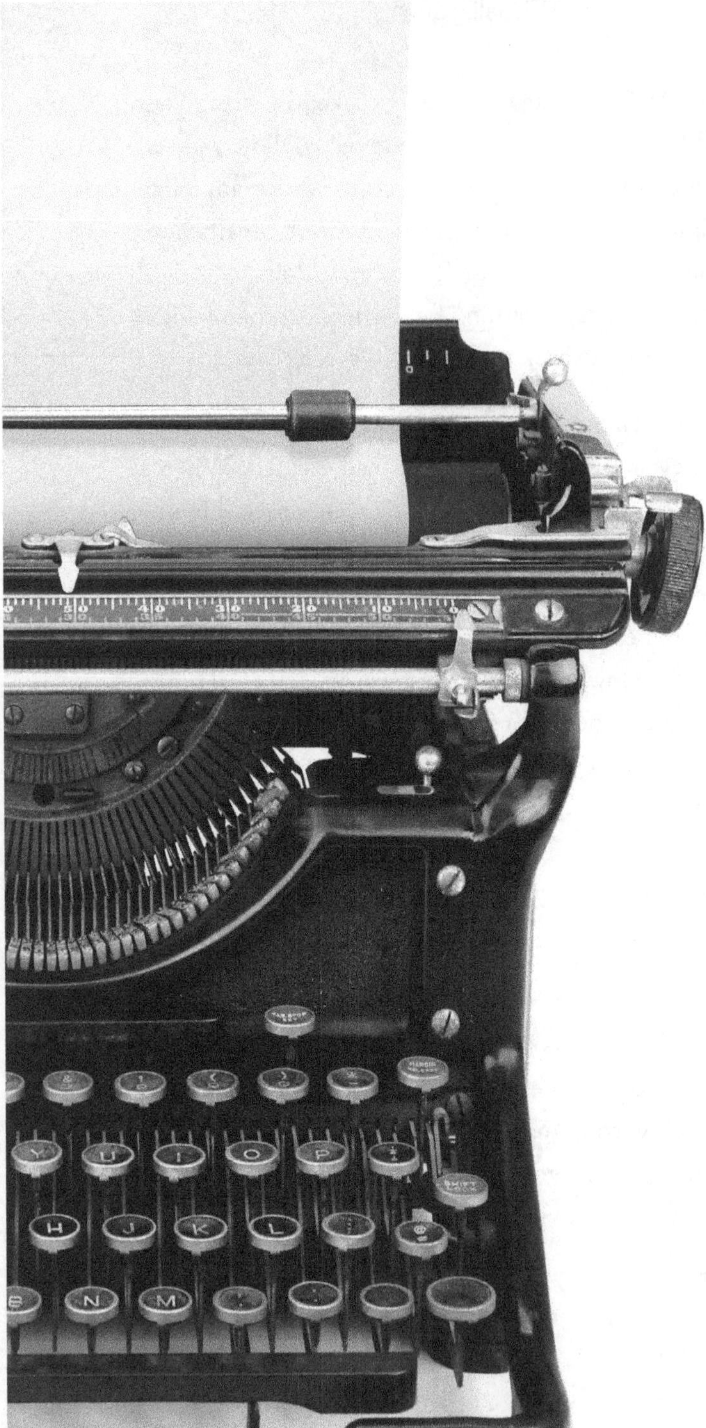

I4
CONSCIOUS CHOICES

"How do you know, right now, that you are aware
of being aware, or conscious?"

— *Henry Reed*

What is the difference between the ideas of conscious and unconscious? In his book *The Untethered Soul*, Michael Singer provides one of the simplest explanations of the difference between the two concepts using the concept of dreams. Let's say that there are two types of dreams: the conscious (often called lucid) and unconscious dream. Singer gives the example that in a lucid dream, if you are flying, you might say to yourself, "Hey, look. I am dreaming and flying in my dream." The point is that you are conscious enough to know you are dreaming. In the unconscious type of dream, you are so immersed inside of the dream that you can't separate yourself from the dream experience and it feels absolutely real.

Let's now apply this perspective to life in general. In much of life, you are situationally conscious. You know when you wake up that you're awake.

You make your breakfast and know that you're eating. As you sit at your desk working, you know you're working. But sometimes when you are driving home, you might remember getting in the car and then be surprised to find yourself at home. There are activities we do where we tune out. Where things can go sideways for you is when, for example, you're unhappy and looking for some outside thing to do or have so you can feel happy again. Well, if the underlying reason you are unhappy is that you aren't feeling connected to your purpose and you're working at a job you hate, then I ask you, "What amount of beer, movies, or fast cars is truly going to make you happy?" Don't get me wrong, those things are fun. But as soon as you're done with the beer, movies, or fast cars, then in the wise words of Buckaroo Bonsai, "No matter where you go, there you are." So when I talk to you about consciousness and awareness, they are concepts about clarity that are bound together.

Remember that super-secret from earlier? *Everything that we human beings do is on a spectrum.* There is a spectrum from unconscious to conscious. I am not saying you must be conscious every moment you're awake. There are many things you do on an unconscious basis that your brain is better at doing without a lot of processing, such as swerving to avoid an oncoming car. In such instances, we want our body to react rather than waste time deciding what to do. But there is an aspect of becoming a whole person and having insight, clarity and conscious awareness where it is very helpful to understand what is triggering you. What feelings are being activated? What beliefs are swirling and how do you feel about yourself as a result? Understanding these qualities is important. Otherwise, you are alive but reacting from an unconscious mind. And that, well, that leads to a lot of unforeseen ramifications that you could be avoiding by being awake.

Unconscious   **Conscious**

Robert Foster Bennett said it well, "Life is the sum result of all the choices you make, both consciously and unconsciously. If you can control the process of choosing, you can take control of all aspects of your life. You can find the freedom that comes from being in charge of yourself." And barring the unconscious choices that keep us alive, it's the unconscious choices that we make, without being fully aware of what we are choosing, that become the sticky widgets in our life stories.

In his book *A Path with Heart,* Jack Kornfield wrote a fable about a tribe in Africa that illustrates the idea of conscious choice. In this tribe, the birth date of a child is not counted from the day of its physical birth nor even its day of conception. For this tribe, the birth date is the first time the child is a thought in its mother's mind. Once aware of her intention to conceive a child with a particular father, the mother goes off to sit alone under a tree. There she sits and listens until she can hear the song of the child she hopes to conceive. Once she has heard it, she returns to her village and teaches it to the father so they can sing it together as they make love, inviting the child to join them. After the child is conceived, she sings it to the baby in her womb. Then she teaches it to the old women and midwives of the village so that throughout the labor and at the miraculous moment of birth itself, the child is greeted with its song. After the birth, all the villagers learn the song of their new member and sing it to the child when it falls or hurts itself. It is sung in times of triumph or in rituals and initiations. This song becomes a part of the marriage ceremony when the child is grown and at the end of life, his or her loved ones will gather around the deathbed and sing this song for the last time.

What I like about this story is it illustrates the connection of mindful intention to the soul. I don't know whether the story is true specifically and I don't know whether many indigenous cultures, including old European cultures, didn't all have a deeper connection to the idea of calling forth a connection to an unborn child or unborn ideas. But I think this story probably resonates because we all have the capacity to be conscious in our desires and choices.

In many ways, this story is aligned with the idea of finding our core essence—calling forth the song of ourselves. Creating the words, ideas and images that reflect the vision of who we want to become. I love the idea of writing my own song—of consciously StoryJacking myself through a thorough exploration of who I am, who I am becoming and what parts of me I need to support to see me through. As you develop a vision of yourself, intentionally instead of accidentally, you are empowered to believe that you are whole, capable, resourceful and creative. This empowerment allows you to connect with your purpose, connect to others, to the world and live a life of meaning.

15
CURIOUSER AND CURIOUSER

"Curiouser and curiouser!" cried Alice (she was so much surprised, that
for the moment she quite forgot how to speak good English)."

— Lewis Carroll

What does it mean to get curious? I love this question! It's like a riddle and its answer all rolled into one. Being curious is exactly that—asking questions. It also involves letting go of knowing the answer. When you are in the mental state of being an expert and knowing, learning doesn't come so easily. When you are curious in the sense that you are open and exploring, you are using your learning mind. Your "knowing mind" is the obstacle to curiosity. You cannot be in the two minds, of curiosity and knowing, at the same time. Knowing something implies you have already decided. There is a type of curiosity, where you are sure you know something, but that is not real curiosity. It's what I call "digging for ammo."

Curiosity comes in a few forms. There is the sort of curiosity that looks a lot like meddling and then there is the sort that looks like developing insights. In StoryJacking, the curiosity is about yourself—the way you think, feel, react, what you want and what is getting in your way of having what you want. It's a completely internal form of curiosity. Can you even be noisy about yourself? What does that even mean? Lyssa was so intrusive, meddlesome and interfering with her own mind that everyone got mad? That's ridiculous, right?

Yet our culture is filled with the negative version of curiosity. Just look at *Aesop's Fables*. It's filled with stories of curiosity leading to danger. Curiosity killed the cat, or the fox and the hare for instance. Mr. Hare's curiosity about Mr. Fox leads him to ask Mr. Fox many questions about his who's and what's, leading Mr. Fox to invite Mr. Hare to dinner so he can truly express his nature. A similar story is The Baby Big Mouth Frog. I loved this one as a kid, so excuse my child voice showing up to share it with you. Imagine a six-year-old telling this story, opening her mouth as wide as she can when the baby big mouth frog is talking. I'll wait…got it in your mind now?

The Baby Big Mouth Frog

Once upon a time, there was a baby big mouth frog. He was on an adventure to explore the world and learn what other creatures might exist. As he hopped along the road, he came across a rabbit. [See my big open mouth talking? It starts here.] "Hello there. I'm a baby big mouth frog, what are you?" "I am a rabbit," said the rabbit. The baby big mouth frog asked, "What do you eat?" The rabbit said, "I eat lettuce and carrots and anything that people love to grow in their veggie gardens." The rabbit and the frog talked a while longer; then the baby big mouth frog ended with, "Well, it was nice to meet you." And off the baby big mouth frog hopped. Next, he came to a cow. As the baby big mouth frog hopped up to the cow, he said, "Hello there. I'm a baby big mouth frog, what are you?" "I am a cow," said the cow. The frog inquired, "What do you eat?" and the cow lazily responded, "I eat grass, clover and sometimes, dandelions." The cow and the frog talked a while longer until the baby big mouth frog was ready to hop on and then he said, "Well, it was nice to meet you." So, this went on for a while and the baby big mouth frog met a cat, a spider, a turtle and a fish. Then the baby big mouth frog hopped up to a crocodile and happily exclaimed, "Hello there. I am a baby big mouth frog, what are you?" The crocodile responded with his gravelly voice, "I am a crocodile." The baby big mouth frog again asked, "What do you eat?" As a lazy smile crossed the crocodile's face, his teeth twinkling in the sun, he said, "I eat baby big mouth frogs." Suddenly, understanding dawned on our little intrepid baby big mouth frog. Then the baby big mouth frog made the tiniest mouth and voice he possibly could make and said, "Oh, really? I don't know any of those..." And he quickly hopped away.

I loved this tale as a kid because it's funny to a six-year-old, though I still laugh at it today. But it also allows the baby big mouth frog to be curious and to change his relationship to his story and make a sensible decision at the end.

These fables illustrate the type of curiosity that is a bit more intrusive. Remember that when you are listening to stories, there is a difference between interesting and important. When you get curious about someone else's story, it can fall into the interesting category if you aren't careful, spiraling into gossip. It's been said that if you poke the fire enough, it will eventually spark. But what if you are looking at yourself? What if you turn that bright light of questioning, searching, inquiring, interest, speculation and personal curiosity, toward your own mind and your own stories? Well, that passes interesting and catapults us into important. Once you develop your awareness of yourself, understanding your beliefs, biases, where you are wonderful and where you have work to do—once you reach that level of clarity, what then might be possible?

SPINNING OR WALLOWING

Okay, who among us has never wallowed? Or spun out about an issue or situation? During every political election, roughly half the country is euphoric and the other half is wheezing about how terrible, awful and rotten the situation is. No one is immune from the seesaw of emotional responses until you start to notice what you're doing. You get so attached to your idea of what's right that when you don't win, it can be overwhelming and frustrating.

I admit I have spent my share of time spinning and wallowing. All those presidential elections where my candidate didn't win—how frustrated I was. And I know I have excessively spun out on a few issues in my life. It's worth noticing where you got hooked that resulted in your excessively spinning around a topic. It's often attached to a negative bent. We don't like something, so we obsessively spin around it. When you spin or wallow, you typically aren't in the spin for solutions. You tend to be in the spin for the "why." Why did such and such happen? Why are people so stupid, or haters, or unenlightened? Why aren't they more like me? Why, why, why?

Right after the 2016 election when Donald Trump was elected as our next president, a lot of people got on Facebook and told people who had voted for him to unfriend them. People were that upset. Right after seeing one of my friends write that very thing on his FB feed, I happened to read an interesting article written by a young woman. She wrote that people shouldn't unfriend her if they voted for Donald Trump or a third party, but rather keep being her friend on Facebook so when she lost all her medical rights and was poor, ill, hopeless and then killed herself, it would show up on their feed so they could know it was all their fault.

I was struck by the level of emotional blackmail and manipulation she wove into her narrative. Remember, it took time and energy to write the article. It takes focused energy to hold on to that level of fear and anger. Just how different might her life be if she focused instead on what she could do to move forward and take care of herself?

I am not saying you don't have the right to be upset when your candidate loses an election. Grieve as you need to. Then get involved in supporting the ideas and the community action around the issues for which you are passionate. If you think social justice, the environment, Women's Rights, or Medicare and Social Security are important, then get busy and activate yourself. Find a march or a community Town Hall and get involved. I think we are often looking for a savior so we can live in our bubbles and not have to take our own time to change our own world. I think it's time to take responsibility and learn how to save ourselves. Personally, I like the idea of turning my energy toward something I believe in. Versus spinning it in circles doing nothing with my energy except being upset. Take the time you need to orient to this moment and then find a path to move forward, in a direction that supports your vision, your essence and your pathway and that allows you to become the person you've been waiting for. No one is coming to save anyone, so save yourself and help the world as you become what you believe the world needs. Put your energy into the work of creating what you believe is important to help the world.

From an outside perspective, it's easy to recognize the young woman in the above story is embracing the victim story. If you voted for Trump, you might think this young woman is overly dramatic. Then I ask you to think back to when Obama won and you lost your shit and started spinning yourself. In either situation, you are focusing on the events happening outside of you—your external locus of control, which I will be talking more about in chapter 26. Basically, you are trying to figure out how to make reality fit your side of an experience and the more painful or difficult the situation, the more deeply embedded in the spin or wallowing you might find yourself.

To be fair, I'm not saying you might not be right and justified about being unhappy over a situation, the outcome of an election, or anything that has happened to you. But if your focus is on a past you can't change, how is that helpful? I don't have the keys to Mr. Peabody's Way Way Back Machine, and I am guessing that you don't either. There is no way I know of to go back in time and make a past situation different. So, to be clear, if you're wallowing or spinning, you're not experiencing curiosity. Wallowing and spinning will exhaust you and offer very little in the manner of a way forward. It can hold you hostage, leave you caught in the gravitational pull of the drama, hijack your brain and keep you from moving forward, let alone envisioning a different story. Interestingly, you may have to hijack yourself from your own mind. Get completely honest with yourself. Be conscious of what you're doing so you can pull yourself out of the spin and up a mountain. Stand in a new spot, with a new vantage point, so you can gain some perspective and clarity about what got triggered inside of you that set you spinning in the first place.

16
THE BEST KIND OF CURIOUS

"Let go of certainty. The opposite isn't uncertainty. It's openness, curiosity and a willingness to embrace paradox, rather than choose up sides. The ultimate challenge is to accept ourselves exactly as we are, but never stop trying to learn and grow."

— *Tony Schwartz*

Human beings have a fluidity of self that is greater than most of us realize. What this means is you have the potential to be anything or anyone you want. I was once in an acting class taught by the actress Barbara Deering. She said something that nailed me between the eyes, "We all carry within ourselves the DNA of every possible story, of every possible role, that can or has ever been imagined." That idea stuck with me and I thought about it for weeks. I don't like the idea that I am capable of being a "bad" person, a cruel one, a murderer, or a racist. I am sure you don't like that idea either. Like most people, I want to be seen as a "good" person, empathetic, compassionate and filled with grace. We put a lot of judgments on words, good and bad. Thus, we often try to avoid one, while presenting the other. Ultimately, our potential to become one thing or another stems from how we choose and manifest our beliefs, choices, focus and especially which of our stories we decide to explore, challenge, choose, or change.

An old folk tale I've often heard called "The Two Wolves" serves as a good metaphor for this concept.

THE TWO WOLVES

The old grandfather was spending time with his grandson. They were sitting and watching people walk by, busy with the doings of life. Then there was a squabble and two people began arguing and fighting. The grandson turned to his grandfather and asked, "Why do people argue and fight, hate instead of love?" The grandfather decided it was time to talk to his grandson about the shadow side and the light side of the human spirit. "Within each of us we have two wolves that are in a constant struggle," he said. "One is the wolf of fear, greed and anger. It hates and judges and it wants to draw you into the dark parts of yourself. The other wolf is the wolf of love, compassion and fearlessness. It wants to draw you into the light parts of yourself. And, in each of us, depending on events, these two wolves can find themselves fighting and at war with each other." The grandson took a bit of time to think about this idea. Then he asked, "Grandfather, if the wolves inside ourselves are fighting, which wolf will win?" The grandfather touched his grandson's head gently and said, "Whichever one you decide to feed."

We all have within us the dark as well as the light. Developing the courage to be honest about both aspects, gives us the power to choose the wolf we feed.

Inquiry and creative curiosity is about starting to explore the stories you have attached to yourself. Being willing to look at your thoughts, ideas about life, limiting beliefs and biases takes real courage. It would be lovely if you could just sit with your good qualities and leave it at that. But none of us can fully grow or know ourselves if we only look to the qualities we like. So, with honest compassion, I tell you that getting curious requires internal courage and a level of boldness, daring and undaunted moxie for you to muddle through the tough parts and come out on the other side with new insights and skills.

I often talk with a client about his or her internal structure. I liken it to the internal scaffolding needed in a tall building. Without the internal structure, any significant wind that comes through has the possibility of blowing the building over. Yet if you are in a tall building in a windstorm, you know there is also a need for flexibility. Your internal structure needs to allow for you to bend and flex so you don't break. The people who struggle the hardest and suffer the most in the change process are the ones who have rigid ideas and beliefs they are so attached to that they are unwilling to get curious about new ways of thinking, feeling, or being in the world. Without the willingness to look at yourself, how will you decide which ideas and thoughts still work and which ones it's time to let go of?

One of the clearest examples of the sort of rigid thinking that will break you is the idea of perfection. There is probably no faster way to stop yourself or beat yourself up than to strive for perfection—because perfection is perfect. Not many people can manage to live in a state of perfection for more than a few minutes—maybe an hour if no one bothers you. Perfect is an unrealistic expectation to have for ourselves or others. I was chatting with a client recently about why she wasn't doing some of the work we had been exploring when this word popped up. "If I define my essence, then I will be forced to live as a perfect person for the rest of my life. That's scary." Okay, well yes, that is scary. Doesn't that idea terrify you? To try to live your life per some idea of perfection and never being allowed to make a mistake. For me, it's scary and exhausting. As we continued to discuss what she meant by perfection, she gave this definition, "Perfection is the satisfaction of completing a task. There may be bumps in the road, errors along the way, but it is completed. There is satisfaction that I succeeded in putting in 100 percent effort." We just looked at each other. Then she stated, "Maybe I need to change my words to something like goal-driven, determined, or committed." We laughed then. In about thirty minutes, she had moved from a rigid, scary and unattainable idea of perfection. One that was stopping her from developing her internal awareness. Shifting into something she already did, which was create a goal, commit to it, take action and, regardless of the bumps along the way, cross the finish line. I asked her what opened up for her with this exploration. "Well, it's a lot more doable now." We then started to brainstorm ideas that would support her in continuing to get curious about herself in a healthy way.

If your stories are keeping you stuck, how can you become creative in your exploration? Look at what might be possible in your family, your community, your relationships and your businesses. Creativity and innovation come from a willingness to be explorers, creatively developing new ways to solve old problems. Many of us come into adulthood with a long list of old stories, old habits and old problems. It will take all your desire, courage and curiosity to explore these old ways of being and ultimately choose the ones that will lead you toward a new ending.

This type of curiosity—creative inquiry—is a way of encouraging your willingness to get inquisitive, to put on your Sherlock Holmes hat and investigate yourself. Personal growth and self-mastery are at the core—a thirst for understanding that can only be quenched by eager and open-minded exploration. When you think about turning the focus of this curiosity toward yourself, it is an expression of willingness to open the closet of your mind, explore the boogeymen living in the shadows, own your baggage and check the fit and feel of the outfits of ideas you have hanging in the dark. It also requires a willingness to start with yourself first, letting go of the idea that your job is to fix other people, rather than growing anyone other than yourself. The mission, should you accept it, is to take full ownership and responsibility for the person you are, gain clarity about the person you are working on becoming and explore everything you toss up like glitter to distract yourself with and that keeps you from the goals and dreams you say are important to you. You are the only person you need to shift into the leadership role of your life.

EXPLORATION AND INSIGHT

As we explore who we are, if we allow ourselves to observe without judgment, we can make insightful connections. We may look at the past, but the purpose is completely different. I have found there are two reasons to look at most events in the past: a) to learn from them, or b) to let them go.

Science is showing us that our memories, the very things we hold sacred as we generate our life stories, are mostly our fictionalized versions of reality. In a study in the department of Neuroscience at Northwestern University in Chicago, Joel Voss, Ph.D. and Donna Bridge, Ph.D. are discovering that when we pull up a memory, we can easily overwrite it. That the contents of our memories can be updated with information from our current experiences, in fact, just by having someone give us new information, even incorrect information, changes our memories. Our memories are not perfect and we waste time when we get into memory-matching arguments with people. None of us remember with complete clarity or absolute correctness and each time we bring up a past event, how we think about it, the focus we spin it with, changes our perception of the memory. We are basically rewriting memories all the time. Wouldn't it be important to rewrite our memories in a manner that helps us move forward? Here is your opportunity to choose wisely.

When we are in the mindset of insight curiosity, we are more interested in learning from the situation. What we did and what happened still show up, but we are also exploring how we felt, what was triggered by our emotions, our perceptions, etc. and how we need to take care of ourselves so we can move forward. Insight-based curiosity is all about getting to the 30,000-foot view—getting outside of the emotional spin and into emotional awareness so we can focus forward. The cool thing about distancing our self from the victim role is that we can let go of attachment to right and wrong and instead of looking backward, we start looking forward: How do I create boundaries to take care of myself? What choices could I have made differently? How might I do this differently the next time it shows up?

The sympathetic nervous system is the system in our bodies that connects our head, heart, lungs, stomach and intestines and sends messages throughout the body. Many of our organs play off each other and trigger chemical communication. They can trigger the fight, flight, freeze response, but they can also be trained to calm and attune to our situation. As we begin to invoke the multidimensional knowing that happens when we learn to listen to the sympathetic nervous system, we develop our gut instincts. Our minds are only part of how we assess, understand and make decisions about things. Our brain is connected to our heart, our lungs and our intestinal system. In fact, there are cells in our intestinal system that are identical to cells in our brain. Some scientists even consider the stomach and intestines the first brain. And, at this point, no one is arguing that there is a clear connection between our brain, our heart and our gut. Have you felt your heart tighten? Maybe you've had a gut feeling? Have you ever experienced making a decision that gives you a stomach ache? Or have you noticed when you are feeling stressed that your gut feels off? Maybe you get diarrhea or a stomach ache?

A primal link exists between our heads, hearts and guts. After all, even a fruit fly has a tiny brain, a heart and a stomach. Our "gut brain" has been with us for a very long time—well before our "head brain" formed into the complex structure we work with today. Finding ways to listen to these internal, physical and emotional "feelings" can help you make better decisions. Our gut helps us notice when things are off and recognize places to pay attention. The more we pay attention to our gut sense, the more we will use our senses to make decisions. All this practice leads to stronger trust in yourself.

Are you ready to listen to your head, heart, guts and any other parts of your body that tie into your internal knowing? Curiosity can help you figure out your truth in any situation and it can help you to formulate a plan to take care of yourself. Be it setting a boundary, voicing a concern, sharing an insight, or just moving along. Becoming aware and listening to your whole self is your best source of your own truth. Maybe a third reason to look at the past and your memories is to rewrite them in a manner that aligns with where you want to go.

EXERCISE:

What's your story?

What is the Story?	What were you thinking?	What were you feeling?	What did you do?

What was the outcome?	Did you like the outcome?	Where did you get hooked?	
		Role in the Drama Triangle: Filters: Emotions: Threats: Defenses:	
	How will you StoryJack?		

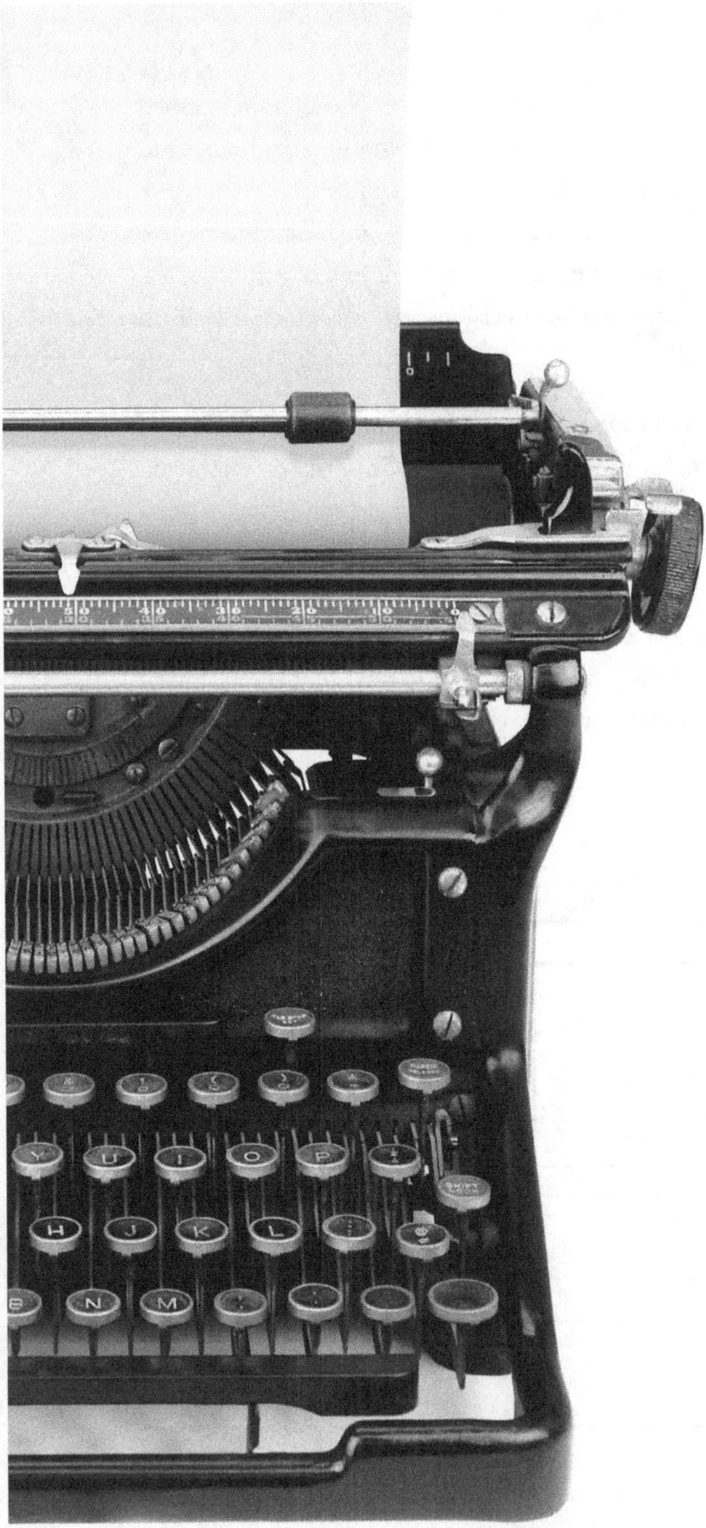

I 7
EXPANDING AWARENESS

"Find out who you are and do it on purpose."

— *Dolly Parton*

Life is about evolving. Nothing stays the same—absolutely nothing. You started off as a baby, helpless, only able to flap your arms and legs in the air. To begin with, you didn't even know what arms or legs were, or that they were attached to the body that your soul landed in. And you were a striver. You wobbled back and forth until you could turn over. Then you pushed yourself forward, learning to crawl, then to walk, then to run and skip. You listened to your parents read to you, excitedly interjecting and wanting to read yourself, knowing that words had power to illuminate, to communicate and to explore. As you grew you learned to read. Maybe you took a toaster apart. You were constantly on a mission to understand more. Curiosity is truly the thing that sets us apart from other species on the planet. No other species has been quite so radically curious. From that curiosity can come, hopefully, awareness.

Now I know I told you a bit ago that everything you say and think is a story and that is still true. Some stories just come with more information—more data points, if you will—that fill out more angles and facets of the story. It's the same with all your stories. Yes, they are all made up, but some are made up with a lot more data points. Like a diamond that has been cut, the facets still must be polished in order to sparkle, and so it is with your internal stories. You must spend the time to polish them so you can sparkle. And the extra clarity that data points give, give some stories an edge. They become a little closer to resonating with a bigger idea of reality. Many years ago, I was watching Dr. Daniel Amen on PBS. He asked two questions about our negative beliefs (i.e., stories). I have adapted them a touch. The first question to ask when you notice a story you're telling yourself is, "Do I know this story to be 100 percent true?" The second question is, "What do I know that challenges the story and broadens my perspective?"

I was working with a client, Tom, who hated his job and decided he was going to find a new one. The problem was that his internal dialogue was slowing him down. He would think, "I can do this!" Then he would flip to being plagued by worries about getting another job that paid him at least the same, where he liked the people, etc. The story in a nutshell was this, "I hate my job, but I don't know if I am really good enough at what I do to be valued anywhere else and at least I have a job." If we take only the negative belief, we are left with, "I am not good enough to be valued."

Let's look at how Tom would reply to these two questions:

1. **Do you know this belief to be 100 percent true?** It might feel true, but let's get curious. Do you know it to be 100 percent true? Now 100 percent is absolute. As in completely true. Do you know this belief to be true at that level? "No," Tom would say. "I don't know it to be 100 percent true. Maybe a little true

but not entirely true."

2. **What do you know that challenges the negative story that you're not good enough?** "Well," Tom would say, "I have a job. I get praise at work. My reviews are fine. I have kept up developing and growing my skills and competencies for my job. I take trainings through work and get training on my own. I am good at what I do. I just don't feel appreciated and I don't feel like I have any growth potential."

"Okay, Tom," I then asked. "Now when you think about looking for a new job, what would be a better story to tell yourself?"

"I am not satisfied with my growth opportunities at work," Tom said, "and I am looking for a new challenge to develop my craft. I have many skills and I enjoy learning how to be better at what I do. I also want to know that I am appreciated at my job."

Tom's narrative had changed and was a far different story than the original story he shared with me. If you were to put yourself in his shoes, how would the shift feel for you? For Tom, the shift was empowering. He took this new story with him back to his office. He ended up having a conversation with his boss, was moved to a new area in the company, was given a raise and ended up staying with the organization for a few more years. His energy had shifted from the depressed, anxious, energy of not being enough and afraid that people would see he lacked value. Transformed into recognizing his value and then sharing that truth. Both energetically and through his non-verbal body language, this truth shone through his actions and his eyes, and people responded accordingly.

Let's sum up awareness as the development of insights into why we do the things we do, why we feel the way we do and why we react and respond the way we do. The willingness to get into inquiry with ourselves—so we can bring the unconscious to the conscious level, or as is often the case, take the conscious and challenge the aspects of the stories we tell ourselves—allows us to explore our narrative, assess consequences and make choices we enjoy living with. Going back to the energy that you exude into the world, your energy shows up for many as confidence. People can feel your belief in yourself, and they respond.

It takes a bit of daring and a splash of fearlessness to develop insight awareness about ourselves. It takes fortitude to get honest and look at what part we are playing in whatever story we find ourselves in. Remember, humans tend to follow Freud's "pleasure principle," moving away from pain toward pleasure. I know for myself that looking at my negative self-talk or having a difficult conversation is more emotionally scary than having a glass of wine. And, because this principle is in operation inside of us and helps us to feel superficially better, it's often easier to drink the wine and avoid the conversation and the work. I mean, really, who doesn't enjoy feeling good? Who wants to seek out discomfort? Very few people enjoy all aspects of the growth process. Most of us on the journey are learning to breathe through our discomfort as we explore who we are and why we are that way. I often tell myself and my clients that we need to master the art of rubbing our tummies and re-

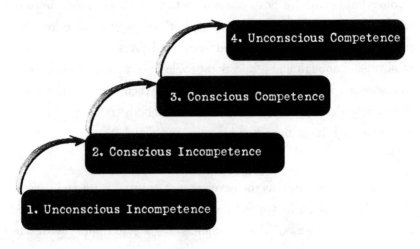

peating, "I'm okay. I'm okay. I'm okay." The prize comes throughout the journey, as we develop mastery over ourselves and gain empowerment in our self-stories.

A concept used by educators in every field is the Four Stages of Learning, or what I call The Learning Journey. This process was developed by Noel Burch in the 1970s. The four steps move in the linear order of 1, 2, 3, 4. As much as we might like to, you can't move from 1 to 4 without taking steps 2 and 3.

Let's look a little closer at how we might use this model.

1. **Unconscious Incompetence:** We do not know what we do not know. In this stage, we may not even be aware that there is something to know or that we are incompetent in the skill.

2. **Conscious Incompetence:** Now we know, but we don't know what to do about it. At this stage, we are at least aware that there is something we are incompetent at doing, but we still may not have the skill set.

3. **Conscious Competence:** Now that we know and have the skill set, we must pay a lot of attention to do the new skill. Most adults bop back and forth between stages 2 and 3. We are aware that something isn't working. Only we may not be clear on "what isn't working" or "how to get it working."

4. **Unconscious Competence:** I know what to do and I do it effortlessly. This is the stage of mastery. We have practiced and learned, questioned and developed to the point that we do what we do unconsciously.

Let's look at this from the perspective of driving a car. When I was a kid, I was driven around all the time. To school, to the store, on errands, to appointments. I was very comfortable in cars. But because I had never driven, I had a superficial understanding of what it meant to drive a car. It seemed easy from the outside. I was very firmly in the Unconscious Incompetent state.

Fast forward to the summer I was fourteen. I had a hardship in my family that required I get an early driver's license. Because my father believed that if I could drive a stick shift, then I would be a "real driver" (notice the story attached to that belief), I was pushed out to the standard transmission vehicle. Okay, seriously, the first time I tried to look in all the mirrors, use the clutch and shift gears, while looking out the front window and keeping my hands on the wheel, I was truly deeply immersed in Conscious Incompetence. I had a full, bright and living color reckoning with reality. Right between my eyes I was hit with: I don't know much about driving.

I kept at it because, well, what else could I do? I mean I guess I could have just quit. My father had dangled keys in front of me, saying, "You can drive this car to school this coming year if you can get your driver's license on the stick." What? I could be a cool kid with a car at fourteen!" Never mind that it was an ugly beater that clashed with my hair…yes, I said that. I could drive my friends to school! I didn't have to take the bus anymore! Freedom! Oh, Sweet Freedom! Okay, I can do this.

I spent a lot and when I say a lot, let me emphasize A LOT, of time practicing. I worked at it, I drove around the block, I drove every time my stepmom needed to go to the store. I generally jumped at every single opportunity to practice. I practiced going slow. I practiced going fast. I practiced going backward. I even practiced parking parallel. Before the summer was over, I went in for my driving test. By the skin of my chinny chin chin, I passed my driver's exam. I had a bit of trouble on the parallel parking. But the rest I could do. I had that driver's license to prove it. I was Consciously Competent.

I drove a lot throughout high school. One of my jobs was driving cars between Austin and Dallas, or Austin and Atlanta and many other places between for car dealers. By the time I was twenty, I had easily put in thousands of driving hours. When I look back on that time, I am not exactly sure at what point I crossed over into Unconscious Competence, but it happened. Today, I feel very comfortable behind the wheel. I easily look in my mirrors. I look ahead and behind without effort or, frankly, much thought. I love driving a stick or an automatic. I can switch back and forth with little or no thought. And all that ease came from practicing until it was effortless.

EXERCISE:

What example can you think of from your own life where you transitioned through the Learning Journey?

_____

_____

_____

_____

_____

_____

_____

What did you need to do to move through the levels?

_____

_____

_____

_____

_____

What are the places that you struggled?

_____

_____

_____

_____

What kept you moving forward?

_____

_____

_____

_____

_____

_____

_____

18

JOHARI'S WINDOW

"When I discover who I am, I'll be free."

— *Ralph Ellison*

The JoHari Window was something I learned about in Psychology 101.
It was created by Joseph Luft and Harrington Ingham in 1955. I believe
the window's simplicity is helpful for understanding ourselves.

1. wide open	3. blind spot
We know & others know The us we share with the world	**We don't know & others know** The aspects of us that we are unaware of and that other people notice
2. mask	4. dark closet
We know & others don't know The us we keep hidden from the world	**We don't know & others don't know** The aspects of us that are deeply hidden

We all have this window and we have these quadrants that show up in different areas of our lives. The window isn't good or bad. It shows you places you are going to have to look at as you explore yourself, investigating your self-awareness.

In the first quadrant is the wide-open place where you share who you are and other people see who you are. Here are your open aspects where you and the people you interact with are all on the same page. For example, Lyssa knows she is a red-headed Irish Leo. She gets mad sometimes and everyone else sees that Lyssa is a red-headed Irish Leo and she gets mad sometimes. Open and transparent. I am not fooling myself or anyone else.

The second quadrant is what I like to call the mask. This is the face or persona that we put on for people or situations. On the outside, I may look happy, in charge and confident, but maybe on the inside I have giant birds flying around my stomach. I remember giving a talk at an event about relationships to a group of about seventy-five people. Before the talk, my stomach was rumbling with all sorts of butterflies, my mouth was dry and I was stress sweating. After the event, another speaker came up and told me how nervous she was and asked how I kept from being nervous…. Well, I don't keep from being nervous. I just don't show my nervous face to the audience. Classic case of what I know and what others don't.

The third quadrant is your blind spot. This quadrant exposes a place where you may not have the same sense of yourself as others do. You may get indicators of this quadrant when someone tells you something about yourself that on some deep level rings true, but you haven't paid much attention to it. It also may be a behavior, attitude, or bias that you have, but you have disowned it because you're not happy with that aspect being a part of you. Let's say someone tells you something about yourself that you don't recognize and it triggers a strong reaction in you.

For example, Lyssa believes that she is a happy, kind and compassionate person. Even when she has some perspective to share, she works hard to bring the concepts of truth, kindness and necessity to the conversation. Her best friend Michele told her during a drive to a party that she was bossy. "What?" Lyssa replied, "I am not bossy! I am just sharing a perspective on the route we're taking. We could get to the party so much faster if you took the exit I just pointed to!" Yep, "Bossy." Great.... Now I can add, "Lyssa is a red-headed Irish Leo, and she is getting mad." "I'm not mad! You're making me mad by telling me this!" Okay, maybe I need to look here. This level of emotional response, either internal or external, is an indicator that something is going on in the blind spot.

There are times when someone tells you something about yourself that doesn't resonate at all with your sense of self. I am not asking you just to assume that one person telling you something about yourself is enough information to go on. You need more data points here too. So consider the source. If the source of feedback is someone who doesn't like you or is mad at you, that person may be sharing his or her perception, and it may be just that—their perception. Don't discount the feedback out of hand either. Find the middle ground, the path between the extremes of "Okay, absolutely you are reading me correctly," and the opposite extreme of "You don't know what the bloody hell you're talking about! You're a jealous meanie." I find it super-helpful to have a few people whom I trust implicitly and who know me well, whom I can bounce any perceptions off of to get a broader frame of reference. If one person tells me I am Miss Bossy Pants, but five say they haven't experienced me in that way, I may question whether this is my issue or not. Here is another of the super-secrets of the universe: *Anyone can say anything they want, so it's my job to interpret the truth of it in a meaningful way for myself.* And once I hear something, I am going to pay attention to my behaviors to see whether and how it shows up.

I had a good friend at one point in my life who got married and disappeared. I kept trying to set up a couple's date, with her and her husband, for dinner. Initially, she was vague about when we could meet. Finally, we agreed on a date and time. When evening came, Michael and I were left sitting in a restaurant eating dinner alone, on what turned into a different kind of "couple date." I was hurt and I bottled my feelings up for a while, trying to figure out what to do. I finally said to her, "Look, I thought we were going to meet up for dinner. Michael and I waited for you at the time and place I thought we had agreed on. Is everything okay?" She told me, "You're needy, and it was too much for me." I sat with that for a while. I had contacted her about four times in four months to set up dinner. Clearly, I wasn't taking the big ass hint she was dropping when she didn't get back to me on her own or by not showing up for dinner. But was I needy? Certainly, I was obtuse. I asked my husband, my best girl Michele and several other close friends, "Am I a needy friend?" The responses were an overwhelming, "No." *Okay*, I decided. *Maybe this situation isn't about me being needy.* I clearly had a lesson to learn about moving on when someone's actions were saying they didn't want to be friends, but needy didn't seem to be my issue. I filed away her perception of me as needy so that if I hear it again, I can explore what I am doing and how I am showing up in some relationship that makes me seem needy.

The fourth quadrant is the one you want to be the smallest and tiniest of all the quadrants. I call it the dark closet. Depending on how much you are storing in your closet, it might be hard to see into its back. There may be lots of clothes, boxes and baggage in the way. In order to explore your closet, you actually have to go in and start pulling all the stuff out, fumble around a bit and see what's hidden back behind that box of old clothes you're still hanging onto, even though you keep saying you're going to give it to Goodwill. When people snap and do something completely unexpected, this is the quadrant those behaviors most often come from. We may find ourselves thinking, What the heck just happened? I didn't know I was capable of that. Again, this quadrant isn't about good or bad behavior. It only holds unexpected behaviors and capabilities.

When I was young, I rode horses every chance I could. One day I was out on a trail in Texas. I was riding alone, loping along on my horse, when I heard a rattlesnake. My horse moved sideways super fast, and I found myself lying face down on a dusty trail. Three feet away from me appeared a HUGE rattlesnake all coiled up and rattling. I had never been in quite this situation. I didn't know I had the capacity to handle the experience. What happened? I calmed my breathing. Then everything my dad and others had ever taught me about being in the wild and coming upon a rattlesnake kicked in. I was able to crawl backward slowly until I was far enough away to stand up. Until that moment, I had no clue I was capable of being calm in the face of danger. I had been hiding this positive quality in the back of my dark closet. That said, you can also hide some pretty destructive qualities in the back of your dark closet. And those are the ones you need to shine some light on, instead of ignoring them.

I think part of our job on earth is to go digging and shine a light on the areas we don't know about ourselves. By doing so, we discover what we are capable of, learn to trust ourselves and can be conscious of our qualities that are both brilliant or not so much. When you have access to your unknown strengths, you have a better shot that you won't get hijacked by your hidden dark side. If you have a brain, you have a dark side. Own it. Shine a light on it. Challenge it. Then choose wisely what you want to do with the insights. This growth happens most efficiently by expanding your first and second quadrants.

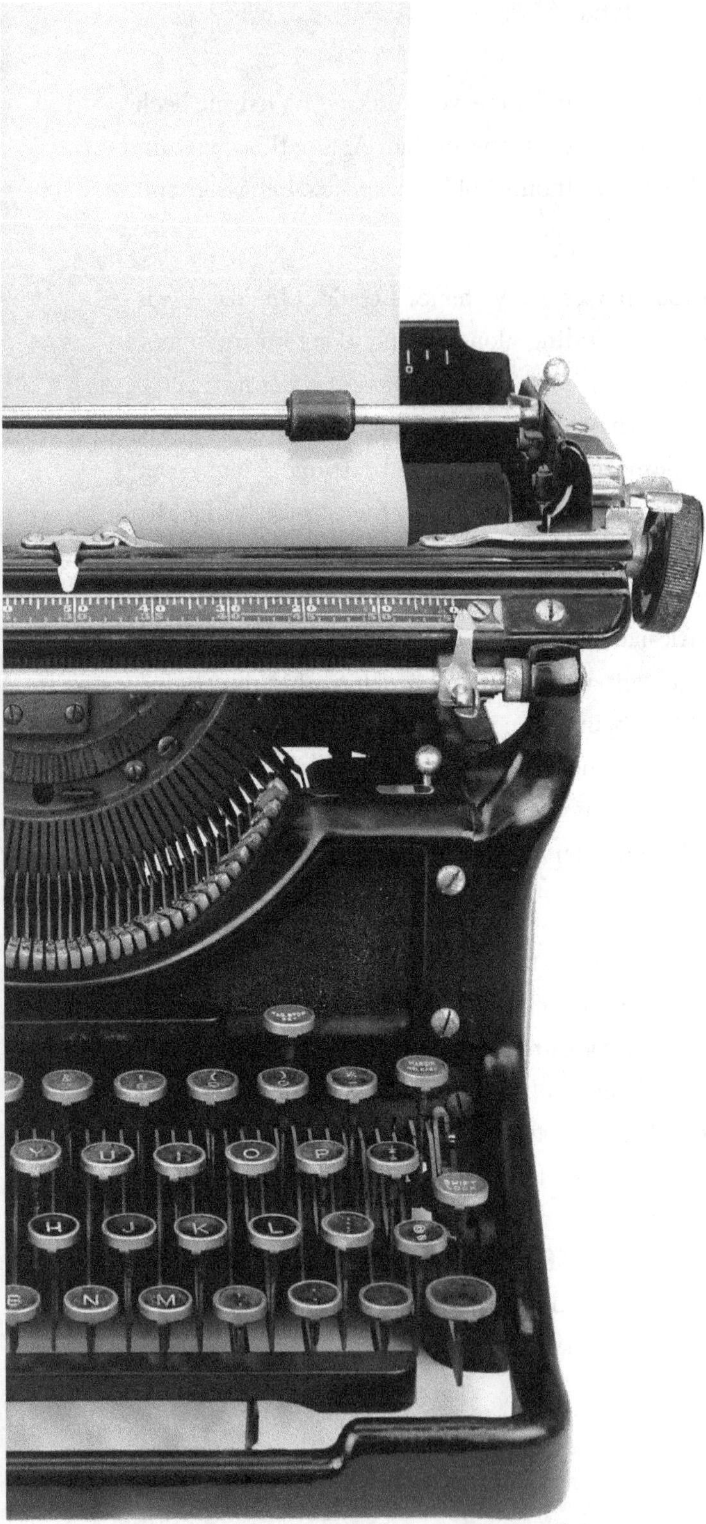
Y
U
I
O
P
H
J
K
L
N
M

I 9
CATCH AND RELEASE

"I believe that everything happens for a reason. People change so that you can learn to let go, things go wrong so that you appreciate them when they're right, you believe lies so you eventually learn to trust no one but yourself and sometimes good things fall apart so better things can fall together."

— *Marilyn Monroe*

Have you ever been fly-fishing? For me, fly-fishing is the most meditative type of fishing. I love standing hip deep in a stream. Feeling the current move against you, feeling the sun on your face and the breeze tickling your hair against your cheek. Working the fishing rod, back and forth, back and forth, breathing and letting the fly dance as you stand within the flowing stream—it's all very tranquil and comforting for me. It's less about catching a fish and more about being in a quiet place. Your mind is at peace, a Zen space, in nature and you are entirely present to the moment. Fly-fishing isn't about a party. It isn't a group activity. It's an act of being intentional and conscious to the moment that you find yourself. The second thing I love about fly-fishing is that the fish stands an excellent chance of sharing a moment with you and still surviving. I tend to fish using the "catch and release" model. The idea of a mental and emotional "catch and release" came to me as I was fly-fishing in Alaska. It's a concept about how we notice things—a situation or experience. We notice the emotions bubbling to the surface, notice the ebb and flow of the current of energy those emotions move through the body, breathe into those emotions and then just let them go.

You may have noticed that certain situations or events can trigger intense emotions in you of joy or anger. The more intensely you respond to the situation, the more likely you are to get caught or hooked by it. When you get hooked by the emotion, either grabbing hold of it because it feels good, or tightening up around it because it is upsetting, hurtful, or overwhelming, either way, you're hooked.

I imagine this is a very familiar idea in regards to negative emotions or situations. You perceive a threat, so you tighten up, your jaw clenches, your shoulders bunch and your stomach might hurt. What you may not have noticed is that you can also be hooked by your attachment to good times. In high school maybe you were the golden boy or the homecoming queen, the smartest, or the most popular. You could be lost in your memories of your first love, remembering the wonderful emotions of joy, hunger, and connection. All that adrenaline is coursing through your body, making you feel on top of the world. You're not alone. We all can get hooked by terrible experiences, and we can also get hooked by the positive experiences too. What is true, for you and me, is that anytime we are hooked by the past, whether it is past pain or joy, we are focused in a backward direction. While savoring an occasional good memory isn't a problem. If we get attached to it, in a clinging or grasping manner, it can drag us below the waterline just as quickly as the negative memories can.

When you are holding tightly to the past, you stop yourself from moving forward. You aren't paying attention to all the new opportunities that might show up so you can have wonderful new experiences. If you're sad and regretful about the past, it can drag you under even quicker. I had a client, Bill, who when he was young wanted to be a Pararescue (PJ) in the Air Force. It was his childhood dream. When he played with his toy soldiers, he had them jumping out of planes and helicopters. They were always rescuing his sister's Barbie dolls, other army men, basically anything his imagination could rescue. Bill, watched every show on PJs— the Navy Seals, The Green Berets—it didn't matter. His focus riveted on becoming one of these brave men. Then, when he turned eighteen, he went to his local Air Force recruiter and signed right up. No questions, he wanted to be a PJ, and he couldn't imagine the world in which that wasn't possible. When you join the military, there are a lot of tests that happen—for your eyesight, physical health, stamina, intelligence, etc.

When Bill got his letter, letting him know what he was qualified to do, PJ wasn't on the list. His health was excellent, he was in top physical shape and he had the right mindset. But his eyesight was the problem—depth perception of all things. He would never be any of the elite paratroopers in any branch of the service. His dream was dead, and this was a life-altering experience for him. He had spent so much of his life with a clear and passionate vision about what he was going to do and what he would be in the world, only to have it blow away like dust in the wind. This is, of course, where Bill's story could have gotten stuck. He could have gotten hooked by his disappointment, pulling his hair and gnashing his teeth over the loss. But inside of him, he accessed his indomitable spirit. Bill licked his wounds, grieved the loss of his dream and then he got on with the practice of creating a new vision.

As Bill and I worked together, he opted to go full "catch and release" and forge a new dream. He explored why he had been so drawn to being a PJ. He discovered his essence and gifts centered on caring, being of service to others, being generous and courageous. The more he developed his insights about his sense of self, the easier it was for him to shift his long-held ideas about exactly how he was going to manifest his gifts into the world. Being a PJ was not the only road upon which he could boldly embrace his essence. He discovered he qualified to work in the Medical Unit in the Air Force, so he then used his GI bill to become an EMT, ultimately joining a Fire Department in his hometown.

Another example of this idea comes in the form of a Buddhist fable about a farmer and his son. It beautifully illustrates the wild pendulum swings that our thoughts about the rightness and wrongness, or the goodness and badness, of things can create. Unexpected benefits can come out of your trials when you learn to let go of your predetermined ideas about how life, things, or whatever ought to be and you learn to be with what is.

THE FARMER AND HIS SON

On a day in early summer, the farmer and his son were working their field when their ox died. The son began to lament, "This is terrible! This is awful!" The farmer replied in a steady voice, "Who's to know what's good and who's to know what's bad?"

As the farmer and his son worked steadily through the summer, giving special attention to their fields and working them by hand, they grew a bumper crop that would fetch a good price at market, so the son sang out in a joyous voice, "This is wonderful! This is fantastic!" The farmer was calm and replied in a steady voice, "Who's to know what's good and who's to know what's bad?"

After the farmer and his son sold their bounty at market, they purchase a horse. As they travelled home, the son fell off the horse and broke his leg. He cried out in pain, "This is terrible!

This is awful!" As the farmer helped his son, he replied in a steady voice, "Who's to know what's good and who's to know what's bad?"

A week later, as the son lay in bed with his leg splinted, the Army swept through the region seeking all able-bodied young men. Of course, they couldn't take the son because his leg was broken. When the army had moved on, the son exclaimed, "This is wonderful. This is fantastic!" The farmer was calm and replied in a steady voice, "Who's to know what's good and who's to know what's bad?"

The story continues, though I think you get the point. We are often tempted to swing wildly back and forth between ecstasy and agony, but what if our gifts show up in both? What if the lessons are in the obstacles and learning to stay steady in the light of the extremes? If you slow down your responses, noticing when your pendulum is swinging and allow it to slow and center itself, you may open your mind to the gifts that will then present themselves to you.

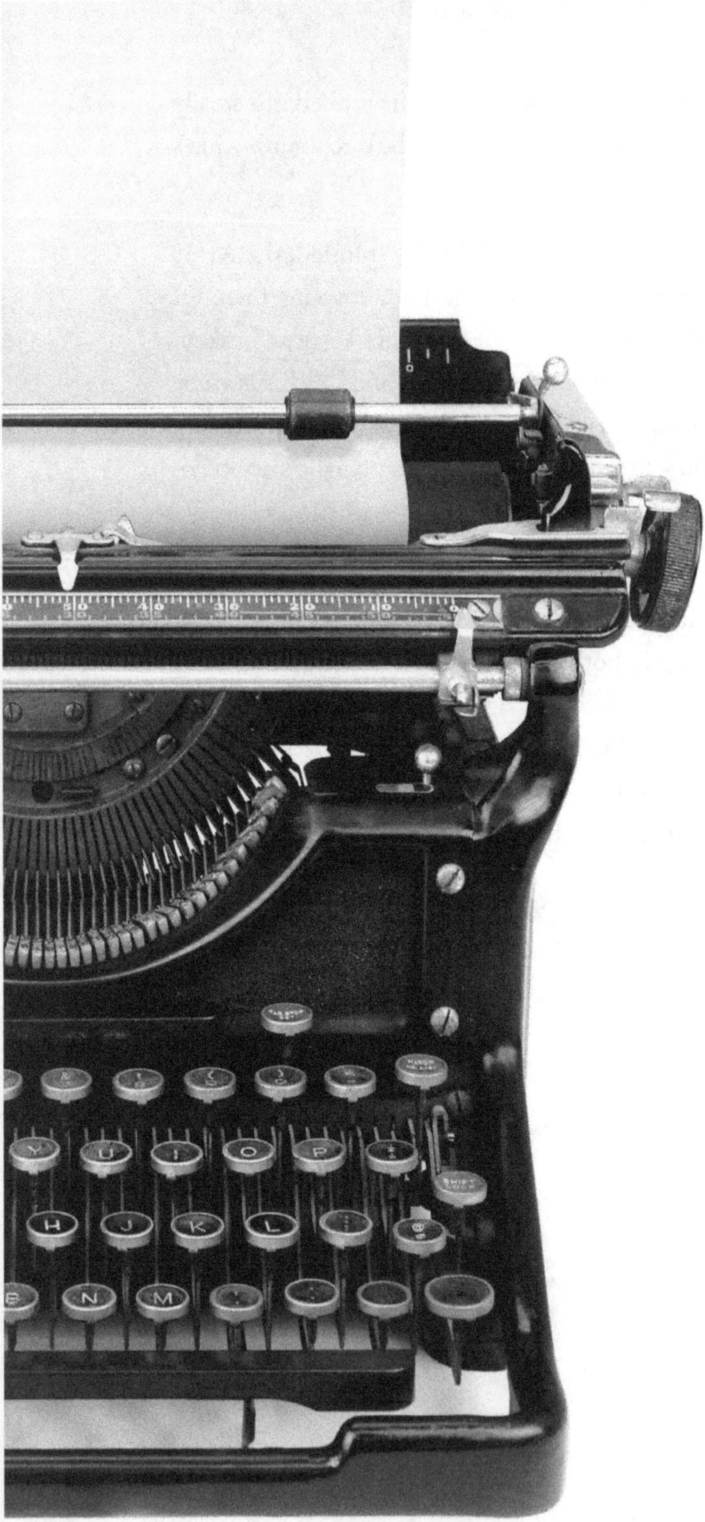
Y U I O P
H J K L
N M

2 0
NOTHING IS PERSONAL

"Nothing others do is because of you. What others say and do is a projection of their own reality, their own dream."

— *Don Miguel Ruiz*

In his pivotal book *The Four Agreements*, Don Miguel Ruiz wrote about the idea that nothing is personal. This idea was difficult for me when I read it, given that when someone dumps a load of anger or is generally snarky, short-tempered, demanding, or condescending, I don't enjoy it…. Do you? And yet, what if it's still not personal? When our new boss is micromanaging us, our neighbor hates us, or when someone cuts in line or traffic, or even runs us over, either metaphorically or in all actuality, what if it's not personal? The longer I have sat with this idea, the more capacity for letting go of my own anger I have had.

I know you feel like it's personal when someone says something shitty to you. Maybe they call you a name or disrespects your opinions. People can do all these negative things and more. They can be offensive, disrespectful, controlling, annoying and generally giant pains in the behind. Please consider that anytime you have more than one person in the relationship, it can be dysfunctional. You can't read each other's minds and you can't absolutely know another person's intentions. And still, nothing is personal. The only thing you can gather from what someone else says, thinks, or does is where that person is at and his or her mental state and emotional maturity. God only knows what's going on in the person's life. You and that person have simply come to a crossroads and he or she has dumped whatever his or her deal is on you. And it's not personal.

I am truly sorry that people come along and dump on you, anger you, or hurt your feelings. I am equally sorry if you chose to take any of it personally, as though what the person said or did was in some manner a reflection of who you are. That is a lot of power to give to people—control over how you feel and, even more importantly, how you feel about your worth. My question to you is: When you give your power away, who is the puppet and who is the puppet master? Who is pulling strings? Who is dancing the tragic dance of bullshit? Here is one of my favorite super-secrets of the universe. I want you to hear it and to sit with it until it seeps into your very bones: *No person on this planet can define your value.* I make this promise to you. You are the only one capable of determining your value. In case you need it, you have my permission. More importantly, I hope you give yourself permission, to control + alt + delete anyone's opinion of you that doesn't resonate with your essence.

That said, you may still need to take a look at what is said to see whether there is any part of you need to address. Your attitudes, beliefs, or stories. You have that permission still and with it comes personal responsibility. You may have unintentionally hurt that person's feelings, so the reaction you're getting is an indicator that you landed poorly on him or her. There may be amends to make. Are you ready to get curious about that?

Intent versus Impact

I know for myself that there have been times when I said something that just went wildly off the rails for the other person. I may have used a tone that triggered something for him, or a word that was neutral for me had great meaning for her. I remember when I was teaching a class for Human Services students. I was discussing with them the term papers they would be writing for the class. I made the mistake of saying, "Please write these papers as though I am retarded to the information. Fill in the gaps for me as you write." That started a shit-storm. I had to apologize and apologize and apologize for using the word "retarded" because it was a trigger word for one of the students. I meant it in an entirely benign manner, as in, "Write the paper as though I have no or limited understanding of your topic." But the student felt like I had been demeaning to people with developmental disabilities.

I wasn't intending to anger her, offend her, or trigger her. I also didn't take her standing up and yelling at me in the middle of the class as a personal attack. I could have since she yelled at me in front of thirty people. An interesting move to make with a person you don't know the first night of class, especially when she is going to be grading you for a semester. But I figured that her reaction was telling me a lot about her. If I had personalized her reaction, she and I would have ended up in a power struggle, at the very least and a screaming match at the worst. And, I ask you, who the heck would that have benefitted? If I had personalized her reaction, what would the other students have thought of me? Would they have thought I was an emotionally stable instructor? Would they have wanted to be in the class? I think not. And, seriously, the worst outcome for me might have been the loss of self-respect I have for myself as I was lectured about my bad behavior on my way out the door. Instead, years later, I still feel good about how I handled myself. I am more conscious of the words I use and I didn't get fired.

I didn't take it personally, but I did honestly sit down with her and apologize. I had never intended to trigger her. Because of how I handled the situation, other students in the class came up to me to let me know they understood my point and hadn't been offended. I won't say that this student and I ever became close, but we were able to work together through the class. Because of this student, I had the opportunity to learn a valuable lesson about how words can have very different intensities and meanings for different people. I needed to be mindful of my impact as well as my intention.

When you go out into the world and do anything—teach a class, write a book, sell a car, or take a photograph, anything—you are going to meet people who don't like what you did, or what you said, or how you acted. You probably cannot hold onto your true self and still please 100 percent of the people you meet. Why would you want to? I mean, really, aren't there people you have met in your life whom you didn't like? And isn't that okay? You are allowed not to like 100 percent of the people you meet, so isn't it okay if they don't all like you back?

It's "catch and release," baby. If you notice yourself tightening up for any reason around someone else's behavior, check yourself. Are you seeing any negative attitude that shows up regarding other people's opinions of you? Seriously, it's been a slough for me because I used to take pretty much everything personally. I was easily offended and got my feelings hurt if someone didn't agree with one of my opinions or didn't like me (for no good reason).

THE GIFT OF CHARLES

When Michael and I moved into our first home together, we bought a small house on a cul-de-sac, which meant we became close friends with all our neighbors. All, that is, except one. Charles disliked us before we even moved in. I have some guesses about why he disliked us, all stories I created. One story was that he thought we bought the house too cheaply and he had been storing his things in the little shed in the back and then needed to move them out. Needless to say, he really didn't like us. And that was hard for me. I was excited that we were going to have our first "real" home together. And I am a connector person, who enjoys getting to know people. To be confronted with a person who was blatant in his dislike was a first for me. If I said, "Hello," he ignored me and turned his back on me. He glowered at me each evening when I drove in the yard. He took tomatoes and chilies to all the other neighbors, but he pointedly didn't share them with us. If we were at a neighborhood party, he either sent nasty looks our way or turned his face so he wouldn't see us. His level of dislike was so above and beyond since all we had done was buy a house next to him. I found myself trying six ways to Sunday to get him to like me. Nothing worked.

So, what was the gift I received from Charles? Charles gave me a wealth of experience to mine for gold. At some point, it became clear that nothing I could do was going to make Charles like me. Michael never worried about it. He just didn't care. And, at some point, I stopped caring too. Not in a shitty, "You're a jerk, Charles," kind of way. But, rather, I came to understand we were just different people. Truthfully, the way he behaved didn't endear him to me either. But here I entered the super-secret zone, and I had a big aha: *His opinion of me is none of my business.*

Being nice wasn't going to change anything, but being ugly, well that would have changed me. Ask yourself, "Am I willing to become the type of person I will have to become if I engage in an emotional or metaphorical war with this person?" Are you? Remember that there are no actions you can take that don't come with consequences. Are you thinking through what the consequences of fighting fire with fire will mean for you? If you're holding onto hurt, falling into the victim role, personalizing someone else's behavior and then ignoring your values and alignment to the core of yourself to win a point, what is the cost of choice for you? How else might you have spent the time and energy? What could you have learned if you had, instead, let go of that person's opinion and noticed your own emotions, done your own work and then moved on with your life? These are important questions to grapple with. Because in the end, you still are going to be living with yourself and deep down, you will know whether your behavior is in alignment with who you truly are, whether you're reflecting your light and bright soul and whether you are manifesting that soul in a manner that supports who you are working toward being in the world. When you close your eyes at night, you know whether you are proud of yourself or not—it's as simple as that.

2 I

ARCHETYPES

*"Life isn't divided into genres. It's a horrifying, romantic, trag-
ic, comical, science-fiction cowboy detective novel. You know,
with a bit of pornography if you're lucky."*

—*Alan Moore*

Our stories seem to come in themes or archetypes. In the last century, archetypes became interwoven with Jungian psychology, but archetypes have a much older history. The concept of archetype was first used by Plato in ancient Greece when he wondered whether ideas in their purest form were imprinted on our souls before we were born. I love this. To me, it means that we are born wired for stories, and in the wiring, we already have the constructs for the different characters or archetypes needed for whatever situation shows up in our lives.

The English usage of archetype began in the 1500s. It was a way of communicating an idea that a story has different characters and that characters themselves play out different parts of a story. Carl Jung believed that archetypes are universal and cross-cultural. They live within the collective unconscious of all people. Jung introduced the idea of the collective unconscious in his 1916 essay "The Structures of the Unconscious." In it, Jung explored the idea that there is a collective unconscious that includes the soul or energy of humanity as a whole and that each of our personal unconscious minds tap into this collective. Within the "collective" are the archetypes: universal characters such as the Wise person, the Hero, the Victim, the Fool, the Warrior, the Muse, the Trickster, the Shadow and the Self. Since these characters seem to show up in mythological stories in every corner of the planet, I think it probable that a "collective unconscious" does exist.

I think it is safe to say that we naturally fall into these different character storylines, in part due to how our brains are designed for stories. The archetypes give us hand holds for exploring character in stories.

I want to share with you two quick examples of the Victim and the Hero archetypes:

The Victim Archetype: In this storyline, the victim is going along through life and through no fault of his own or participation on his part, something tragic or bad happens to him and he ventures into or gets tossed into a drama. He is harmed in some way and is helpless to activate any sort of change or have any positive impact on his story. He is often lost in the story and powerless to transform it or its outcome. Victims spend a lot of time complaining and/or blaming the wrongdoing of others for the circumstances they are stuck in and they often are looking for someone outside of themselves to save them.

The Hero Archetype: The hero ventures into, or sometimes even gets tossed into, some sort of adventure. She may not yet have the tools for the adventure and she may feel overwhelmed or scared, but she pushes through the fear and begins the work of changing the story's outcome. The hero often collects allies and wise guides along the way. She seeks courage and, ultimately, willingly, walks into the fire and is transformed by the experience. The hero is often not in the adventure for herself alone. She is doing what needs to be done for the greater good. Win or lose, she learns from the experience and continues moving forward.

In Orson Scott Card's book *Treason*, the following line captivated me: "The difference between a hero and a victim is the mood one is in when circumstances take a turn for the worse and require action." I have used this quote with myself and my clients for the past twenty-five years since I first read it. The mood that we are in, the story we have attached to our belief in our ability and our emotional states all play into which role we will choose to adopt in our own story. Think about that—you are in control. You may not be in control of the universe, just to be clear on that, but you are in control of your responses to the universe. That's power.

There are many more archetypes to explore. Part of getting curious is taking your first step into the exploration of what archetypes you notice showing up in your own stories. What characters resonate with where you find yourself right now and how might you mold those characters into roles that take you more directly in the direction you want your story to travel? What are the voices that these characters' manifest in your mind? You will often have competing voices, much like the light and shadow wolves. It's up to you to decide which to feed. It becomes part of your journey to explore which character's voice you are feeding.

For the purpose of being curious, in the next chapter, we'll look at this idea of archetypes as the different parts, voices, or characters we play within our own minds and lives.

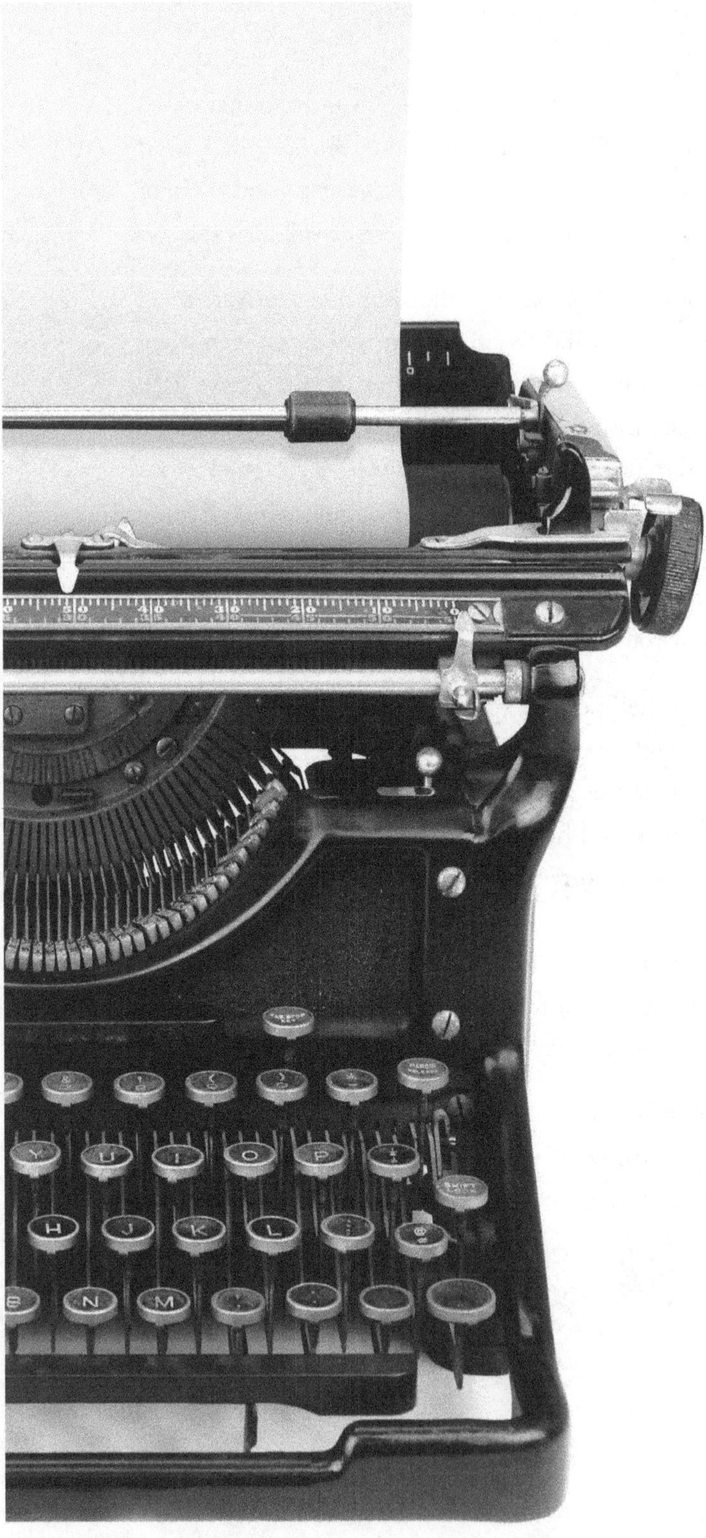

2 2

YOUR VOICES AND YOUR PARTS

"Until you make the unconscious conscious,
it will direct your life and you will call it fate."

— *C. G. Jung*

As is evident to you by now, we have many voices that show up and tell us stories. Some of the voices are drivers, pushing us forward, while other voices show up and thwart us. One idea of these parts of ourselves comes out of Ego State Therapy, which was explored and developed by John Watkins and his wife Helen. EST looks at how these states or parts of ourselves integrate or dissociate within us. What I have found in myself and with my clients is that these parts developed from our experiences, our perceptions, our beliefs and, as a result, they affect our moods and how we organize and use these different parts either to help us or derail us. With many of my clients, I have used the idea of the boardroom or kitchen table so that when a situation shows up, where someone is in a negative story, we can aim toward getting the parts to work together better. We visualize a space where all these parts can come together and have an opportunity to speak. Often what happens when people are stuck or struggling with an issue is that one part of them sees the vision of where they want to go, while another part is sabotaging the works.

Here is where archetypes come in and can be very useful. We can begin to see these parts as characters in our internal story. Some archetypes show up repeatedly. One benefit to having a Jungian psychologist for a mother is that most of my life was steeped in the theory of archetypes. I've had time to be curious about how they work inside of me. Our parts help us to navigate the world. They color how we view situations, how we react and respond, and ultimately, how we show up and make decisions. There are a few archetypes familiar to most of us. Not positive or negative, they do, however, have qualities that are strengths and shortcomings. If we become over-identified with any one part, we run the risk of overuse. For example, if the only part of you showing up when someone pisses you off is the angry and rebellious part, you might just find yourself in many arguments or tussles of opinion that lay waste to your relationships. By the same token, if the only part that shows up is the peacemaking part, you may not stand up for yourself. It's a complicated balancing act that we navigate internally and in the words of Carl Jung, "What you resist, persists."

Carl Jung described these archetypal figures as the primary characters: the mother, the father, the child, the wise person, the trickster, the devil, the god and the hero. Honestly, there is no actual limit to the labels we can generate for different archetypes. These are just the primary common types. While our internal voices are similar to archetypes, what I have found more often is that the parts or voices that show up are: the critic or judge, the scared part, the child or kid part, the angry part, the pleasure seeker, the creative, the wise self, the doubter, the taskmaster, the blamer, the rescuer or enabler and the dreamer. But again, there's no limit to the names we call these voices. These are just some of the more common voices I see in the work I do.

This idea of voices or parts is a big part of the Eye Movement Desensitization and Reintegration (EMDR) training I have been doing since 2006. When someone has experienced trauma, he tends to disassociate from it. When the trauma occurs over a long time from early childhood, the psyche must help the child find a way to survive his life situation. A child who was sexually, mentally and/or severely physically abused within his or her family has to be able to survive the abuse and then sit at the dinner table with the abuser. To do that, the mind can create distinctive parts that might not even know that the other parts exist. Much of the work I did when working with complex trauma from childhood abuse, relationship abuse, PTSD, or other traumas was connected to understanding that we normally have the different voices, but under traumatic situations, we disassociate from them so that the bad things that happened didn't happen to me, my primary self, but rather to someone else—one of my other selves. It's a complex system that the brain creates to help the child survive.

I no longer work with complex trauma, PTSD, or severe dissociation of the parts. I spent twenty years working with family trauma and eventually, I was exhausted. Yet I loved working with clients using EMDR. I loved working with the different selves. Because most people are whole, capable, resourceful and creative, they have enough internal structure to get curious and explore themselves. When playing with our voices, the work became fun again. I learned about Voice Dialogue and began to play with my clients, helping them develop deeper insights by accessing their own internal processes.

Captain Adventure and the Taskmaster

I had a client I loved working with named Scott. Scott was genuinely funny, even when he was working on some painful issues and trying to understand himself at a deep level. He is a writer and director, working on a screenplay. It's an audacious goal and one he wanted to make sure he had completed before he missed his window. One day we were discussing an issue that was vexing him. He was struggling to stay on point with his project and was juggling all manner of details. In his mind, this was an attention/inattention issue. He was frustrated with himself. He felt he was too distractible. "Squirrel! Okay, come back. Sparkles!" Scott and I discussed using the Voice Dialogue technique. Hal and Sidra Stone developed Voice Dialogue as a way to explore the world of Selves, or the voices that inevitably show up that can support us or cause us problems. The process is grounded in Ego State Awareness, so I was familiar with the idea of the Primary Self and the other parts or voices. I asked Scott whether he would like to try the technique to see whether any new insights showed up for him about why he was struggling to stay focused. Because he's an open-minded fellow, he said yes." He was very curious about exploring the issue in a new way.

As we began the conversation, I explained to Scott that he would be fully in control and that his "Aware Ego," his primary-self, was in charge. I would be asking him to invite forward other parts in response to the issue of distractibility. But I would be checking in with his primary-self regularly throughout the process. Scott agreed, and we began. The first insight he noticed was the internal narrative of the Taskmaster. As we talked about the taskmaster part, this part explained why he must be so firm and tyrannical—to keep Scott from starting too many projects and frittering his time away. This part feared nothing would get done. The taskmaster felt like if he didn't regularly remind Scott he was wasting time, then Scott would just do fun things. The taskmaster was "full on pissed" because there wasn't enough time in the day to be wasting. The taskmaster kept bringing up the rationales and killing the joy.

The second voice that showed up was Captain Adventure. Capt. A wanted life to loosen up a bit. This part wanted to have some fun, be creative, go out to play and have an adventure—all things that Scott loved to do—the things that filled his creativity and helped him innovate new ideas. There was a distinct conflict going on between these voices. One was a manager and the other a creative muse.

Scott reaped many benefits from this exercise. Starting with clarity about the internal argument that was keeping him from doing either work or play well. He recognized that it was affecting his focus. He wasn't getting work done, and he wasn't enjoying his time off when he was exploring and playing. His other big insight was that he needed both parts to show up because they had different jobs and both helped him to be successful. When his primary-self became witness to the voices, his awareness grew and, ultimately, opened the door for him to choose consciously. He was then able to tell the voices, "Now I am going to play, so Taskmaster, you need to sit this one out," and "Now I am going to focus and get the work done. Capt. A, please take the bench."

The exploration of insight and awareness is what conscious choosing is all about, and it's where you have the power to choose wisely.

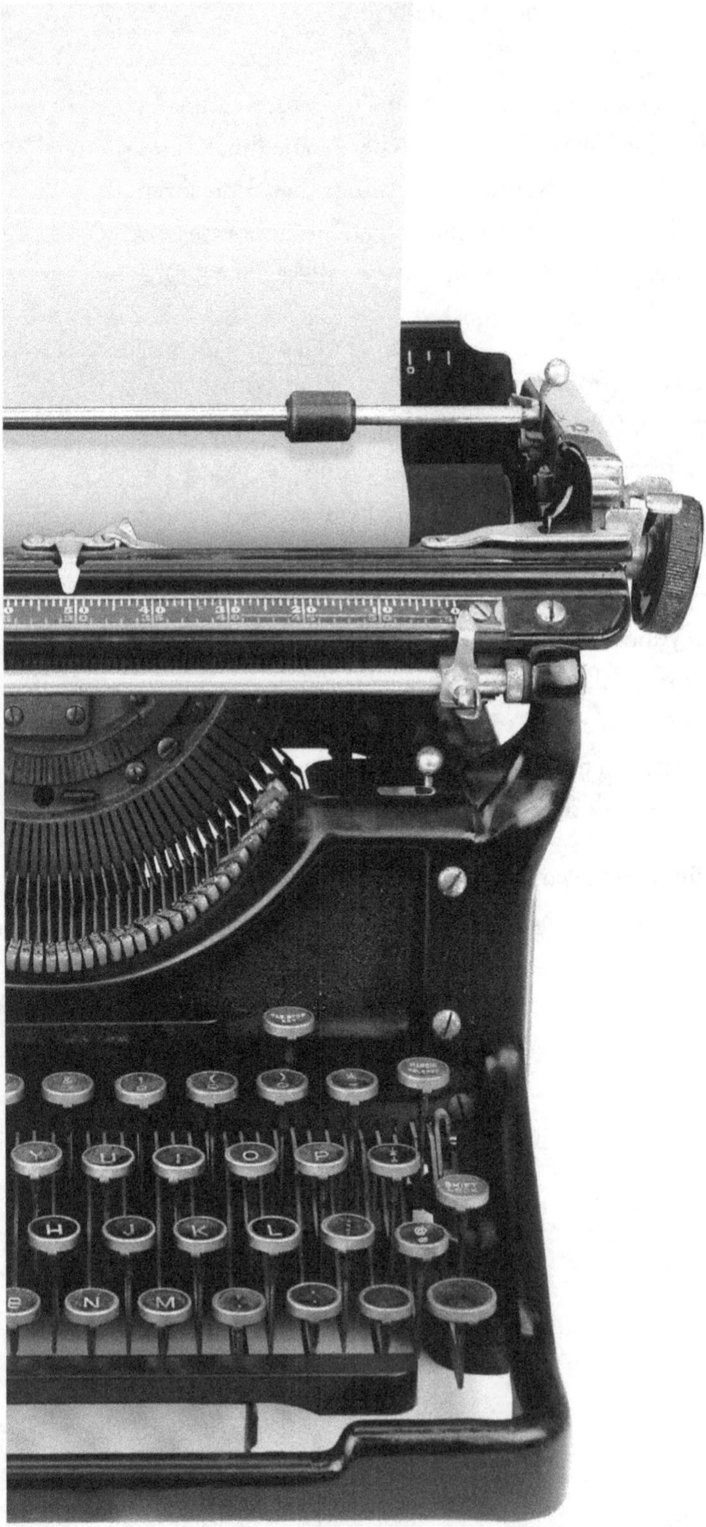

23
RECOGNIZING YOUR STORIES

"People think that stories are shaped by people.
In fact, it's the other way around."

— *Terry Pratchett*

I have taught and trained on several different personality assessment tools through the years, including the DiSC, Meyers-Briggs, EQi 2.0, Tilt365, and even the Enneagram. My most important insight is that personality assessments are subjective since we are answering them for ourselves and we can skew the tool based on how we respond to the questions. My second most important insight is that we are all more than our personalities. We have the ability to change everything and anything we wish about ourselves. We choose our change in terms of how we think about situations. How we react and respond to circumstances, and how we feel about ourselves in relation to the situation. Is the change easy? No. Old habits take time to change. But given enough desire, time and determination, any change you can imagine is possible.

Laurie came to work with me because she wanted to lose weight. She was 300 pounds and 5'5". She had health issues, her knees hurt, she felt a lot of shame about her body, and she also felt humiliated by others who could be cruel. Just before we started to work together, Laurie's mother passed away from weight-related issues, heart disease and diabetes. This created a powerful desire on Laurie's part to shed some weight. Through the support of her family, friends, a support group and coaching, Laurie lost 100 pounds in about eighteen months. It wasn't easy, and she had to commit fully. No one was sitting with her 24/7 monitoring her decisions. If this was important to her, it was a process she had to generate from the inside out—as it is for us all. Laurie joined Weight Watchers, went to meetings regularly, created accountability partners, helped others and lost a lot of weight.

Then something interesting happened. As Laurie lost weight, we unearthed deeper triggers about how she felt about herself. Laurie had to be willing to explore the fears that losing weight revealed. And that was the place where Laurie and I began working on StoryJacking. Looking at the stories that she had created about thin people—how they were all shallow or skinny bitches. Her stories about not being attractive were triggered as men notice her. She was no longer the walking invisible. People started to see her, and she had work to do to accept attention. Laurie then noticed that some of her voices showed up to try to sabotage her goal: "What's one cookie?" "You've been good, really sticking to your diet. You deserve a treat." "People should like you as you are. You shouldn't have to change for them!" "This is too hard."

Laurie had to acknowledge that these voices were not only showing up, but trying to derail her. A great deal of courage was required to stick to what she said she wanted. She had to acknowledge that she had parts that liked being invisible. Parts that wanted the wiggle room of being a victim. They wanted an excuse not to show up bravely in the world, and the weight, she determined, was a symptom of the deeper stories. If she were going to keep the weight off, she would need to keep noticing these stories, keep being curious about them and if they were the truth for her, deepen her awareness and hold determinedly to what she wanted for her life. Laurie lost a lot of weight. The majority of the weight she lost was the emotional baggage she had been carting around for a long time.

For each of us, it is different. Some people can very happily live a full life while overweight, loving their bodies and being bold in the world. For others, it's the story of not enough education, or not the right boyfriend, right girlfriend, right job—you know the one. It's whatever story you are telling yourself that keeps you unhappy and feeling stuck. If you do manage to change yourself on the outside, trust me, you still bring yourself with you to your new life and your triggers will get sprung. If you want to move forward with a healthy relationship or a career you love, there is some very deep work you will need to do so you can show up in this new space with the best tools to stay in your new you. What baggage are you willing to get curious about?

We are, all of us, more than our personalities and we are far more flexible and capable than most of us imagine. I hope we can agree that we are made up of many different parts and that our personalities are not fixed. Who has not shown up as different people in different situations? We may be our professional self at work, our parenting self when around kids, our bossy demanding self when paying a lot of money for dinner, our funny and lighthearted self with friends, or our best loving self when curled in our sweetie's arms. These are all different aspects of who we are. As mentioned before, these aspects of ourselves have their own voices. They may say things inside our heads like, "I love this person" while a warm feeling washes over us. Or "These kids are driving me crazy" when spending time with rambunctious, screaming kids. Maybe we are saying, "I am having such fun!" when spending time with people we love to laugh with. Or "I hate this job" when we are in the middle of a hard patch at work. Each of these stories comes from different aspects of our person—there is the part that is telling the story, whether it's a story of love or annoyance or a story of what we can or cannot handle. We even give ourselves roles in the stories we tell—maybe the victim, the rescuer, the creator, or the muse.

When you take some time to listen to the voice in your head, do you recognize that as soon as the voice starts talking, you are telling yourself stories? In fact, in any given situation, there may be more than one voice showing up. There might be the voice that is asking "What voice?" Or possibly the voices that argue both sides of any or all situations—the devil on this shoulder and the angel on the other. It's the voice that is telling you what you can or cannot do or what you should or should not do. Each and every thing you say inside your head is a story. "I can't do that," "I hate my job," "I like this, but not that," "I am not good enough," "No one gets me," "I'll never find a boyfriend/girlfriend," "I need more education," "I have too much education," "No one cares what I think," "I am right," "I am stuck," "I am smart," "I need help," "I can do this on my own," "I have no self-esteem," "I am broken," or "I am empowered and capable." All of these are stories and they are all manufactured by the voices in our heads. These voices and stories come from what we have been told, what we have experienced and from the perspective we have adopted about the experience.

Because in our heads is where we have become wired for stories and where we spend time talking to ourselves as we make meaning, it is crucial to notice the voices. In fact, I would argue that everything you think, believe, say or don't say, is all in your head. If you see a picture in your head, that is a visualization of an image. When you add meaning to that picture, you have just taken the leap into humanness and created a story. Stories, at their core, are narratives, either true or fictional, that help us determine the meaning of a situation, an event, why we are here, what is happening, what just happened, how we should feel about what happened and what we should do about what just happened. Stories are deeply woven into the neurology of our minds. More often than not, we have more unconscious stories running wildly around our noggins than we have conscious stories. And this can create blind spots that limit what we believe possible.

Have you ever started off on a new adventure, project, job, relationship, or dream with so much excitement and enthusiasm that you can't even imagine it won't be accomplished? Have you ever felt like the passion and excitement you're feeling is so profound that you will always feel this way? Have you ever found your resolve wavering somewhere in the middle of the adventure so that you madly wished you had never even started down this road? Maybe the job became a drudge, or the project went sideways so you feel like you are stacking sandbags for a river that has flooded and you are working so hard to save something that you're exhausted, but no relief is in sight. If it's any consolation, we've all been there. That spot that started off so sunny, but somewhere in the middle, all the shit hit the fan and the only wish is that the merry-go-round will stop so we can get off and find another ride. Have you ever felt like that?

All the way through the journey, we are choosing stories. The story of possibly getting sandbagged by the story of exhaustion. The truth in my world has been that, the more open to awareness my memories, beliefs, biases and interpretations are to all stories, the more likely I will explore them to see whether they fit what I want from my life.

Change can be hard and exciting. Whether you decide to love or hate change, it is inevitable in any life that lasts long enough. You may think you are unchanging, though I am not sure that is even possible. As we age, we may get more attached to the steady state, but even from the steady state, when we look at our life and we notice that things need to change. We are all on the road to shifting and rewriting our stories.

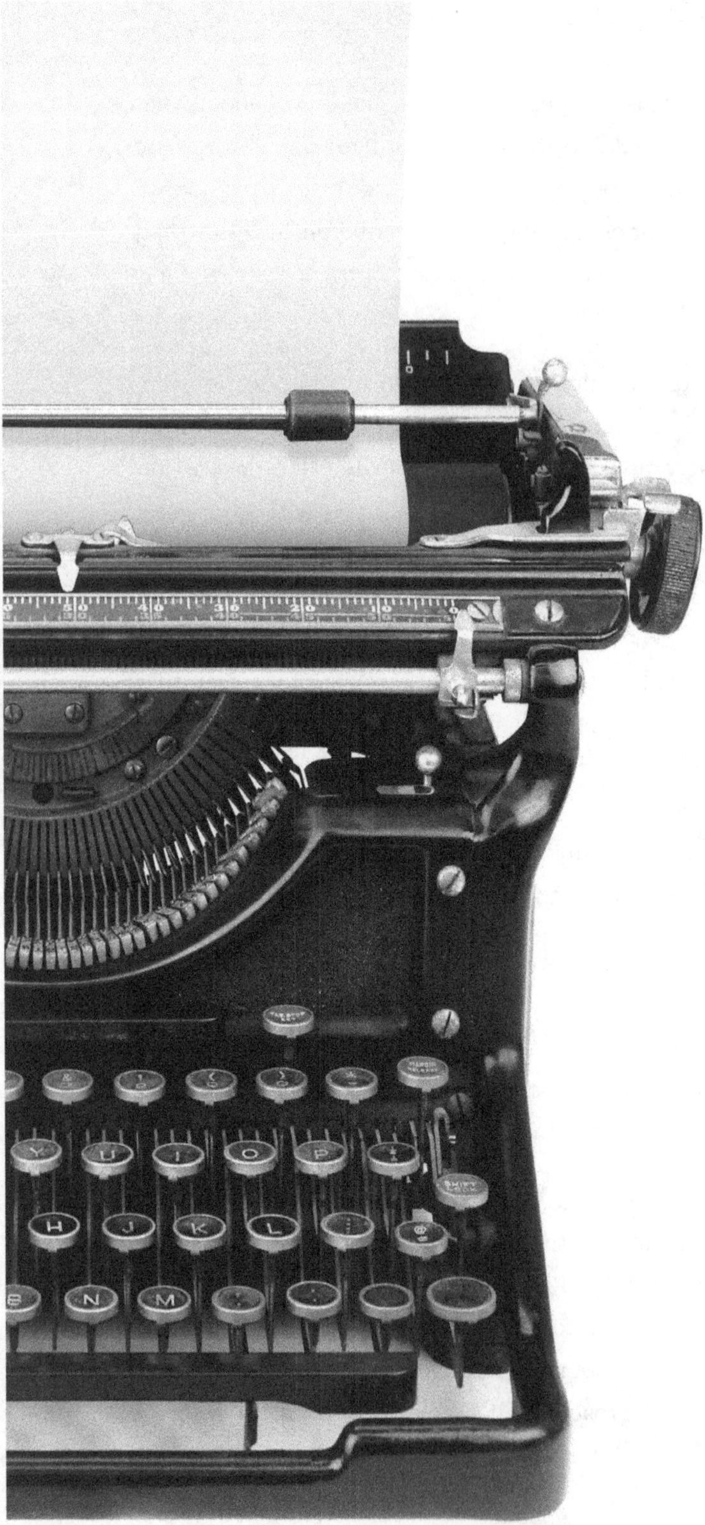

24
SNAPSHOT STORIES

"What happens is of little significance compared with the
stories we tell ourselves about what happens. Events matter
little, only stories of events affect us."

— *Rabih Alameddine*

While we all have stories that are long recitations of our experiences, we also have supersonic stories that whip into our minds and start the story ball rolling. These are not always negative. The positive stories sound like: "I can do this," "That was a nice person," or "I love my life." There are, however, snapshot stories that often needle at you and work to sabotage what you want. They get in the way of what you need to be doing. Like a photograph's negative, these snapshots are hard to see unless you hold them up to the light. It's only when you begin to be aware of what you are saying to yourself, in the privacy of your head, that you can begin to challenge these short and quick stories. When you turn these snapshot stories inward, they often end up sounding like "I can't handle this," "I am a failure," "I am a fraud," "I am stupid," "I don't have any real friends," "I am unlovable," or "No one likes me." And none of these snapshot stories are helpful to you, not even a little.

When you externalize these snapshot stories, they often lead to judgments, biases, defensiveness, or victimization. "You aren't a nice person," "You can't handle this," "That was a failure," "You're stupid," "They're idiots"—truly the list is long and I could go on all day, writing little snippets of stories. What's important, though, is to begin examining these snapshots. Several things may emerge from this examination. One is that these stories are the tip of the iceberg and a deeper story lies below the water line, submerged just out of eyeshot and by getting curious, you can continue to understand yourself better. The other important insight from examining these snapshot stories may be that you begin to notice an imbalance toward the negative in these stories. People often have an imbalance toward the negative. You may notice those things that bother you, so if you are bothered by aspects of yourself, guess which things you'll create negative stories about? For example, if I call someone else stupid, I am often telling myself how stupid I am…and a lot more often. You may not use the word stupid with yourself. You might dance around the negative self-talk, with a whole host of other descriptions about your inability to function at the level you think you should be functioning.

Which then leads to the story of "should." When I worked for the Children, Youth and Families Department (CYFD) in Albuquerque, New Mexico, I eventually joined a small group of clinicians working in Family Preservation. This program was designed to keep children at home with their families, by providing intensive in-home services to support families in addressing the issues concerning to CYFD. I remember talking with my supervisor about what she called the SWCs —"shoulda, woulda, coulda's." Those powerful words that leave us helpless because they are all about the past—that place we have no ability to change. I made a point to get curious with my clients when these words showed up. What do these words mean in relationship to this situation? Circling the SWCs is about as helpful as a hammer in a china shop. Little forward motion happens, and often an enormous amount of judgment is attached to these unmet expectations. "You should have done…," "I could have done…," "If only I would have done…." Have you ever tried to walk forward into a new room, while looking backward over your shoulder? It's probably not the most efficient strategy, right? I think you get the picture. These are classic snapshot stories, and they will leave you disempowered and focused on the past. Your attention is focused on unrealized expectations, fighting with the reality of the here and now, instead of developing the vision you might work on moving toward in your life.

To illustrate how snapshot stories ride below the surface, I once worked with a client named Mallory. She was a lovely twenty-nine-year-old woman with a Master's degree in Psychology. For all intents and purposes, she appeared to be someone who was moving forward in her life. She seemed filled with options. When we started working together, I asked her, "What brings you to my office?" Mallory began to tell me how she still lived with her grandma. She was working at a little dress shop in the mall, and she didn't have the confidence to get a "real" job. She was scared, anxious, and most of all, depressed. Mallory had stories about how her parents were critical and frustrated with her because she had an excellent education and they felt she was wasting it at the dress shop. She felt a lot of external judgment. For wasting time and not getting on with her life. As part of our work together, I asked her what she was saying to herself. Her response was classic, "I'm not saying anything to myself. I want to move on. I am just not able to. I don't know why. I think I'm broken." She then rattled off all her diagnoses. And, there it was, the underlying snapshot story, "I'm broken."

After Mallory and I had talked about the idea of snapshot stories, I asked her whether she would be willing to play with me around this idea of noticing her internal dialogue. She agreed, so before our next appointment, Mallory decided to write down all these little thoughts that were her snapshot stories. Two weeks later, into my office came a very different person. Mallory sat down and handed me her journal. It was almost full. Mallory looked at me and with all seriousness, said, "If I heard someone speaking this way to another person, I would call it emotional abuse." Ding, ding, ding! Now that's an insight! This first insight didn't change a long-standing habit overnight, but it was the step that led to her taking charge of her internal dialogue. And, it knocked out about 85 percent of her anxiety, depression, and fear right out the door.

Over the next six months, Mallory created new habits about how she could talk to herself. One recommendation I gave her was to stick Post-it notes up on her bathroom mirror. The post-it's said all the things she knew to be true about herself. "I can try." "I'm allowed to make mistakes." "I'm allowed to fail and learn from it." "I am capable." "I have gifts to share with others." "My ability to work through my depression and anxiety will help other people." And, in the end, "I can learn to trust myself." You get the point. She had some work to do, but I am happy to say she had a clear goal of where she was going and she decided to do the work to get there.

EXERCISE:

What resonated for you in this section? It could be a positive or negative feeling? Get curious about the feeling. _____

_____

_____

_____

_____

Is there even a small part of the section that you could relate to?

_____

_____

_____

_____

_____

What, inside of you, would be important to inquire more deeply into now?

_____

_____

_____

_____

_____

_____

What's your goal?_____

_____

_____

_____

_____

Is the story you are telling yourself helping or hurting your ability to reach your goal? _____

_____

_____

_____

SECTION III
You Are Resourceful

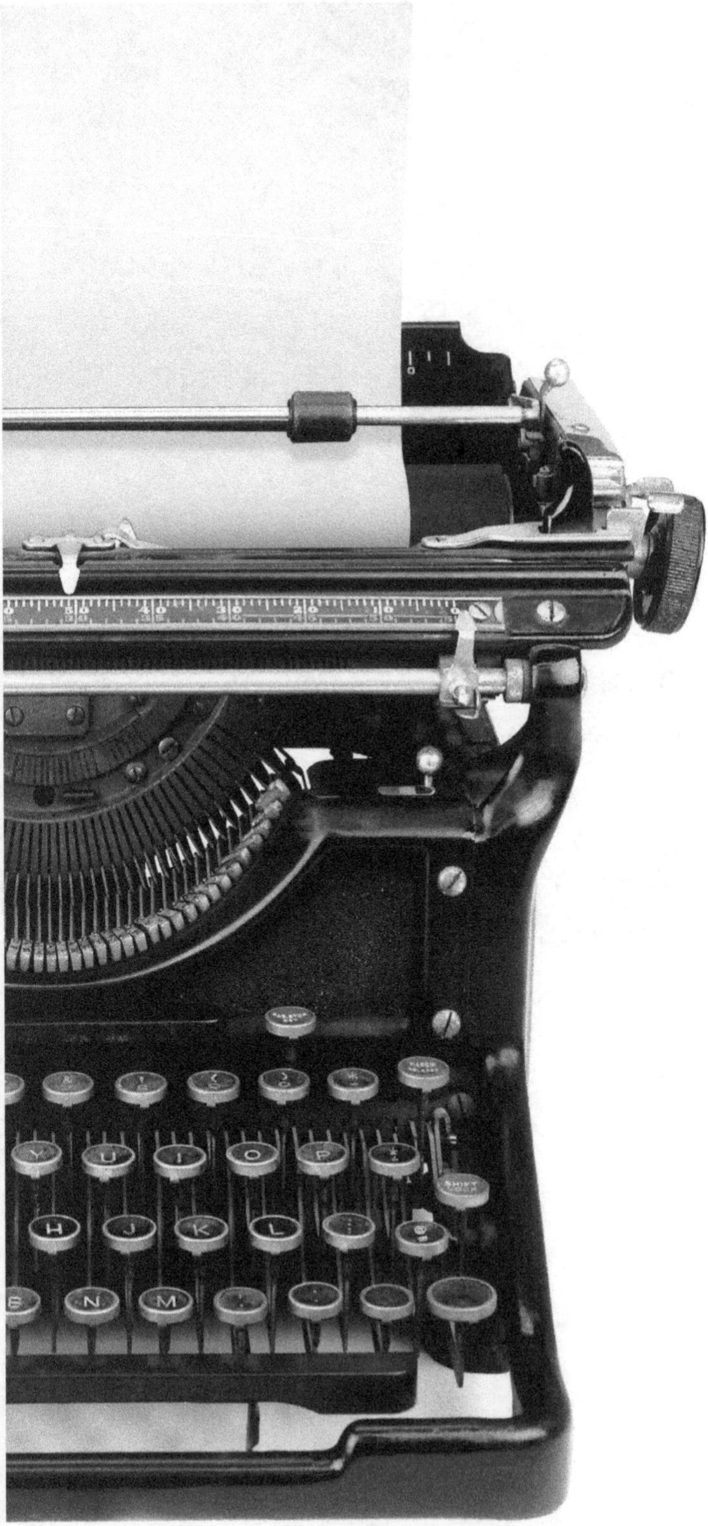

25

HOW WE MAKE SENSE OF THE WORLD

"Don't believe everything you think."

—*Allan Lokos*

You live in a multidimensional world. Information comes to you through all of your senses. You see, hear, touch, taste and smell things. In your world, you can pick up objects and move through space and time. Yet, in any given situation, your brain has to process thousands of bits of information and sadly, your brain can't handle as much information as the world tosses at it. Your brain has a solution. Your brain filters the information, rapidly and unconsciously, through its filtration system.

The world around you is sending you copious amounts of data all the time. It is relentless. The human brain can, on an unconscious level, process several thousands of bits of data at any given moment, which is great if you're driving down the road because you don't consciously have to think, brake, accelerate and notice, "Tree. Dog. Oh, wait, there is a pedestrian and a line. There's another driver. What's my route? My speed is XYZ." Your unconscious gives you the ability to swerve quickly to avoid someone turning in front of you.

To be fair, how much information is coming at your brain depends on where you are and what is going on. For example, if you're sitting in your bedroom in the dark on a quiet night, it might be a lot less information than if you were climbing Mt. Everest or driving in Seattle during rush hour. But for fun, start to attend to everything in the room. Notice every picture, bump of paint, the texture on the walls around you, all the papers, pens and wires on your desk. Pay attention to the clicking of the typewriter keys, the buzzing of a chainsaw in the distance as a tree is being cut down, the light in another room, the dog scratching, and a garbage truck rumbling by. What's that? Your boss talking to you, the loud music your neighbor is listening to, cars driving by, a noisy Vespa or the buzz of a motorcycle, even possibly sirens. Maybe there is a conversation taking place in the cubicle next to you, the little itch on your back, your sore knee, the conversation you're still thinking about from last night, plus anything else that might be going on such as hunger pangs or a headache. This information is coming directly at you, and you are sensing all the information through multiple levels, sight, touch, taste, sound and smell. Your brain, however, has no way to process all these random bits of information and focus. So your brain starts to make decisions about all these bits of information, basically racking and stacking them by importance. A few studies have shown that we can hold in working memory about seven items, give or take two. This ability is referred to as Miller's Law, named for George Miller's research in Princeton University's Department of Psychology.

What is your mind to do with all this information? Well, it must whittle down all the random noise by filtering and focusing on the data points of information that your brain decides are most important to your survival. The brain begins a process of filtering to decide what you are going to pay attention to. To reduce the influx of info, your brain must make assumptions, fill in blanks, generalize, speculate, delete and distort what it pays attention to. This is the simple reason why no two people ever see the exact same situation the exact same way. We take in the bits of information and funnel them through our own filters.

The following diagram illustrates this process:

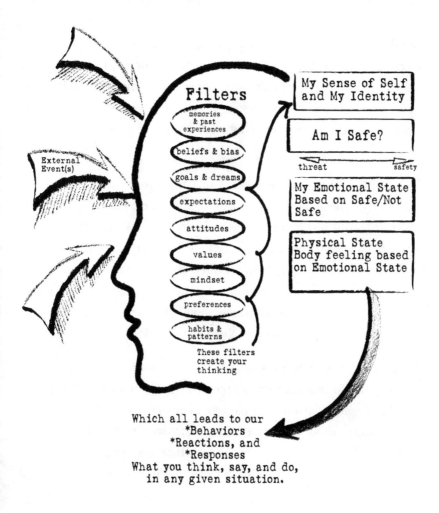

My filters—experiences, beliefs, expectations, etc.—are probably not going to be identical to yours. Let's say I am standing on a corner when a dog runs by with another dog hot on his heels. My past experiences, biases, expectations and attitudes are going to influence what I see. Those filters are rapidly going to decide whether what I am seeing is scary or exciting. Add to that the other filters like attitudes, expectations, values, habits and mindset and you can begin to see how things can be different very quickly for various people. What if the two dogs are scary-looking (whatever my bias is that determines what qualifies as a scary-looking dog)? Where might my attention and my mind go then? What if it's a small dog being chased by a big dog? Or if the two dogs look friendly or fierce? What if I don't even like dogs? (No worries; I am a total dog person.) Or what if I just dropped my purse on the ground, it spilled open, and I am focused on picking up all the change that fell out with my credit cards, makeup and tampons—am I even going to notice those dogs?

What's important to understand is that from your filters and focus of attention on the situation, you are going to create a story. Again, it's not good or bad, it just is. Later when you tell yourself the story, you are going to believe it. Your story may or may not be objectively "true," but it will feel subjectively true. How we interpret the story then leads to how we are going to feel in the situation. And how we feel activates our sense of self. We begin to make decisions about what we are going to do and what we are going to remember about the situation.

When you start to notice the story, barring immediate actual danger that requires instant reaction, it's the perfect time to bring out the Sherlock hat to get curious about what you are noticing and what story you're confabulating about your experience. Start working through the questions: Do I feel safe or unsafe? What emotions are triggered by the experience? Where am I feeling the emotion in my body? If I can look objectively at the situation, what makes me most curious? What is causing me to focus on X and not on Y? What tools do I need to gather to expand my perspective? And what would help me challenge the story if needed?

Here's the deal: Our minds do this with or without our choosing it. Then add to these filters the chemical cocktails that lead to fight, flight, freeze, or freak-out, and you are in the perfect storm for a story. And I don't want to discount that some events you are going to react to instantly—and you should—but those events are when you are in real danger. We are not talking about shutting down your safety mechanism. We are talking about when you notice, as you're sitting in a restaurant, your dinner partner says something that rubs you the wrong way, that there is not a real danger. What's gotten triggered? Is there a preference not met, or just your opinion that you're latching onto, or a bias or a belief that isn't helpful? Would it be useful for you to take a deep breath and get curious? Maybe, just maybe, we can agree that none of us see the entire picture and that we may need to question our assumptions, generalizations, and presumptions about what we think the story is all about. By looking at our filters, we can expand our personal awareness, get conscious and challenge our habits of thinking.

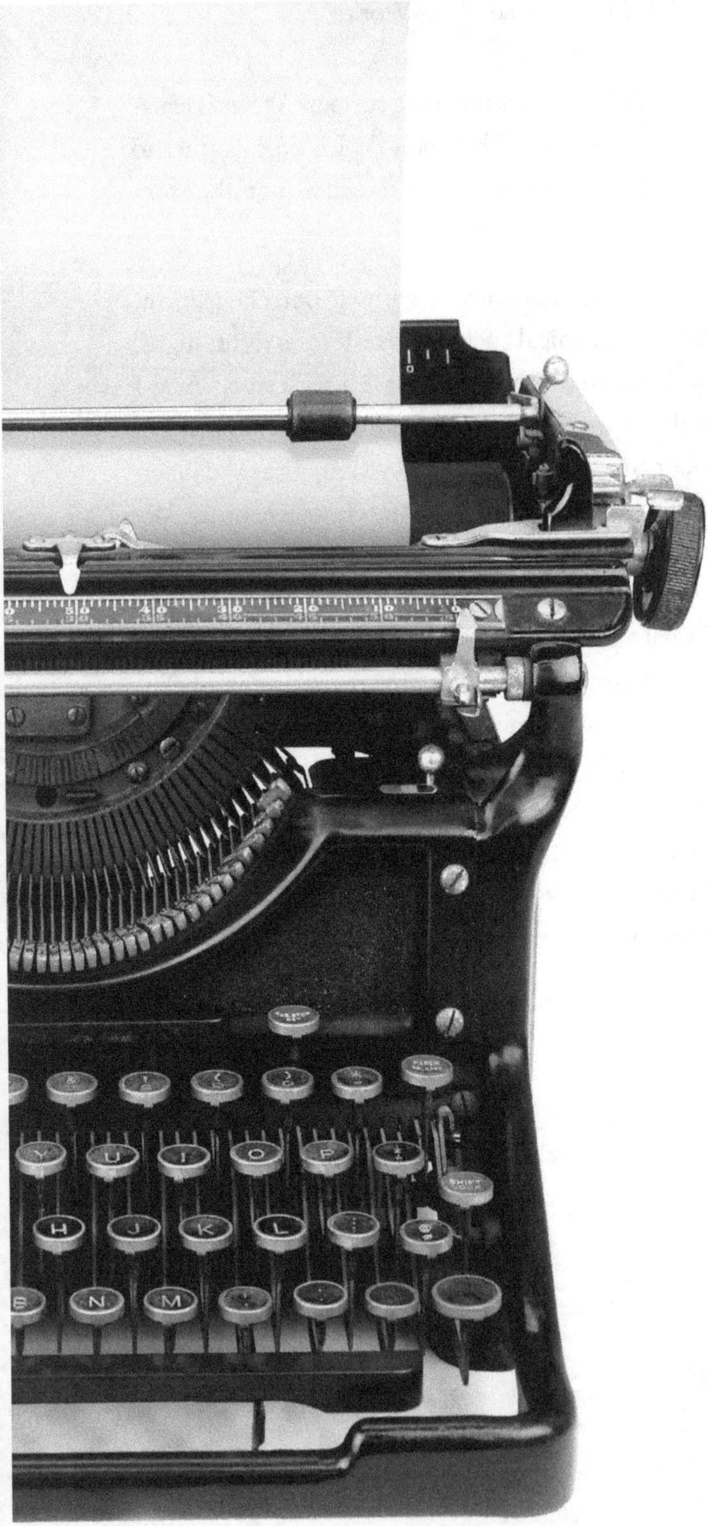

2 6

LOCUS OF CONTROL

*"Becoming fearless isn't the point. That's impossible. It's learning
how to control your fear and how to be free from it."*

— *Veronica Roth*

One of the most important shifts in my own story came with an understanding of Locus of Control. Let's look at this from the perspective of two circles. The inner circle is the Internal Locus of Control and the outer circle is the External Locus of Control. Here's how each of these circles work. See the diagram on the next page.

EXTERNAL LOCUS OF NO CONTROL

When you think about what things cause you to feel bad, stuck and angry, what comes to mind? I sum it up this way—other people, the world and time. The external locus is the outward focus. You may be focused on how other people make you feel, on how external situations impact you, or you may be focused on the past. Let's look at each of these three items separately.

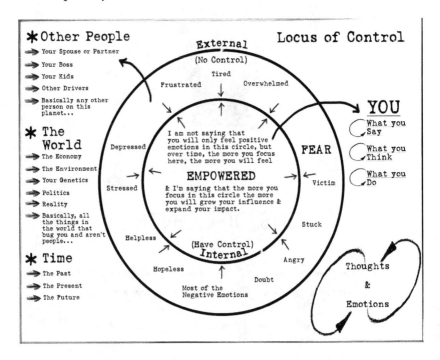

Other People: This is a massively big group that includes our spouses/partners, kids, friends, neighbors, bosses, other drivers and all the other people out in the world who vex us at times. As much as we might like to be in control of them, their decisions, etc., we don't have absolute control over anyone. We might be in physical control of them, but we can't make them like us or what we are doing to them. We can't make anyone like anything, or see our point of view, or see our genius in fixing their lives. This applies to about 100 percent of the people on this planet—you may have some godlike power on some other planet, but on this one, you don't. Now, this isn't to say that you can't influence people, you can. If you are honest with them, more often than not, they will respect you or trust you. And if you lie, steal, or cheat them, they will often decide they dislike you. But you might be the nicest person on the planet, care deeply for all humanity, be compassionate, honest, fair and caring and regardless, I can promise you that somewhere, someone is going to have a problem with you. You can't please everyone, nor should you try.

The World: This is all the big stuff on the planet, like governments, politics, the environment, the economy and even our health—whatever is not within our absolute control. Yes, absolutely there are things that we can do to influence these big issues—we can vote, sign petitions, donate money to causes we care about, exercise and change our diet, but very little has ever changed by our focusing solely on how much of a problem these items are or how much we dislike something. And then there is *reality*. I hate to bring up reality because we seem to love it when it's supporting our worldview or our dreams, but when it is in direct conflict with us, we hate it, we fight it and we suffer. That's because none of the big issues will change or do what we wish without us committing ourselves to what we can say, think, or do to effect and influence them to be different.

Time: I add time into this diagram because we spend a lot of time, pun intended and energy on this section. Wasted time spent being mad about things that have already happened, wasted worry on what is happening at this moment and then the worry or anxiety around what the future holds. Time is an interesting concept. It is a moving experience, steadily marching forward. Let's look at "time" in regards to reading this book. The past was when you purchased or were gifted the book. You wouldn't be reading these words at this moment if you hadn't already done something to be holding the book in your hands. As soon as you read these words, they shift from being this moment into being a past moment. You could put the book down and impact the next moment. But the present moment and the past moment are what they are. Done. The future is a little more flexible. Again, you could put down the book, never pick it up again, or pick it up again later. You have some choices over your actions here. But the future in the bigger picture of the world is not completely within our control.

In this context, I think of the Black Swan theory by Nassim Nicholas Taleb. At one point in time, people couldn't imagine a Black Swan. They had only ever seen White Swans, so they couldn't know or predict the possibility of something that was completely unknown to them. They wouldn't have thought a Black Swan was possible up until the moment when someone saw and photographed the first Black Swan. Forces are at work in the universe that exist regardless of how much you think you know, or how hard you have worked to create a different outcome. For example, people didn't foresee the housing bubble of 2008/2009. The common logic/story was that buying a home was always the smartest financial decision because housing prices would always rise so you would make money when you sold your house. When the bubble burst, a lot of people woke up to experience a very different reality. It was a Black Swan event for many of us as we sat in our overpriced homes with few options and tried to get out from under the burden. Black Swan events are hard to predict. If we deny they are possible, it can make us blind to what all the potential consequences might be in a given situation. In this regard, the future is not absolutely controllable either.

INTERNAL LOCUS OF CONTROL

Let's take a look at the inner circle, the *Internal Locus*. This circle focuses on where you have control. *You*. You have control over what you say, what you think and what you do. You can choose each of these things and thus, you can impact outcomes. In the diagram, I added in arrows to connect thoughts and emotions because these two aspects play off each other. If you are feeling a powerful emotion, look at your thinking. Get curious about how your thinking is affecting your feelings. For example, I am feeling angry as I drive down the road: I'm stuck in traffic, running late for a meeting and feeling a lot of anxiety. As the feeling rises in my body, my chest might tighten, my head might hurt, and the thoughts that are attaching themselves to the situation might be: "These stupid drivers!" "I hate this feeling!" "I'm going to be late! Can't you people move?" Maybe you add in, "Jiminy H. Christmas, what is wrong with these people?" "Aaarrrggghhh!!!!" Possibly you call your appointment to say you're running late, but the conversation doesn't go well because your tone is angry. Now you have an upset receptionist or client, and you are still running late for the appointment. Or the person cancels because you've rubbed him or her the wrong way. Does any of this sound familiar?

From the outside, we can see that these thoughts are only going to amplify the negative emotions. But for fun, let's say you are in the same exact spot, you notice the plot twist, forget the easy drive to your appointment. You're stuck in traffic, watching the minute hand tick off time, knowing you are going to be late and feeling all the same angst. What if you step back? What if you notice where your focus is? Traffic, other people, bad drivers, time? Which circle is that? Do you have any control over making this situation change? A magic wand maybe? No? What if, in stepping back, you ask yourself, "What do I have control over?" Your response might go something like this: "I can breathe. I can start counting and focus on my breathing. I can force myself to laugh for two minutes. I can rub my tummy and repeat, 'I am okay. I am okay. I am okay.' I can roll with the plot twist." Does any of this change the external situation? No. But if you can change the internal situation, then you change your responses to the external situation. You are still running late, you still call, but you're lighter in spirit. You laugh with the person on the other end, letting him or her know you are stuck in traffic. Maybe you can even start the conversation on the phone. You relax, you shift your energy and the other person energetically changes with you. Maybe the person needs to reschedule, but he or she is relaxed with you. The question then is: What changed? The situation only changed because you did—that's a StoryJack.

Then there is the other side where your thinking helps you navigate the emotions. As described above, there are clearly situations where our emotions overwhelm our thinking and spin us off into anxiety and fear. Same thing happens with the power of thoughts. If you are thinking how awful, terrible and horrible something is, what emotions does that engage? If you are thinking about what you are grateful for, or how much you are enjoying yourself, what emotions show up then?

Putting this into action, let's look at a relationship issue. Let's say you are mad at a coworker. You can choose to focus on where your power is by looking at how the situation is impacting you and what you need to say, think, or do to impact the situation positively. Or you could beat your head against a wall, trying to control what she did or said in the past that has annoyed you beyond measure.

A friend of mine once told me a story of waking up in the middle of the night to the sound of water running. She had been out of town for a week on a vacation. She looked high and low, checking everywhere—outside faucets, inside faucets. Well, her son had visited her before she left on her trip and he had taken a shower. Unknowingly, he didn't turn the water completely off—not only was there a slow drizzle of water in the shower, but it had been running for over a week. She had two choices in that moment: She could choose to focus on him, his behavior, his carelessness, his whatever and the cost or waste of water and get angry and dump all over her son. Or she could reorient into her own internal Locus of Control. Where was her power? What did she need to do? Turn off the water. What else? Make sure to get the knob fixed so it easily turned all the way off. What else? Let people know when they used that bathroom to make sure the water was off because it didn't always work perfectly. She had two choices and each choice would lead to a very different outcome.

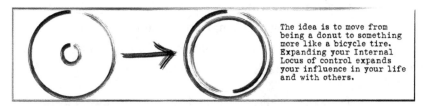

The idea is to move from being a donut to something more like a bicycle tire. Expanding your Internal Locus of control expands your influence in your life and with others.

Your job, if you wish to StoryJack your life, is to move your focus intentionally from what you can't control toward what you can. You can expand the inner circle so you move from being a donut into a bicycle tire. What do you think? Which circle would empower you more?

Most of the ongoing negative emotions you feel grow very easily in the petri dish of the external circle of No Control. We tend to be mad, frustrated, helpless, or victims. We can generate a story about being unimportant when people don't do what we want them to do. "I mean really, if you loved me, you would do XYZ. It's such a little thing, right?" Truly, we can get exhausted fighting with reality. It's the leading cause of suffering, this fighting with reality.

One day, I was walking with my friend Anna. We were discussing her teenage son and my mother who is in her seventies and lives with me. Both of us were dealing with our unrealistic expectations about these other people. We both wanted the best for our family members. Anna wanted her son to go outside, enjoy fruit, exercise more, do well in school and have a bunch of friends. All good wishes. I wanted my mom to get outside, exercise more, spend time with her friends, do art and find ways to enjoy her retirement. Nothing wrong with this either.

What we both noticed was that the more we pushed our agenda of what we wanted on either person, the more our actions created resistance in him or her. And we were so busy fighting reality that we were both exhausted. I said, "I have to remind myself every day that I am only in control of myself and my actions. I have to let go of my expectations of my mom. My mom is who she is and that is reality. And reality is like gravity, it's not going to change just because I don't like it." Anna responded, "Maybe we need anti-reality boots? Because I think the anti-gravity boots work." Then we both laughed.

I am not saying that in the Internal Circle you will always feel happy, light and joyful because getting real with yourself and noticing what circle you are spending too much time in is about you getting clear about what is going on inside of you and how you are either embracing or abdicating your power with where you choose to focus it. It requires that you challenge yourself and call yourself out when you shift circles. Get curious—not about how to make everyone and everything different, but on what you are going to say, think and do. How are you going to choose to show up in your life—as a victim or hero? Ask yourself, "What am I about to say, think, or do and will it take me one step closer to my goal or one step farther away?" This is a simple question, yet shifting your focus to where you have the power to make changes is one of the super-secrets to being empowered in your life. It doesn't always feel good, but what I have seen over and over again is that the more you focus on this inner circle, the more empowered you end up feeling over time. Real power and influence come from getting clear about your life from the inside out. And that, my friend, is pretty cool.

27
IF YOU HAVE A BRAIN, YOU'RE BIASED

"Your assumptions are your windows on the world.
Scrub them off every once in a while, or the light won't come in."

— *Isaac Asimov*

A bias is a tendency, trend, inclination, feeling, or opinion, especially one that is unreasoned. You can have strong biases toward something as well as against it.

At the NeuroLeadership Conference, I heard a statement I liked: "If you have a brain, you're biased." In case that makes you feel in anyway less than. Remember that every other human being alive on the planet, regardless of whether you think he or she has a brain, also has biases. The differences show up in your awareness of your biases. What are your biases? Are you unconsciously biased or consciously biased? Thinking back to the JoHari Window, what biases do other people believe that you have and that you are unaware of having? Here's the kicker: If someone thinks you have a bias, I promise he will form his own biases about you. Depending on what bias he thinks you have, he may just take his opinions and biases, pack up and go play somewhere else, or not hire you, or not choose you to be on the kickball team, or...you get the point.

So how do you increase your awareness of your own biases? The first step is to breathe as you recognize that you are probably far more biased than you think you are. You may be saying in your head as you read this, "Not me! I may have a couple of biases, but I am completely aware of all my biases, so technically, I am not really biased." Yet, sadly, if you are reading this and you have a brain, I'm willing to bet dollars to donuts that you have a few biases you might not even know about. Welcome to the club called, "Being Human." You're biased just like everyone else, only you're biased in your own unique way.

Again, because I like saying it, if you have a brain, you're biased. Let's not dump a bunch of judgment on this idea. It's not a good thing or a bad thing to have a bias. It's just an important thing for you to understand and develop insight around because your biases are among the important filters your brain uses to assess what bits of information need your focus. If you have ever made a hasty decision between two choices, you can thank your brain's biases for making that happen. And there are literally hundreds of biases that your brain will leap to—so many more biases than the common biases you might be thinking of, such as:

Group Attribution Error: Here you might have a biased belief that the behavior of an individual reflects that of the entire group. For example: "That woman was overly emotional, so all women are emotionally hysterical," or "That man was an insensitive jerk, so all men are insensitive jerks who don't care."

Stereotyping: Stereotyping happens when you expect a member of a group to have certain characteristics without knowing that individual.

This bias shows up regularly. You'll recognize it when you notice that maybe you think white people are XYZ, or black people are XYZ, or Muslims are XYZ. If you watch the news, you see these generalizations showing up all over the place. You may also notice that if you're the one making the generalization you feel good about it. But, as soon as the generalization is about you, you usually have a pretty adverse reaction. "That's not true! All white people don't XYZ!" It doesn't matter which group you self-identify. As soon as you generalize another group, you're stereotyping.

In-Group Bias: This bias occurs when you give more preferential treatment to people you see as part of your tribe. For example, I will help my sister, kid, or friend to get a job in my office, over a stranger, who might actually be a better match for the job. Or I give my own dog more treats than I will give yours. This syncs up with **Selection Perception Bias** where your expectations affect your perceptions.

Expectancy Bias: Here's an example of how we might expect certain behaviors from certain people. If my mom regularly eats oatmeal for breakfast, I may be surprised when she makes an egg. That's a benign example, so let's look at something like politics. Here is an area where we get locked into our powerful beliefs and start making sweeping statements. Then we look for those statements to be true. For example, if our statement is "All Democrats waste money," we will look for examples and say, "See, they wasted money here, here and here." Or you might have the reverse expectancy bias and say "All Democrats care about people," and then you'll go find evidence so you can say, "See, they took care of people here, here and here." Basically, if you're looking for it, you will probably be able to find evidence to support your perspective.

If you were a member of only one group of people, it would be hard enough to figure your biases out, but most likely, you are a member of multiple tribes of people. You have your family tribe, your friend tribe, your cultural identity, your gender identity, your volunteer group, your work team, and your church and religious orientation. It's endless. Because of life's complexities, you might have biases that get in your way that you have never even considered. Like the bias that you apply to yourself that keep you living small, such as, women should be sweet, or you must be a "good daughter." So what is unconscious bias and how do we notice it, especially since it's unconscious? There are too many biases to write them all down here. I recommend you go to Wikipedia (https://en.wikipedia.org/wiki/List_of_cognitive_biases), where you can get the whole long list and start exploring biases at a deeper level. Thanks to DesignHacks.co, Buster Benson and John Manoogain, there is a cool image there that has organized where biases fit on a wheel. If you're an organized or design-type person, you'll like this image.

Bandwagon Bias: You probably can guess this one. Yep, it's the tendency to think certain ways or do certain things because all the folks in your tribe think and do the same thing. In my house, we all take our shoes off at the door, so obviously, that's the right thing to do. If you don't, you're going to trigger my bias about what the correct behavior is supposed to be. We can get fairly judgmental with this bias because we feel like we have the support of our crowd behind us.

Confirmation Bias: This bias happens when we do something, such as buy a car and we need to justify our decision, so we start searching for information or seeking interpretations that support our decision. That's fine when it's about a car, but what happens if we get mad and yell at an employee, kid, or friend? Then our brain scrambles to justify our bad behavior. "Well, he is not doing his job," or "She didn't clean the bathroom like I asked…a million times," or "He yelled at me first." We may even add information to our memories to make it all feel better.

Endowment Effect: If you have ever sold something, you have probably experienced this bias. Let's say I am selling my old car because I now have a newer one. I may demand or expect to sell it for a much higher value than I would personally be willing to pay for it. If I am selling the car, it's worth $5,000. Yet if I am buying the same car, it's worth closer to $2,000. We can't help it. We get attached to our stuff. We are hooked by all the memories, or how much work we have done to make it great. All the time and energy matters to us when we are selling, but when we are in the buyer's shoes, we might not care as much.

Illusion of Transparency Bias: You may overestimate how able other people are to understand and know you. You might think you're an open book—that it's obvious why you did whatever you did—but other people might not understand at all. The flip side to this is that you overestimate your own ability to understand others, assuming why they think or do the things they think and do. This can be a place where conversations jump the rails and go off to bushwhack through all manner of dysfunction.

Shared Information Bias: This is the tendency for groups of people to spend more time and energy discussing information that all the individuals in the group are familiar with and less time and energy discussing information that only a few members know. If you're going to take a risk, risk telling people what they do know, versus not telling them something they need to know. This bias can leave people feeling out of the loop and, at worst, shut out. It can slow down innovation and ideas. Plus, it leads to people feeling disconnected and excluded. And once you trigger exclusion, it takes a lot of work to bring people back to the team.

There are many more biases to explore. You are born with a brain that is going to look for ways to short-cut, generalize and focus your attention. Some biases you are born with, so you don't even need another person to help develop them in you, like the bias against things that smell of decay. You and most people you know, tend to be innately biased not to like the smell of rot. It's a survival function, and it helps us avoid eating rotting food that might cause us to be ill or even kill us. There are other unconscious biases you share with most people on the planet. You probably don't like to get burned. You may have a bias against a bear eating you, I do. You may have a bias against hanging over the edge of very high cliffs or a bias about tossing yourself out of perfectly good airplanes. You can, of course, work through these, lots of people do. But survival biases are integrated into our DNA, for survival purposes. Then there are the biases like the ones I listed above that have little or nothing to do with survival. These biases develop in our childhood through our experiences and in relation to our tribe of people. What they said they believed and what they said as the spoke. Biases are often communicated non-verbally, such as when we see what other people say, think, or do and decide unconsciously that's what we are going to say, think and do too. To bring the unconscious to the surface and get conscious only requires you to open your mind and get curious about what your automatic pilot program is doing. Harvard University has a great website for exploring unconscious biases relevant to how we implicitly react to different people, genders, colors, sexual orientations and more. Visit www.implicit.harvard.edu and play there, while also developing your awareness around what some of your unconscious biases are.

Project Implicit

implicit.harvard.edu

Discover your Unconscious Biases

Social Attitudes:
take a few tests & write down what you learned.

There are assessments on skin color, gender, disability, age, culture, and even one regarding Presidential Popularity, so have fun!

What Biases are you aware that you have?

What Biases did you discover that your weren't aware you have?

What was one unexpected Bias that you are willing to get curious about?

What are 3 things you are willing to do to challenge these biases?

1.

2.

3.

What are your most important take-aways?

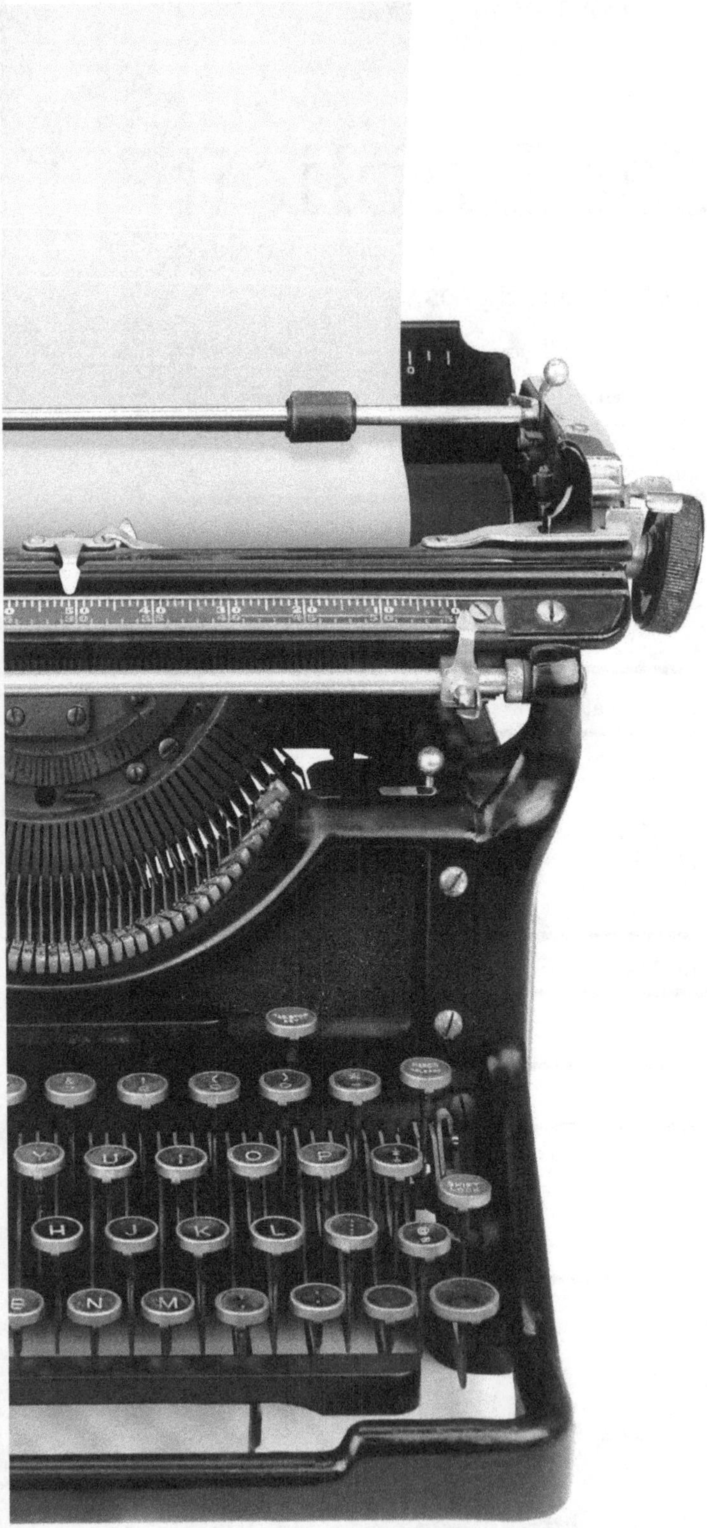
50 40 30 20 10
Y U I O P
H J K L
N M

28

THREATS AND OTHER TRAUMAS

"The only way to deal with an unfree world is to become so absolutely free that your very existence is an act of rebellion."

— *Albert Camus*

Many years ago, I took a class about trauma and working with people with severe PTSD. One of the insights that came from the class was that we all have windows of tolerance inside of us. For some, depending on the level and duration of the trauma, the window may be tightly shut. For others, the window might be a little bit open. Before we can delve deeply into our stories, we need to make sure we have coping tools in place so that it's safe to open the window and let in some light. To open the window wider, we need to work on our internal grit or inner strength to be "okay" when we feel the emotional discomfort that is part of emotional growth. This inner strength allows us to make choices from an entirely different space than the choices we make when we are feeling anxious, scared, or angry. Giving ourselves breathing room by expanding our window of tolerance means that we can choose from conscious awareness.

This wasn't a new idea to me. When I was teaching anger management, I noticed in myself and others that if we didn't feel safe in a conversation or situation, all our defenses were activated. So I thought, *What is the opposite of "safe?"* It's obviously "not safe," and I believe another word for it is "threatened." Given the nature of how the brain responds to the perception of a threat, which is to spring into Fight, Flight, Freeze, or Freak-Out mode. I think the addition of freak-out came from Raphael Cushnir and I liked the addition to the overall response because who hasn't seen someone absolutely lose his or her "shit" about something trivial? Anyway, I call these the Four Fs and they get turned on anytime we move from the feeling of safety to one of feeling threatened. When I visualize it, I see a line that has Threat on one side and Safety on the other.

Threat   Safety

The Four Fs, in a nutshell, are the unconscious brain's response to a life or death threat, or even just a perceived threat. Fear often comes with the threat, especially the life and death versions. But we might have other feelings that show up when we feel threatened, like helplessness, anxiety, annoyance, anger, frustration, depression and being overwhelmed. Pick some emotion that shows up for you when you feel a threat to your person, happiness, survival, or belief system. Safety doesn't mean that everything is golden. Safety just may be a more comfortable place to be. Safe is the body-brain connection to feeling okay. The feelings that show up may be calm, comfortable, excited, hopeful, or empowered.

The Four Fs are the survival mechanism we humans developed and that evolved from a time when lions, tigers and bears were a very real hazard to our ability to live another day. Today, this survival response more often gets turned on and fully locked and loaded over bad neighbors, other drivers, our exes, our kids, our spouses, our bosses, the credit card company, the checkout clerk—basically anyone who seemingly threatens us, our worldview, our rights, or our strongly held beliefs. And here's the funny thing—the threat doesn't have to be about actual life and death anymore. I'd guess 90 percent of the time our threat sensor gets engaged for completely non-terminal issues like: a difference of opinion, differing religious beliefs, or political party preferences, but it also gets activated when someone cuts in front of us in traffic or doesn't use his blinker, which is where the "freak-out" comes in.

Long story short, when your brain senses a threat, it releases the hounds, which are named things like cortisol, adrenaline and norepinephrine. You can read more about them on Wikipedia. Their purpose is to help you survive a life-threatening situation. Your ability to think is overrun by your capacity to react, and hopefully, when the lion pops out of the grass, it helps you run faster than the slowest member of your group.

While we don't have nearly as many life-threatening situations happening around us today, we use this powerful protection on all sorts of... trivial situations. That would be why we need to learn: Don't Sweat the Small Stuff.

But let's say a non-life threatening but still threatening situation happens. For example, your ex-someone (wife, husband, boss, business partner, friend) calls and says he/she is taking you to court for something. Is this going to kill you? Probably not literally. Of course, the fact that your head feels like it might blow up and your heart feels like it's going to burst out of your body could lead to your death. Just the words, "I'm taking you to court," will release the Four Fs.

Where do you think the words, "I'm taking you to court" fit on the Threat to Safety Spectrum?

- Do you feel safe or threatened?
- What emotions get generated for you?
- Where in your body do you feel the feelings that show up?

What if someone makes a snarky comment about you as a person, or your beliefs? Do you just let it roll off you, or does it click on a defense mechanism? What are defense mechanisms? Well, keep reading; we will take a closer look in Chapter 31.

29

EMOTIONS ARE LIKE ROAD SIGNS

"A mind all logic is like a knife all blade.
It makes the hand bleed that uses it."

— *Rabindranath Tagore*

You are an emotional being. It's part and parcel with having a brain, neuro-chemicals and a body in general. There is no getting away from it. Threats and traumas will always set off intense emotions. And, if you are like most people, you may be overwhelmed by those intense emotions at times. You might also have adapted a few ways to tamp them down, subdue and control them, so you don't have to feel anything painful or uncomfortable. People tamp down anger or suck it up. But in doing so, they also tamp down love and build walls to keep their hearts safe. I will argue, however, that emotions, either pleasurable or painful, are not bad. And protecting yourself from the ones you don't like shuts you off to life. I will agree that some emotions don't feel so good. In fact, they can downright suck. But each emotion is your psy-che's attempt to help you work through something important. The emotions are only giving you indicators of what is going on inside of you.

You're not buying it. I can hear you saying, "There are bad emotions and I must protect myself from them!" or "I can't handle these feelings!" Well, I disagree. All that work and effort you put into protecting yourself from your feelings often comes at the cost of energy, hurt or destroyed relationships, addictions and the invention of snapshot stories about all sorts of things. Our negative emotions don't go away if you ignore them or avoid them. They're a little like the hot molten lava under Yellowstone Park. At some point, the pressure builds and then you may encounter them as they bubble up and spray super-hot poisoned water on you.

As you know by now, I love analogies. Let's say you're driving down the road when you see a sign—maybe it's "children crossing," or "stop," or "no right on red." Maybe it says, "Photo enforced intersection ahead." Which of these is the "bad" sign? I mean, each sign, regardless of whether you like the sign or not, is just giving you information, right? It is the same with emotions. You may dislike feeling angry, scared, or sad, but all these emotions are doing is indicating that something has hit a trigger for you, so you might want to pay attention.

Of course, the emotional road is a bumpy one, so it's going to take more than reading this once to get it. It takes practice, getting curious instead of sliding down the rabbit hole of emotions, to start to learn what your emotions are telling you. It takes using your tools of calming down so you can get some perspective on a situation and your emotional response to it. Once I began the real work of getting inquisitive about how I was feeling, instead of running, building walls and defaulting to getting angry, I was able to use my emotions to help me make better choices for myself. It will be the same for you. Emotional awareness isn't rocket science. Okay, yes, it's brain science, but it's not impossible. You can learn to improve your emotional radar.

I'm offering many tools and techniques in this book—working to get clarity, reasoning with yourself, looking at where your focus is internal locus or external locus, figuring out what filters you are running the experience through, breathing—plus, all the skills that you already possess and use with great adeptness. Use them and apply them to calming your brain down.

One of my favorite tools is the Emotional Distress Road Map. I adapted it from Redford Williams's Hostility Road Map because it works for all distressing emotions, not just anger or hostility.

Emotional Distress Road Map

What is the situation or plot twist that triggered
your disturbing thoughts, feelings, and or actions?

There are 3 questions and 2 outcomes... let's go

1. Is this matter worth my continuing attention?

YES

2. Am I justified?

YES

3. Do I have an effective response?

YES → **YEAH!**

NO

Are you still wallowing or spinning?

No   Yes

What StoryJacking skill will you use?

adapted from Anger Kills by Redford Williams

The way the Road Map works is to think of an upsetting situation, then trundle down through the three questions.

1. *Is this matter worth my attention?*
2. *Am I justified*
3. *Do I have an effective response?*
4. If you get all the way through saying, Yes, Yes, YES! Then yea you! But if you hit a hiccup and find yourself saying no to any of the questions, it's a sure indicator that you either need to work on finding an effective response or letting the situation go: Figure it out, forgive it, forget it, or just move on. If along the way you get to "No" and you're still spinning or wallowing, then engage some of your other tools.

StoryJacking Skills:

- Try reasoning with yourself – Do I have a realistic expectation here? Am I letting some small plot twist get to me?
- Meditate and quiet your mind
- Take a time out, maybe walk around the block
- Talk to a calm friend
- Find what's funny about the situation
- Figure out what is underneath the situation that you need to address
- Listen to where the other person is coming from
- And my favorite of all time: Ask yourself, "If this were the last day of my life, is this what I want to be spinning or wallowing around?"

My final point about this road map is that if you say something is important to you, then you owe it to yourself and the situation to find the effective response or let it go.

Exploring Your Emotions

On the Emotional Distress Worksheet, Question 3 is important, "Do you have an effective response?" Because if you are going to take all the time and energy to be distressed about something, don't you owe the situation, if it's so important, the exploration on how to be effective? You can use your emotions as the door into awareness. It's a bit of the chicken and the egg debate—which comes first, emotions or thoughts? I have a theory that they take turns showing up first. Some moments, the flush of an emotion cascades over you and the thoughts come directly from the feeling. Other moments, you are talking yourself into a feeling. I am comfortable in believing that they are connected. If an emotion gets triggered, it leads to thoughts, which lead to more emotions, which tumble into more thoughts. What is probably the truth is that our minds have reactions to situations on a deeply unconscious level that lead to the releasing of the brain cocktail or chemicals that then lead directly to feelings and thoughts.

Here's the part that's important: When you start feeling a powerful emotion, notice it. Let go of the judgment that it's good or bad. Just allow yourself to notice what you are feeling because emotions are like a doorway into your story. The story is connected through our entire body and is an opportunity for you to explore what is going on internally. Some people can get to the deeper issues by thinking their way to insights, but for many of us, it's the emotions that are key to discovery.

Take a look at these emotions. Choose a situation that causes you annoyance at a level of 2 or 3 on a 1-5 scale, where 1 is no annoyance and 5 is watch out!

What is the situation? You can run the situation through the Emotional Distress Road Map, but to explore what's below the emotion and work on getting to a place where you have an effective response, you need to understand what is getting triggered.

Notice the emotion that goes with the situation:

Anxious	Small	Angry	Confused
Curious	Shut Down	Cautious	Overwhelmed
Disappointed	Frustrated	Scared	Confident
Determined	Helpless	Hopeless	Excited
Annoyed	Suspicious	Surprised	Embarrassed
Shamed	Guilty	Disgusted	Enthusiastic
Hopeful	Lonely	Hurt	Hostile
Jealous	Sad	Proud	Sorry
Relieved	Positive	Negative	Peaceful
Safe	Pressured	Thoughtful	Regretful
Humiliated	Depressed	Empowered	Happy

When you notice the emotion most connected to the situation, what is the belief underlying that feeling?

EMOTIONS AND THE UNDERLYING STORIES

My husband has ridden some form of two-wheeled vehicle on and off for years. Consequently, I pay close attention to bicyclists and motorcyclists. So it won't surprise you that one day when I saw this huge SUV riding on the bumper of a little motorcycle, I was instantly upset. I started in with all the stories about the driver being a jerk, about careless driving and "Who does he think he is tailgating a little motorcycle with his big bad SUV?" Yep, my anger bubbled to the surface pretty quickly.

I then took a step back. I looked at the motorcycle driver. He didn't appear concerned in the slightest. What was going on with me? I started digging. I was feeling angry, but also protective. What was that about since I didn't know either driver? Well, honestly, when cars hit motorcycles, it's harder on the motorcycle than the car, most of the time. Okay, so there was some validity to my feeling protective. But what was below the anger? Deep down, I noticed a sense of people treating other people without respect. I was feeling very much like the SUV driver wasn't respecting the space or breakability of the motorcyclist. Which, if I were completely honest, led to thoughts about times when I felt like people were not respectful of me or my needs.... What?

The insight was like a light bulb flashing in my head. I was personalizing this situation, and much of my anger was really about my experiences, not what was happening in the lane next to me. Now, don't get me wrong. There is still the issue that we should all be careful of other drivers or riders on the road. And, if I feel strongly about motorcycle or bicycle safety, I can notice that. I can start a movement, offer classes, write stories, shout my opinion out into the world. Clearly my anger at that moment wasn't just about the two people next to me on the road. It was about me. My internal narrative was getting hooked. Once I realized that the underlying issue was that I felt disrespected, then I could explore what was happening on a deeper level. Once I knew what that was, I could decide what I wanted to do about it. If I had stayed in the place of spinning out my anger, about the badness of the other driver, I wouldn't have figured out what was going on with me.

What is important to take from this is that you can use that big brain of yours to get curious and use your emotions as a doorway into knowing more about yourself. Notice the emotion and try to stay neutral to the feeling. I know it's difficult to look at a negative emotion and not say, "That's bad." The problem with deciding whether something is "good or bad" is that we are judging it and not being curious. You can always judge later. If you can set to the side the rightness or wrongness of the feeling or the situation, then you open yourself up to noticing what the emotion is trying to teach you.

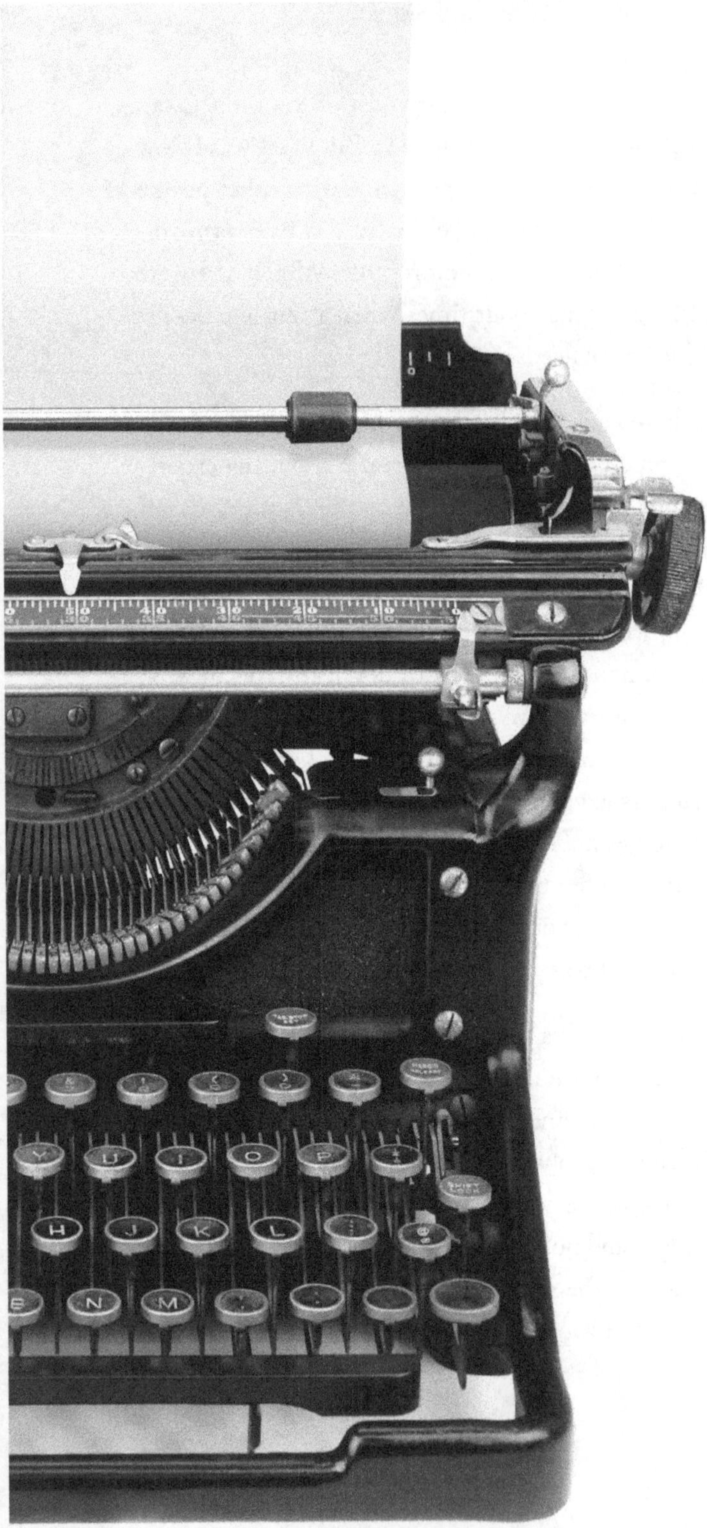

30
CLARIFYING VALUES

"Be sure you put your feet in the right place, then stand firm."

—*Abraham Lincoln*

You have values. I have values. Each person you meet has values. Your values are important to how you look at and operate within the world. Your values tell you about the aspects of yourself that are most important to how you show up and behave in every relationship you have, be it with a person, an animal, or a situation. Your values are the concepts you use to help you choose a partner, job and your friends. They help you light the way into the dark places that you will probably have to explore if you are going to challenge and change your stories.

A few things tend to come up when you start thinking about your values. You may be using these words to express in broad strokes your conceptual values, yet we often have vague definitions about what our values mean in a practical way. If you say that a value is important to you, then might it also be important to have clarity about what it means to you? How do you recognize when you are living in alignment to the value? How do you feel about yourself when you are out of alignment with a significant value? Are you holding other people accountable for your value, but then not holding yourself accountable to it? How, if you haven't worked out your meaning of the value yourself, will you be able to use the value to help you move forward? People often hold other people to their definition of the value, vague as it might be. They use the value as an indicator of what is right or wrong with the other person. What if we are both using the same word? When you and I say honesty, how do you know we mean the same type of honesty? Isn't honesty on a spectrum, like pretty much every other thing in the world? Without personal insights into the deeper meaning of your values, it's going to be a tad difficult to know where your values fit with other people's values.

Have you ever had a conversation with someone where you are both using a word to describe a value, but then you get the idea that the other person is not talking about the same value, even though she's using the same word? I have had a lot of conversations around values through the years. What I have discovered is that most of us give great import to the word, but we have little idea about where our meaning and someone else's sync up—if they don't miss completely. And this requires you to think about what the value means to you. How would you describe it to a friend? How do you apply the value to yourself? Or to others? Is there a person who represents the best qualities of this value for you?

What do you do when you find out that maybe you and I have a slightly different take on this value of honesty? It's not cut and dried. There are a lot of facets to the meanings of these words that we assume everyone understands the same way we do.... Thinking back on your life, when does misunderstanding ever happen? Oh, you might think you are in complete agreement, but I am going to guess that unless you have explored your own thinking and then had a meaningful conversation about what you both mean, you may only be operating on a shared assumption.

Let's play with the value of honesty because it seems to be important to a lot of us. What does honesty mean to you? Is it when a person always tells the truth, under every circumstance, never lies by words or omissions and is completely transparent in all circumstances? Or is it something else? Some descriptions I have heard are: "Honesty is about truthfulness; I have to know you're honest; otherwise, how will I trust you?" "People should tell the truth at all times, even if it's hard." "Honesty to me is sort of black and white, 1s and 0s." The dictionary describes honesty as: "The quality or fact of being honest; upright and fair. Truthfulness, sincerity, or frankness. Freedom from deceit or fraud." For my part, my version of honesty includes integrity, which might be different from your version.

Let me just say that I don't know anyone who always tells the truth. Good, bad, or indifferent, the fact is that everyone tells lies, half-truths and muddles up the truth in a myriad of ways. We can't help it; just go back to your filters and understand that if I am running my experience through my filters and you are running your experience through your filters, we both may be sharing our "honest" interpretation of events, but we may be sharing different versions of the truth.

Personally, what I have found is that people are more often honest in actions than in words. If I am going to trust in other people's honesty, I am more comfortable trusting when their actions and words are saying the same thing. What you might want to pay close attention to is when people's words are out of alignment with their actions. For example, when I was in college, I was in love with a nice boy. He, while lovely on a lot of levels, was not in love with me in return. Because of my great love for him, I worked diligently to ignore this truth. His heart had been broken by his last girlfriend, so on one level, I think my love and enthusiasm about him helped him to feel okay and start the process of healing from his own broken heart. To keep me around, along with my sharing my feelings about how great he was, he had to encourage my continuing adoration of him. Truthfully, we had a lot of fun; we shared a funny bone and laughed a lot; we had fun debating and thinking about all manner of ideas and we were good friends, so he encouraged my belief in our "being together" and that he loved me too. I loved those words—"I love you," "We're best friends," and "I can't imagine not having you in my life." All those words fit perfectly into what I wanted and desired most—to be in a relationship with him that was leading somewhere. Yet I was plagued by doubts and often felt crazy and manic; I sensed something was just not right. Then when I caught him with other girls, flirting with my friends, or better yet, when a particular young freshman girl came knocking on his dorm door in the middle of the night, I realized his behaviors were out of alignment with those words that I was staunchly holding onto. Now, mind you, I was twenty-two; this was my "first love," and I'll admit, I spent a lot of energy making all these situations okay, but seriously, I knew on a deep level what was what. In hindsight, it was one of my most painful lessons; my heart cracked in two. But then I dusted my broken heart off and dived into what I had learned. And, here it is folks, another super-secret of the universe: *If words and actions are out of alignment, you are not getting the truth, no matter how nice the words are.*

When you start to riffle through what honesty actually means to you, maybe it's closer to: Someone is honest when he doesn't lie about important things, or doesn't lie to cheat, steal, or harm another person. For me, I live by whether words and actions are in alignment. But, on a daily basis, I am totally okay when you tell me my new haircut looks terrific, even if you actually hate it. As long as I like my haircut, your opinion is none of my business. Just say some nice things about my hair. In other words, I don't need unfiltered brutal honesty about my haircut or how my outfit looks. How about you? What do you need when you're on the receiving end of someone else's "honesty?"

To circle back to values, the overall point here is that if you have a value that is important to you, how are you defining it? How are you holding other people accountable to it and even more importantly, how are you holding yourself accountable to it? And how does this value work with the other values you may have, such as kindness or family? Lastly, remember, you are going to need different values for different situations. Some values support healthy relationships. Slightly different values may help in raising your kids. Then there are the values that help guide you as a courageous human being on a journey to challenge your stories. Some of these values may be the same, but you may discover a few differences that would be interesting to clarify.

Here is an exercise I have used with clients through the years. Look at the list of values below and circle all the ones important to you. If there is an important value you have that isn't on the list, go ahead and add it as well.

Adventure	Balance	Happiness	Personal Growth
Creativity	Confidence	Education	
Freedom	Friendship	Grit	Power
Fulfillment	Fun	Family	Self-Respect
Responsibility	Curiosity	Health	Humor
Independence	Influence	Honesty	Self-Trust
Integrity	Spirituality	Harmony	Appreciation
Gratitude	Vulnerability	Passion	Being Right
Loyalty	Peace	Knowledge	Serenity
Purpose	Pleasure	Love	Autonomy
Choices	Exploration	Security	Self-Worth
Diversity	Wisdom	Generosity	Perfection
Congruence	Authenticity	Self-Reflection	Effectiveness
Nature	Awareness	Simplicity	Achievement
Optimism	Flexibility	Openness	Faith
Empowerment	Compassion	Awareness	Empathy
Wholeness	Intuition	Career	Insight
Acceptance	Belonging	Transformation	Relationships

Now, while there are no right or wrong values and you will undoubtedly have more than five, it's helpful to distill your values in order to develop some clarity around what you truly believe is important to you. Therefore, let's winnow your list down to your top five values. Because you can choose different values for different areas of your life, my clients will often winnow the list down to their top five values in an area of their lives such as relationships, their professional life, or their personal sense of self. For this exercise, I want you to choose the five values that would best help you when you challenge the narrative of the stories you are ready to shift.

The more you understand and clarify what your values mean to you, the better able you will be in communicating them to others. This clarity is uber-important when establishing new relationships, whether they be friendships, work relationships, or intimate relationships. The more you understand yourself, developing your own sense of self-trust, the easier it is to recognize values in others. After all, isn't it helpful when we at least know where each person is coming from and how he or she understands the "shared" value to be defined?

3 1
DEFENSE AND SAFETY

"The most courageous act is still to think for yourself. Aloud."

— *Coco Chanel*

Any strategy can become a problem when it's overused. To begin looking at your safety strategies, you need to understand them. Anytime you feel that energetic contraction in your body, you are in the process of battening down the hatches and probably looking for some way to stay emotionally or physically safe. When the feeling of fear or anxiety gets triggered in a situation, you might feel your whole body contract. Your chest and shoulders might come down and around your core in a protective posture. When our hearts open, and our shoulders return to their normal position, our bodies are feeling safe again. We close ourselves down to stay safe. This may work in a physically dangerous situation, but it is overkill in an emotional situation. And trying to stay safe doesn't work to help us develop awareness. The more we close or shut out our emotions, the more the pressure cooker builds up pressure. How do we become leaders in our lives, in our organizations, or our communities, if we shut down our senses, instead of learning to explore them? What often happens is that when we share our emotions, if we choose to protect ourselves by attacking outwards, we are going to get an entirely different response than if we honestly explore what is getting triggered for us and speak to that.

Let's look at what Sigmund Freud developed when he first explored the concept of defense mechanisms as an unconscious method for reducing anxiety and discomfort from situations that were either unacceptable or possibly dangerous. Defenses come directly from the internal sense that you need to protect yourself. Some incident or situation happens (the stimulus), you don't contemplate it too much and instead, you have an instant unconscious response (the reaction) in hopes of protecting yourself from the perceived threat. Again, this unconscious response is great if someone wildly swings into your lane of traffic, or you just noticed the tiger in the tall grass. But what happens when the situation is not so wildly dangerous, but rather psychologically uncomfortable?

In this context, the defense mechanisms are responses to situations that impact us on a psychological level. They become our ego's way of keeping our mind or sense of self safe. Defense mechanisms can be unconscious in the moment, but not always. Defense mechanisms are also not good or bad, but rather fit on a scale of healthy to not healthy. It's only when we back up a bit, looking from that 10,000-foot view and get curious that we can see whether what we are doing is helpful or not.

Quick story: In anger management, I had a client, Kevin, who challenged me about his behaviors with his boss. He felt completely justified in his anger because, from his perspective, his boss was a complete idiot and didn't realize the insight and genius that Kevin was demonstrating. As we explored the story of Kevin's rightness and his boss's wrongness, I asked, "What are you attached to in this story you're telling right now?" Kevin's response took a few minutes. "I want to be acknowledged and appreciated and my boss never does that." I then asked, "How do you manage to live with that?" Kevin took some more time as he thought about it. "I guess I am trying to get even by ignoring him when he tries to be friendly, I work slowly and I think about how much I hate him." And, boom, there you are. This is how we use defense mechanisms to feel better in a difficult situation. What might have emotionally and situationally changed for Kevin if he had spent the same amount of time noticing when his boss was being friendly or positive toward him? How might Kevin have behaved differently then? Going back to the internal locus of control, Kevin was also influencing his situation by his use of his defenses.

Let's now explore a few of the common defenses we tend to use to protect ourselves from a reality we don't like. These are stories we create to make sense of the world and make ourselves feel better. Note that there are probably as many defense mechanisms as there are people in the world, so this is not an exhaustive or complete list.

Distraction: When I was in third grade, I didn't like my teacher. She seemed critical, I didn't think she liked me and I felt a lot of shame for not being good enough in her class...so I tuned her out. I couldn't leave the class because I was basically a kid who didn't want to get into trouble and, being eight, I didn't have a lot of choices. So I gazed out the window for almost an entire school year. The teacher even had my mom take me to get a hearing test because she thought I was possibly hard of hearing. Well, physically, I could hear in the range of an average dog, but in her class, I was totally deaf to her. To survive what felt like a difficult situation, I had drifted so far into a fantasy of spending all my time riding horses in my head that I couldn't hear her voice at all. I missed a lot of learning that year. But when we feel helpless, or don't believe we have a lot of options in each situation and we feel stuck, we often fall into a distraction-type fantasy. Distraction on the healthy end of the spectrum can help us catch our breath and shift our attention from something bothersome to give us time to make a different choice.

Projection: This is classic. We do this by kindergarten effectively: "I know you are, but what am I? I know you are, but what am I?" This behavior happens when we are avoiding something we don't like about ourselves and instead of dealing with it, we see it in the other people around us. Basically, we point out what someone else is doing that we don't like. Often the stuff that bugs us the most is the same stuff we are doing, either in fact, or in how we are thinking about people and situations. This isn't always the case, but when we are bugged by something, it might be a good place to get curious about how we may be showing up with something similar. Judgment is a great example. I haven't met anyone who enjoys being judged, but we all tend to love to judge others. It gives us a sense of security in superiority. If we don't pay attention to our own judgments, when someone judges us, we may project onto that person all sorts of negative feelings, instead of looking at our own behaviors and how we may be sitting in a high and mighty seat of judgment ourselves. In other words, "When I judge you to be judging me, I am in effect judging you." Some call this a circle jerk—I think you might know what I mean.

Denial: It's not just a river in Egypt.... Sorry, I couldn't help myself. Denial is a rejection of reality. If we don't like reality, we strap on our anti-reality boots and deny, deny, deny. "It wasn't me. I didn't do that. It's not my fault. You're making too much of this XYZ. I didn't do anything wrong. That's not what happened. I reject your truth." In all its forms, denial is the rejection of some reality or our part in any situation that we are upset about. I have seen denial in every relationship, but it especially shows up in marriages that are having problems. Denial is like the dialogue of the deaf. Everyone is talking, and no one is listening.

Exaggeration: Exaggeration is often accompanied by global language.

For example: "You always do XYZ! I never do XYZ! I have to do everything!" Over-exaggeration is the blowing up in our minds of the reality of a situation. It isn't just a great meal, it's the best meal I have ever had in my entire life. It isn't simply that you hurt my feelings; it becomes, "You always hurt my feelings; you never cared for me." We all do this sometimes. We might even think when the story is positive that it's okay to exaggerate; for example, "You are the most wonderful person on the planet." Yet what I have found is that if we overuse exaggeration, people stop believing us. The extremes of always/never, great/horrible, absolutely right/absolutely wrong are often signs that we may not be paying attention to either unrealistic expectations, or we are talking up drama to sway another to agree with us. It rarely works unless we are co-opting someone with no dog in the fight who is willing just to agree with us. It can be funny to exaggerate; I personally love to use big language in telling stories, but it's only works for the long-term when everyone knows it's a fish story.

Passive Aggression: When I worked for the military, this was the number one reason why people ended up in my anger management group. Okay, technically, it was the second stage of this defense mechanism, when the passive shifts into active, that sent them to my group. But I think it would be fair to say that most parents and bosses have experienced being on the receiving end of passive aggression. When we are feeling overwhelmed by someone else's words, demands, or expectations, we might begin to work s-l-o-w-l-y. Because we don't feel safe or free to say "no" in a direct manner, we then say no passively. Passive aggression shows up when, instead of just coming out and owning that we don't want to do XYZ or we feel we have no choice but feel obligated to do XYZ, we say what the other person wants us to say and then we do something differently or very slowly. It also shows up when we are experiencing a negative emotion and direct it at someone, but we aren't direct and clear with that person about what's going on. Instead, we hide our negative emotions behind passive comments or actions.

Rationalization: Have you ever made up a story to avoid taking responsibility for something? For me, it might be eating dessert. I don't need sugar and fat nestled in a warm chocolate cookie, really, but...I might tell a story about how it's just this once, my birthday, a holiday, or I deserve that cookie after the day I've had. Basically, rationalization is an excuse wrapped in permission and we can be excuse-making machines. Another way rationalization might show up is when we do something we don't feel good about and not wanting to sit in the discomfort or apologize, we come up with why it's not our fault that we did whatever the "it" is that we did. "It was my boss," "I had a bad day," or even better, "Maybe I will instead project the blame onto you...." Wait, that's when rationalization becomes projection.

Asymmetrical Warfare: This is a military concept, but we use it with people all the time. Someone says "ABC" to you or does something to you and you come back with "XYZ" and hit the person harder. The idea being that if you are willing to hit hard enough, you will eventually get what you want; maybe to get the person to shut up, to agree with you, or to leave you alone. It's a tactic for "warfare." If you are going to adopt this tactic, you need to realize you are engaging in a war. You may have made yourself the victim and are taking full advantage of all the rights you believe victimization gives you. But the other side—you know, the one from the other person's perspective—doesn't see you as the victim but the offender. Perspective is a curious thing. Couples often come into couples counseling because they are participating in this version of fighting. It's not fair fighting; it's warfare. And while they may win the battle, their relationships have a great deal of difficulty surviving long-term with any real affection.

Withdrawal: This one is the "I can't hear you" of strategies. We withdraw in many ways. I shared earlier about my third-grade experience; I retreated into fantasy to avoid a teacher I felt didn't like me. Withdrawal might show up when, within our group of friends, people's perspectives change until a point comes where we don't have enough in common anymore, and we withdraw from the friendship. In relationships, if we are engaging in asymmetrical warfare, we regularly are having the same argument repeatedly. Usually, we're upping the ante until at some point when we've bounced back and forth between each other, making points, rationalizing, showing contempt, calling names, not listening and not being heard, one person finally just shuts down. You might then think you've finally "won" or convinced someone of your brilliance, but often once the person has time to catch his breath, he either comes back harder or withdraws from you completely. With couples, this happens when one person doesn't want to escalate the fight and needs to calm down, so he or she just stops participating in the argument. Between people in close relationships, withdrawal often has the opposite and unfortunate consequence of intensifying the other person's behavior because he or she feels disconnected and wants to hook you back into the "conversation." John Gottman, Ph.D., talks about the Four Horsemen of the Apocalypse of a relationship: Criticism, Contempt, Defensiveness and Stone Walling. Withdrawal is classic stonewalling.

THE ANTIDOTES TO OUR DEFENSES

Acceptance: When we are willing to allow the reality of life to be known, even when it's not to our liking, we can either fight it or accept it. I don't know whether we should accept all things. That's not my place to decide. I do know that in my life there are some hard realities I have had to accept to move past. Acceptance isn't necessarily the acceptance of someone's bad behaviors or our own. Rather it's the acceptance that if something has already occurred, it's in the past and no amount of worrying or being upset will undo what has already happened. That's where acceptance is most useful. The acceptance that the past "is what it is." That if we don't like it, we need to shift our attention away from the past, and onto what we are willing to do to change the paradigm.

Courage: My perspective on courage is twofold. There is the type of courage that is our emotional, mental, physical and spiritual willingness to confront our external fears, obstacles, uncertainties, or anything else the world provides that overwhelms us. The other type is the internal strength that we have—a certain type of inner scaffolding that gives us backbone and grit in pushing past our limiting beliefs and stories, holds firm to our willingness to trust in the universe or God or our Higher Power and allows us to see ourselves as both wonderful and flawed as part of our journey.

Internal Regulation: The ability to manage our emotional states is epically important to how the story will play out. If I am super-angry, which has happened a few times in my life—after all, I am a red-headed Irish Leo—and I react without giving myself a breather, then I am more likely going to have a negative consequence. My ability to self-manage my emotions gives me power over my reactions and responses. Stephen Covey talked about Reactive versus Proactive in his book *The Seven Habits of Highly Effective People*. Below is a chart illustrating the differences.

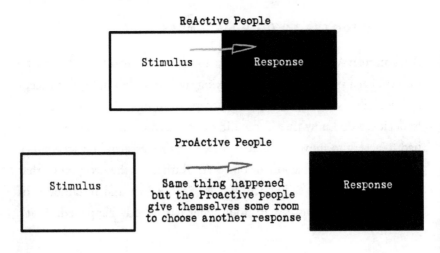

When you encounter some situation, event, or stimulus and you choose to be proactive, you have given yourself space to take a breather. This time allows you to contemplate your response. It might even be the response you were reactively wanting, but when you've had some space, you just might choose something you couldn't have considered when your brain was first on fire.

Gratitude: I know I have a blessed life. I see myself as very lucky. At the end of 2014, I was living with my mom, my husband and my mother-in-law. That December my mother-in-law was diagnosed with end-stage pancreatic cancer. As a result, our entire household went through the end-of-life process with her. It was a painful and sad situation on many levels. None of us had ever envisioned being in our situation. What we were going through had never been a wish we had when we thought about our lives. None of us came together in this situation by choice. But I learned so much about compassion, love, caring for others and surrendering to the impermanence of life through that journey. It was a gift to have been allowed to participate in this experience. We had the opportunity to figure out some necessary truths about life. And death taught us about appreciation of the moment, not taking each other for granted and letting go of anger. Life is short. And finding my gratitude in the situation changed the experience from one of drama and sadness to one of connection and a recognition of just how very lucky we are to have each other. During this time Michael said, "We aren't living in a box on the side of the road. We have it better than the majority of the people on the planet, and if we sit in misery, we aren't appreciating what we are so blessed to have." So be joyful.

Humor: I am a self-described member of the tribe of funny. I have had some ups and downs—some very far down. What I know is that if I can find the humor, I can find my way through the tragedy. In March of 2005, I quit my job with the Air Force so I could continue to grow my private practice. In May of 2005, I slipped while hiking and shattered my leg. I spent the next six months slowly learning to walk again—no sick leave, no job, no shit. It sucked and I was in a lot of physical as well as mental pain over the situation. It took a bit of time for me to find the funny in it. But as I did, it helped me to recalibrate my emotional state. I journaled about my pain, which helped my mind stay busy and not focused on the pain, but it also engaged my funny bone.

Here's an excerpt from my journal:

- **Numbing Pain:** This is a strange combo effect where an area feels numb and it is also a dull ache. This pain can play tricks with your mind because you start to worry about why it is numb. "Why, why, why?"

- **Curling Pain:** This form of pain works by curling through an area like smoke through a still room, gliding through bone and muscles like a slick, hot, vicious beast.

- **Ripping Pain:** This pain feels like something with sharp teeth or talons is ripping and tearing at you. When you look down at your leg/foot, you expect to see some blood or a stump.

- **Gnawing Pain:** This is much more painful than throbbing pain or aching pain. This feels like gerbils are gnawing at the marrow of your bone.

Mindfulness: Seriously, mindfulness is everywhere lately, which is great. It's not a new idea, but it has swept through the media like a whirlwind in the past few years. I don't mean to overuse the idea, but while it has become the "it" word of the decade, it also is the antidote to many issues. In a nutshell, mindfulness is a series of tools, ways you can talk to yourself, calm yourself down and learn how to be in the moment. Mindfulness can come in the form of meditation, breathing, or prayer. Mindfulness is developed by focusing our attention purposefully. I have found that when I garden, cook, knit, or do art, my mind quiets. And that's the key—it is a way that we quiet our minds. Maybe for you hiking, petting your fur baby, or playing with your child relaxes your mind. Mindfulness is a state of being and awareness that comes from allowing and acceptance. For instance, when I was experiencing pain after I broke my leg, I didn't want to take medication all the time. I allowed myself to feel the pain and breathe through it. It's the same for emotional suffering. Mindfulness is the path to moving through the suffering, instead of becoming stuck.

Patience: If I could build one muscle in my mind and my stories, it would be patience. A lack of patience is an area where I am in regular practice mode. It is easy to have a flash of irritation at someone or some situation. I notice it when something isn't going fast enough, or if I am making repeated mistakes, or something is driving me crazy. I have wrapped judgment to impatience, so letting go of judgment is relevant to my experience of impatience. When I notice myself feeling impatient and see the judgment stories, I can ask myself, "Is what I am thinking 100 percent true?" I have yet to come across a lot of negative internal self-talk that is 100 percent true. This question opens the door for me to challenge myself and reframe the story to include patience.

Empathy: Empathy is one of the most important antidotes to our defense strategies. We spin a lot of stories out of our preferences. Preferences are not right or wrong; they are just the way we prefer life to be, or how we prefer people to behave. When we attach sharp right and wrong, black and white thinking to our preferences, we can become quite intolerant of differences. In every great religion, there are quotes and passages about acting with humility, gentleness and patience. We need to allow that people have different perspectives. Empathy is the antidote to intolerance. Empathy doesn't equal agreement. It means that we are willing to see from another perspective, to accept that there is a spectrum of variety in the world and we are not all going to show up the same. It's the putting of yourself into another person's pair of shoes and attempting to understand a situation from his or her perspective. It is also an inside-out experience. I may not agree with your position, opinion, or external locus of control. If I can see that you have the right to your perspective, as do I. Then I can, at the very least, let go of the idea that I need to change you. I don't know about you, but I haven't found that trying to force my opinions down people's throats has worked very well.

If you capture anything from this chapter, I hope what you can walk away with is this: If you have a brain, you're defensive.... Okay, just kidding. Seriously, though, we are all self-protective. We react and respond with defensive strategies to feel safe from any perceived threats. Thankfully, there are antidotes to our defenses since most of the time we aren't under serious threat and the defenses aren't all that helpful. Using an antidote becomes one of those opportunities of choice. Is what you're about to say, think, or do, going to help you get one step closer to your goal, or one step farther away? You decide.

3 2

JUDGING YOUR INSIDES BY OTHER PEOPLE'S OUTSIDES

"We judge others instantly by their clothes, their cars, their appearance, their race, their education, their social status. The list is endless. What gets me is that most people decide who another person is before they have even spoken to them. What's even worse is that these same people decide who someone else is and don't even know who they are themselves."

— Ashly Lorenzana

Many years ago, I had a coworker at Kirtland Air Force Base who used to say, "Too many people judge their insides by other people's outsides." I loved the simplicity of that statement, so I stole it and have used it ever since. It fits for most situations. Too often, we spend an inordinate amount of time comparing ourselves to other people. We look at them and think to ourselves how they have it all together while we are lacking or failing in some way. The other side of this is when we look at someone else's life and feel superior to that person. Either way, we are judging our internal experience by someone else's external presentation.

Clients have told me many times something along the lines of "I hate my life. Everyone I look up to is doing so much better. They are happier, more successful and more put together than I am. I, on the other hand, am a freaked-out mess. I am stressing over my relationship. I am stressing over the amount of work I must do. I am stressing over my mortgage. I am stressing over my kids. Basically, I'm stressing out over most of the important aspects of my life. What is the secret? Why do I feel this way and how do I become successful like these other people?"

It's a common complaint. When we judge people solely by external appearances, it's easy to leap to self-judgment with little, if any, information. When we do that, we are making assumptions about what is happening in those other people's interior experiences.

When you're out in the world, to whom do you show your real internal workings? Do you share with every person you meet how freaked out and stressed you are? Or do you pull yourself together and present a mask to the world? If you don't create a mask, with how many people do you share your every internal freak-out?

When I worked with the military, many of the men I worked with told me that guys often wear a mask. The mask is whatever you want to show the world and for a lot of men, it's a tough guy mask. "I wear the mask to protect myself from other men so that they won't bother me. I also wear it with women so they can't hurt me." This was the general flavor of the mask story. "If I wear the mask, then it's 'that' guy who's acting that way, not me. I can stay over here, safe, where no one can touch me. If I say or do something you don't like, I can disown it, because that was my mask acting that way, not the real me. You don't even know the real me."

Personally, I don't think mask-wearing is a gender specific issue. Both men and women wear masks. We spend a lot of energy pretending how we feel about ourselves and our lives. We may have a few confidants that we share more of our true self. With much of the world, we share the mask we want people to see. Take a look at Facebook. People fill their FB walls with happy pictures, moments in time that show whom they are and whom they want us to believe they are. There is nothing wrong with any of this. It's how we find the gratitude or joy in our lives, by sharing our best moments and staying in touch with others. The opposite—only sharing depression or angst—isn't any better. It's just a different spin. Here's the rub. If you look at these external expressions and assume they represent that person's totality and then judge yourself harshly, you are making decisions about yourself without all the information.

I have had clients think they know all about my life. What they see is whatever they are looking at. Maybe they see my car or house and decide something about my life. Or if I share that it's possible to like as well as love your partner, they assume my relationship with my husband is easy. Then they look at their lives or relationships and think there is something wrong with them. There isn't.

I'm not saying they may not have work to do. Very few people have it all together. Let's say maybe 5 percent of the entire planet is that good. They have it clicking all together, all aces, on every level. That percentage might even be high. But I believe the only way they got there was they pushed through the fear when it showed up in their lives. They didn't stick their heads in the sand. Instead, they stood up and looked directly into their anxiety, fear and uncertainty. They didn't flinch from self-awareness. They didn't run from being open, honest and learning from their mistakes. They owned it. Maybe they did it at age twenty and became a shining star, or maybe they are doing it at fifty. Just possibly, they do it again and again as they discover more about themselves, making themselves a "work in progress" from fifteen to fifty-five. So think about this: If you're going to look at something, look at where you started ten years ago and see what you've accomplished since then. Maybe you had kids and are raising interesting people, or you went to school, or you left a destructive relationship, or you kicked an addiction. Maybe you decided to "get real" with yourself and start looking at some of the places that stop you from having honest and loving relationships with others. Look at what you have done because I am going to guess you are not the same person you were ten years ago. And some of those changes may have happened by sheer accident. So what would be possible for you if you consciously chose to make shifts in your stories and beliefs with a clear intention toward an outcome? What would be possible then?

How you handle your issues determines what you learn and what you take with you into the next difficult situation that shows up. It determines your attitude and the mindset that you will bring to challenges. Get curious and look at how you are feeling when you're stressed and freaking out on the inside. Don't spend too much time looking at what others have done and using that to tear yourself down or build yourself up. Instead, focus on how you are feeling and what you need to do about your situation. Then you're on the right path to StoryJacking. The only focus that matters is how you think about yourself when you lay your head on your pillow at the end of the day. How much you respect your choices and how well you align yourself with your values. Ask yourself, "Am I choosing the focus that empowers me to be at my best?"

3 3
LETTING GO OF JUDGMENT

"Never look down on anybody, unless you're helping them up."

—*Jesse Jackson*

In her book *A Great and Terrible Beauty*, Libba Bray wrote:

> In each of us lie good and bad, light and dark, art and pain, choice
> and regret, cruelty and sacrifice. We're each of us our own chiar-
> oscuro, our own bit of illusion fighting to emerge into something
> solid, something real. We've got to forgive ourselves that. I must
> remember to forgive myself. Because there is a lot of grey to work
> with. No one can live in the light all the time.

I can't think of a more truthful statement about the growth process. I
would add that this need to forgive and not judge ourselves applies to
everything in our lives. It is unrealistic to expect you will only have fun
and good times.

To that end, if you look around, you will see that a lot of people, maybe all people, spend their time gazing out of windows instead of looking at themselves in the mirror. Sitting in judgment on other people is a slippery slope, and when you do that instead of doing your own work, you disempower your journey. By comparison, we become empowered by expanding our internal process, taking control of what we say, think and do. Judgment is an external locus issue. Each time your focus turns to another person and away from your own behavior, you have sidestepped progress and come full stop at a judgment.

We are all just one bad decision away from an entirely different life. Seriously, who here hasn't done something that only by the grace of God you survived without hurting yourself or someone else beyond repair? And to boot, we get totally spun up over some minor things—the loud neighbor or the jerky one, this news station or that one, dirty dishes or laundry on the floor. There are so many non-important issues that we spin out over.

We sit in these seats of judgment when we call the driver who speeds past us "reckless" and the slow driver in front of us "timid." Do we honestly believe that whatever it is that we are doing is okay and of no consequence, but everyone else is wrong? The greatest StoryJack you might need to do for yourself is to develop awareness of your hypocrisy because if you are human, you have been a hypocrite—yes, you and yes, me too.

The path to resolving this situation is to work on owning your actions, your thoughts and your words. They matter because we have no influence to bring about good when we sit in judgment. If you want to have a life where you aren't angry or suffering, you might just owe it to yourself to do the work of self-awareness and learn to be okay with reality.

FORGIVENESS

Very few of us make it to adulthood without suffering at the hands of someone else. But if I hold onto the past, along with blame and bitterness, I stay stuck. Moving forward is seriously compromised when our heads are looking backward. Forgiveness is an act of freedom we give ourselves. When we let go of the blame, the anger, and the bitterness, we free ourselves up to move in new directions. When we hold onto those negative feelings, we generate the patterns repeatedly. It's a little like the movie Groundhog Day. We wake up and repeat the same day over and over until we get past the hurt. I think we choose situations that push our buttons to force ourselves to learn. Forgiveness for ourselves and others gives us the bandwidth to change our story's trajectory.

My father is in his seventies and still trying to figure himself out, which I admire. Recently, he told me, "I don't feel good about the relationships in my life." He described even feeling worried about being around people because he might say something rude or careless and because in the past, he has held grudges and been angry for a long time, sometimes that anger came out unexpectedly on strangers.

A little back history on my dad is needed here. My dad experienced a lot of emotional and physical abuse at the hands of his mother. She lost custody of him when he was three and then she kidnapped him from his father. She didn't want him. She just couldn't stand the idea of anyone else having him. He bounced around. He was sent away to Catholic school, to his disinterested grandmother and back to his self-centered mother. He rarely felt loved, cherished, or wanted. And I would guess that the adults around him didn't do much to show him that he was loved. However, while he and I have had our issues, he has been a better parent to me than his parents ever were to him.

I was interested that my dad would say he was struggling with bitterness and holding grudges since that was something I was struggling with also. Instead of being comfortable with himself, he was questioning all his behaviors. He was afraid to interact with people because his anger often came out inappropriately. He was isolating himself because he never knew what he might say. Knowing what his childhood was like, I told him, "Dad, at some point you are going to have to forgive Grandma for being a terrible mom because I think you are still reacting to all those old hurts and it's keeping you stuck. If you learn to forgive her or allow yourself to forgive her, the forgiveness lets you move on." He told me he wanted to move on, but it was hard to let go of so much pain. I asked him, "Who do you think you're punishing with your anger and bitterness?" "I don't know," he replied. Here is where I was talking to myself as well as him, "You're punishing yourself. In this case, Grandma is gone. You're the one still holding onto and living with the pain. If you could forgive Grandma, it could help you to enjoy your life. Letting go of your anger at her will lighten you up. It's a type of freedom you can give yourself." He replied, "I've heard that. I just don't know what to do."

I was feeling a lot of empathy for him because letting go of grudges is hard, especially if you haven't been exercising your forgiveness muscle much. "You forgive people for yourself," I told him. "In this case, she's dead, so who on earth do you think you're hurting?" He took some time before he responded, "I haven't ever thought about it like that." I replied, "Well, take some time to ponder that because you get to choose."

Which, of course, led me to reflect on my life situation. As I have mentioned, my mom lives with my husband and me. She and I have had a very complicated relationship over the years. When I was seventeen, my story is that she chose my verbally and emotionally abusive stepfather over me because she was going to live the rest of her life with him. Now she lives with me and hasn't had a relationship with him in years. But a part of me—perhaps the seventeen-year-old part—still hurts from the belief that I wasn't important enough to her. I didn't feel protected at that time, and that gets swirled into my story. I wish when I was forty-seven and she moved in with me that I could have just let go of this story, but that didn't happen. I am now fifty-one and still wrestling with it a bit. The feelings of resentment and hurt compound now that my mom has health and memory issues. I oversee her finances and generally, I am responsible for many of her needs. This is not the place either of us ever expected to be.

One weekend, as I was cleaning my mom's space, I thought, "Lyssa, you keep wanting your mom to love you the way your seventeen-year-old self wanted to be loved, cherished and chosen. Remember you have no control over any of that because it's in the past. Ask instead, how do you want to love your mom?" Despite everything, I can't make my mom different than she is. I know she loves me and is proud of me, so somewhere along this journey, I must forgive her and myself for who we were and who we are. I must take the same advice I gave my dad, only I get to do it while my mom is alive. I love my mom, so how do I let go of the hurt so I can live the love and share it with her?

I once saw a bumper sticker that said, "Let go or be dragged." It made me visualize my anger as my hand clutching at the tattered pieces of my past hurts. It was such a great visual that it stuck itself inside my psyche. It continues to help remind me why I am working on letting go of the past—I don't want my bitterness to become my rut or my grave.

The whole point of forgiveness is—the letting go, the surrendering of the past so that you can move forward into your future with grace and energy. Letting go doesn't mean denying that some bad shit probably went down in your life. But it allows you to decide whether you will remain a bitter, angry, grudge-holding person over something that happened in the past and can't be undone. When you choose anger and blame, the person you become is not a lot of fun to be around. Often, you don't even enjoy being around yourself. Maybe you try to tune out the discomfort of living with hurt, anger, and blame by using drugs, alcohol, sugar, or shopping. Once you come down off the high, you still feel bad. All you've successfully done is create a crazy tilt-a-whirl of issues, broken relationships, shame, blame and lost opportunities to play and feel joy. Because the tools you use to avoid pain can lead to bad decisions, ultimately your bad decisions will catch up with you.

Personally, I am glad that I never accidently hurt someone in an angry fit. I did destroy a beautiful purse once, at least it was mine. That action was an eye-opener for me on how rage isn't thoughtful. Rage is reactive rather than proactive. I am very glad I never hurt someone while driving recklessly and in anger. I don't judge you if you also have struggled with letting go of your past hurts. I can only encourage you to explore what it will take to shift your mind so you can work through it and then let it go. Catch and release, baby—it will free your mind and improve your life.

EXERCISE:

What about you? What do you need to let go of?

_____

_____

_____

_____

_____

_____

What old story are you still holding onto?

_____

_____

_____

_____

And what support and tools do you need so you can open your heart and let go? So you don't have to be dragged around by your own upset anymore?

_____

_____

_____

_____

_____

_____

Take a few minutes to ponder that.

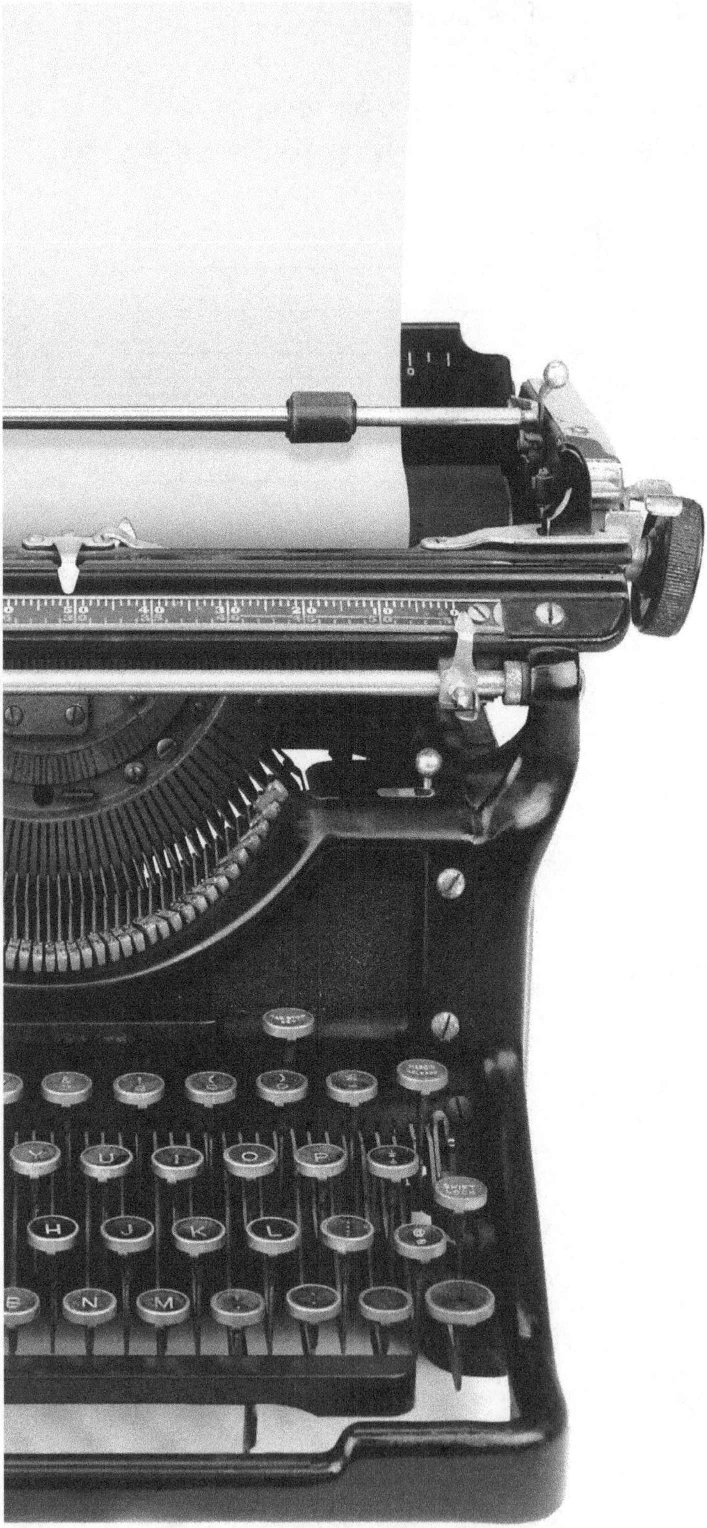

3 4
THE DRAMA TRIANGLE

*"You can't save others from themselves because those who make
a perpetual muddle of their lives don't appreciate your interfering with the drama they've created. They want your poor-
sweet-baby sympathy, but they don't want to change."*

— Sue Grafton

When I was in my late twenties, I dated a man who told me, "I never trust anyone until I have had a fight with them and see them angry." I wrestled with this idea. There seemed to be so many emotions to explore that it stumped me that he would use anger as his litmus test. But the longer I sat with his words, the more sense they made. It's easy to get along with people when everyone agrees. When we all taste the cookie and agree it's amazing, it's easy, simply put, to get along. We may have deep philosophical discussions on how much to cook the pasta, or what we like to add to it—butter, olive oil, pasta sauce, pesto—but if we aren't too attached to the situation or we agree, we do fine. The rubber doesn't meet the road in a relationship until we have a meaningful disagreement.

Michael and I met not long after I started thinking about this idea of trust and conflict. As we got more serious and decided we were going to live together, the inevitable happened. One morning, Michael said something he thought was funny and I heard as a criticism. Suddenly, my defensive, angry, critic voices were spinning and I spent an entire day stewing. My avoidance-of-conflict part even joined the fray because I went to the bookstore after work and meandered around for several hours before going home. It was a vain attempt to avoid having to show up with my chaotic feelings pinned so clearly on my face. I was by turns hurt, then angry. Who the hell does he think he is? Who the hell does he think I am? What's funny right now is that I don't even remember what he said—just how I felt, and it was bad.

After meandering and malingering as long as I possibly could, I finally went home. I wanted my apartment back so that I could avoid the conversation. Wanting it didn't make it true. So, through the front door and into a "difficult conversation" I went. I knew I didn't want to handle the situation the way all my wild, angry emotions were pushing me to respond. I knew I wanted to stay in the relationship, not damage it and to be honest about what was going on inside of me. Those two wishes were the rub: how to be honest and not destroy the relationship. Frankly, I had done damage in my past relationships. They had often ended poorly.

As I came through the door, Michael moved toward me. He had no idea I was even upset. He still thought he had been funny. Mostly he was worried about where I had been for several hours. When I looked at him, I just started to cry. I had no clue how to navigate forward in the conversation. I didn't have a lot of practice having conflict in a healthy or productive manner, and I didn't want to shag things up with him. As I sobbed, he wrapped his arms around me until I could form whole words again. We sat on the couch, and I started to explain what had happened and the story I had concocted. I told him how I had gotten my feelings hurt. How I had felt mad. How I took what he had said and made a story inside my head about what it meant. I explained I was afraid he would think I was a crazy person. And, that I was at a loss about the next step to take, so I had avoided coming home.

He confirmed that I was probably a crazy person, but that he was sorry he had hurt my feelings. We spent about thirty minutes talking. He didn't take any of it personally, and I didn't blame him. We talked, sorted it out and muddled through. It went well. In hindsight, I think my defenses began to come down because we both handled it well. I finally understood what that young man had been telling me, it finally made sense.

Not long after, I came across the work of Stephen Karpman, M.D. Dr. Karpman came up with an ingeniously simple tool he calls the Karpman Drama Triangle. It diagrams what is happening during a conflict, what roles we play and when a conflict goes sideways. The model explores the connections between where responsibility, power and the roles of victim, rescuer, and persecutor are found in conflict. It's worth noting that we can play all three roles in different situations and within the same argument, we may bounce between the roles.

The roles make up the triangle's three corners as pictured below.

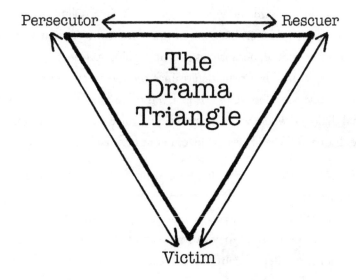

Here's how the process works:

The Victim Role: In this role, the victim's voice screams that "Something bad has happened to me! There I was, minding my own business when you—life, the universe, whoever, or whatever—came along and harmed me. I hurt because of this terrible situation or this horrific person. I am powerless, oppressed and well, victimized. In most cultures, victims have rights. Something bad happened to them, so they have the right to justice. This viewpoint keeps victims from looking at how they participated in the situation. No responsibility is taken when we are in the victim role. We tend to flip from the victim role into the persecutor role pretty quickly. I mean, you harmed me, and now I want to protect myself. These plot twists are happening to me, and I am helpless unless I attack.

The Persecutor Role: Every person on the planet has played this part and learned this voice by age five. This voice declares, "I'm rubber. You're glue. Whatever you say bounces off me and sticks to you" and "You're stupid! You big meanie, you're the one to blame! It's all your fault. I never would have done this if you hadn't started it." This is the critical, blaming, angry voice. Full of vim and vigor, this voice sits in absolute judgment of the situation. This is a problem when the voice is directed outward, say at your boss or spouse, because it's probably going to trigger the person's drama triangle until he or she determines the role to take in response to you. Typically, they choose "victim." Even more problematic can be the internal dialogue where we turn this critical voice on ourselves, spinning up the drama and then beating the crap out of ourselves.

The Rescuer Role: This role tends to want to "save" the victim. This voice either wants to rescue the other internal voices, or externally, it might be another person or the situation. For example, if I think you're helpless or need my help, I may swoop in and try to rescue you. Or if you are experiencing internal conflict, the rescuer voice is a way of rescuing the person from feeling bad, or having a difficult conversation. In my situation with Michael, my rescuer voice had me meandering around the bookstore for several hours while my victim and persecutor voices cried and raged respectively. This is our enabler part. We get to ride in on the white horse and try to save the day. I usually swoop in with a glass of wine or a brownie. But whatever our method, the rescuer helps us avoid taking responsibility for our part and soothes away our discomfort. By focusing on saving the victim, we can shift attention away from whatever we are trying to avoid or distance ourselves from—the conflict, uncomfortable feelings, etc.—and redirect our energy into blame or helplessness.

This drama triangle shows up in almost every conflict, whether it's a marriage, a friendship, siblings, parents and children, at home, at work and around the world. When the voices we are using are these three, we will avoid conflict or bring it on so hard it will rock the world. We have the capacity to choose different roles and ultimately change the story, which leads nicely into the drama triangle's antidotes.

Along Came TED

I recently read *The Power of TED: The Empowerment Dynamic* by David Emerald. David's wife, Donna Zanjonc, generously shared some time with me and brought me a copy of the book. In *TED*, David explores an antidote to what he calls the Dreaded Drama Triangle (DDT). He calls the antidote The Empowerment Dynamic (TED). The beauty of TED is that it very simply makes sense of the DDT by way of a fable. As I was reading David's book, I could see how I still engage in the DDT.

One Sunday Morning

As mentioned earlier, my mother has been living with Michael and me.

She moved in with us in 2013, due to health issues and the need for more support. Because of our complicated relationship, I am challenged daily with falling into old patterns of moving between victim and persecutor. One Sunday morning, which also happened to be my wedding anniversary, I went downstairs to make sure my mom was awake because her ride to church was coming in a couple of hours and she needed the time to get dressed, have breakfast and be ready when her ride showed up. She isn't the best at time management. When I checked on her, she was already up, so we chatted a bit. I started a load of the laundry, and then I went back upstairs.

Fifty minutes later, my mom still hadn't come upstairs to eat. She still had an hour before her ride was going to arrive, which would be plenty of time for an average person, but my mom tends to be slow. She doesn't see well, so things take her longer. I went downstairs to check on her and my laundry, which should also be ready. She was only now getting dressed. "What have you been doing for the past hour?" I asked. She responded, "Meditating. I am now meditating on Om Mani Padme Hum, the Buddhist chant for compassion." As she was telling me about this compassion meditation, I feel my frustration building. My internal dialogue was: If she isn't ready and people are coming to help her or give her a ride, and she makes them wait, they may stop. Then all the responsibility will fall on me! From this mindset, I said, "What? You have to be ready for people to pick you up in an hour! You haven't finished dressing. Hell, you haven't eaten! You need to choose your activities in a different order. Like get ready and be ready to leave, then meditate in the time you have left."

Okay, I was now in full shift out of helpful mode and smack into another role. My focus was on my external locus (my mom), and I was not feeling any compassion at that moment. My frustration continued building up, so I piled on a few more concerns. The thoughts swirling in my head were things like: "I am going to have to clean up after her. She is going to be late again and annoy her ride. At some point, she won't get rides, and I'll have to be a chauffeur, on top of everything else I have to do for her." I continued thinking, "It's my wedding anniversary, and she hasn't bothered to say, 'Happy Anniversary.' Instead, she is ruining my morning and my day is starting all wrong. All I want is just to live alone on a deserted island with no responsibilities. How the heck did I get here?" You get the idea. My mind was spinning with all the reasons I had to justify my negative feelings. I had stepped fully into the victim role. I knew all these thoughts were not going to help if I said them, so I kept a lid on it. Instead, I asked her a bit more about her meditation and silently started thinking that my meditation needed to be, "God, grant me the serenity to accept the things I cannot change, the courage to change the things I can and the wisdom to know the difference." I moved the laundry to the dryer and went back upstairs.

About twenty-five minutes later, I heard my mom coming upstairs to make breakfast. She had things that would be fast to eat—her oatmeal, a few hard-boiled eggs—which would have been good choices because now she had about thirty-five minutes to make breakfast, clean up, brush her teeth and be ready for her ride. This amount of time was feeling like an unwinnable number. *But I am not going to solve it. I am not going to solve it. I am not going to solve it. It's not my job to micromanage her.* I reminded myself of this several times. Within five minutes, I heard the fan over the stove turn on. My husband and I looked at each other. This sound is connected to things burning in the kitchen. I got up to check. Yep, the kitchen was filled with smoke and the smell of burnt butter. My mom hadn't opened a window. Instead, she was making an omelet in a room filled with smoke and the microwave fan blowing on high. OH, HELL! An omelet? What happened to the quick meal? She had also managed to get cheese on three of the four surfaces in the kitchen. There were dirty bowls and eggshells laying around. Now my vision of cleaning up after her had fully bloomed. I was no longer feeling only like a victim. I was now mad, so I flipped into the persecutor. I was cleaning up her mess and discussing all that I was doing as I was doing it. I was annoyed, and she knew it. In fact, the part of me that was talking out loud wanted her to know it, while the part of me that wished I was a better person wished I would stop talking. I got the kitchen cleaned, walked out and said to my husband, "There, I just turned into both the victim and the persecutor all at once." He smiled, but it was mostly in sympathy for my internal drama.

I was glad I could see the dynamic. By not turning away from my roles and my experience, I could work to let go of my anger a bit faster. I also knew I needed to chant the serenity prayer, but I didn't, and then the situation escalated. Since it is never too late to start doing helpful calming behaviors, I began to repeat the prayer about four times slowly. I calmed down, my brain stopped firing angry chemicals, and I was able to breathe calmly again. I went back into the kitchen and apologized. Then we had a nice chat until she was done eating. She had five minutes left. So much for my timing concerns. She said, "I am really glad I had the omelet." I could have reacted, but I reminded myself, I'm okay; I'm okay; I'm okay. I said, "Good. I am glad too, and it will tide you over until lunch. I just appreciate that you hustled." She said, "Thank you." We both knew that the thank you was "Thank you for not haranguing me anymore." I said, "You're welcome," and we both knew the "You're welcome" was about my shutting up.

My mom went downstairs, brushed her teeth and then was sitting on the front patio waiting for her ride. They showed up and swept her off to church. I sat down and wrote this story so I wouldn't forget it. The morning was saved and I had yet another reminder of how I create my own hell.

By getting curious about my own behavior, focus shifts from the situation itself and instead becomes about where you are choosing to put your attention. In the above story, my focus had become about time and getting my mom ready in time for her ride. (Which locus of control was I in? Internal or external?) Then my enabler showed up. TED asks that I look at the situation and notice how it affects my Inner State. As the pressure of concern rose, my anxiety or frustration shifted into high gear. My Inner State in this situation went from calm, when I walked downstairs the first time, to one of frustration and annoyance. This emotional state then impacted how I behaved. In my case, my tone was shifting. I was speaking in a curt manner and ultimately, I fell directly into lecturing and justifying why I was behaving the way I was—the classic persecutor just arrived in the house.

Here's where it got more interesting for me. I knew deep inside my heart that I didn't want to behave the way I was behaving. I don't like it when I acted out in ways that made me feel bad about my behavior. I didn't enjoy being angry, and I didn't like it when I was overreacting. What made this even worse was the reality that I was overreacting. I was getting all wound up about something that wasn't that important, and I didn't make the situation better with my reactions. Finally, what I was noticing about the situation was that it was a habit or pattern of response. It was the reincarnation of a pattern that my mom and I had been going around and around with for at least the past ten years, probably longer.

Fortunately, once you know something, as in deeply understand it, apply it to yourself and get curious about it, it is very difficult to "unknow" it. Once we recognize the DDT, it's difficult not to see the ways we are showing up with it in our stories and in our negative interactions.

David's antidotes to each of the roles in the DDT are:

- The Victim shifts to the Creator—Moving out of blame or

shame and into seeing yourself as capable of choosing your responses. Looking forward toward your passion and purpose. And not getting waylaid by life events or plot twists.

- The Persecutor shifts to the Challenger—This is a shift of mindset; you do not need to be the angry interrogator. Instead, you move into a state of mind of curiosity, provoking the Creator to take his or her own actions. Letting go of attachment to the choices that the Creator will take.

- The Rescuer shifts to the Coach—In this dynamic, the Rescuer/Enabler shifts his or her focus, similarly as in coaching in general. In this role, you see yourself as whole, capable, resourceful and creative. You also see the other person as whole, capable, resourceful and creative. It's a supportive role that still allows the Creator to be fully empowered to own his or her story and journey.

We have a choice in how we respond. An important mental shift occurs when we decide to look at our life and adjust our perspective. For instance, the Creator perspective is about creating a vision, a direction that you want to go. And my guess is that you have done this multiple times in your life. For example, when deciding on a career, whether to enter a relationship or even what to do with your off-time. There is a decision, and we create a vision of our life. For me, as long as I stay in the DDT with my mom, I will spin in circles. Because parent-child relationships are terminal and no matter what happens, my mom will always be my mom, I have a reason to work on my part of the situation. I have to ask myself, what is the vision that I want for this relationship?

In *The Seven Habits of Highly Effective People*, Stephen Covey talks about this very thing—in fact, it's his first habit: Begin with the end in mind. I like to use the analogy of taking a trip. If I have a destination—say

I'm driving from Seattle to Portland—I have a goal or direction. At any given time on this trip, I might take a side trip to the gas station, or a scenic route and be slightly off course. But if I know my destination, I can adjust my course throughout the trip. Ultimately ending up arriving at the destination I wanted, Portland and not somewhere else, like say Spokane.

In my story, shifting from the persecutor to the challenger means that I maybe challenge my mom to think about what she needs to get done. I can ask her in what order she would like to do those things so she can be ready on time. Or in my internal process, I might need to challenge myself when I know I am going to get annoyed. I can ask myself how I want to show up in the situation. I can breathe and then ask my mom about the time frame. A key factor here is that in the challenger role, I let go of attachment to my mom's choice. She either has a plan, or she can create a plan. What I am challenging myself to do, is to behave in ways that support what I say my goal or vision is—in this case, to be more compassionate.

One important lesson I have been developing as a coach is to become comfortable with not knowing. Coming from a place of curiosity and allowing people to expand their awareness without my attachment to what they are supposed to do or how they are expected to be. The coach is an objective observer, not trying to "fix" the person or the situation. Again, it's about being curious about what is going on. Noticing what story we are telling ourselves, and what actions or behaviors generate as a result of the story. Exploring if there is alignment with our stated goal. In my own situation, it might look like shifting attention from my frustration with my mom and her time management. Stepping out of the drama triangle and instead noticing what feelings are coming up for me. I maybe need to sit with them, explore what they mean for me, probe whether they are even true or just victim/persecutor/rescuer voices and then deciding how I want to move forward toward my deeper goal.

HOW DO YOU EAT A MAMMOTH?
ONE SMALL BITE AT A TIME.

At each step of this process, we need to know that we can make little adjustments and take small bites. It's okay to make little adjustments since few of us make epic changes overnight. When we do make these micro-adjustments, we build new neural networks, and that is exactly what we need to make the changes stick for the long haul.

In my relationship with my mother, if my vision is to be kind and respectful to her and her situation, then when I feel myself slipping into one or all the drama voices, I can choose to get curious. If I am not able to get curious right away, I can step out, walk away, take a breath, calm down and then remind myself that my goal is to be kind and respectful. In this moment of awareness, I get to decide whether what I am about to say, think, or do will take me one step closer to my goal, or one step farther away. Then I can choose whether to complete that action or take a different route.

35
COURAGE IN THE FACE OF OUR CHOICES

"It is our choices, Harry, that show what we truly are, far more than our abilities."

—J.K. Rowling

Interesting intersections happen in each of our lives. Someone shows up and has some great gift to share with you. This person is usually unexpected, so it is up to us to listen to providence and pay attention to what is happening. By leaving ourselves open to possibilities, opportunities, and experiences, many interesting characters will show up. We have only to notice them.

I have a friend, Nanny, who is a connector. She often pulls together all the women she knows and creates a Ladies Day, involving food, exploration, laughter, general getting to know each other and having fun. One day, I decided to join her outing, but because I also wanted to spend time with Michael that day, I only signed up for the gallery tour and lunch in Poulsbo, Washington. I decided that meeting up with Nanny and the gang would be fun and I wasn't going to put pressure on myself to be anything other than open and choose to have a good time with these women, many of whom I had never met before. Poulsbo is a small town close to where I live. It has a sweet downtown that is all of one street and five blocks long. It has the air of a little Viking seaside village. When I arrived, the ladies were at the farmer's market, so I decided to step into the Front Street Gallery and look around while I waited for them to finish up and head toward the restaurant. As I was meandering about the gallery, enjoying looking at how creative people can be, I noticed a gentleman behind the counter, who was quietly sitting and stringing beads. Soon we were chitchatting about the artists. He introduced himself as Joseph Fourbears. With a name like that, I felt drawn to know more about him. I told him bears were my spirit animal and showed him several of my grizzly bear photos. He asked me what I did. I said, "I'm a recovering PTSD and Complex Trauma Therapist and was now I'm transforming myself into a Narrative Coach and author." When I told him about this book, providence stepped in.

Joseph shared some of his story that day. I have learned more since then because we have developed a friendship. Joseph is a Native American and a Vietnam Vet, who struggled with PTSD for many years.

In the late 1960s, Joseph had consciously chosen to join the Army to fulfill his childhood dream to be a paratrooper and ultimately tested for Green Beret. Much to his dismay, he found himself stationed in Germany, far away from the action. Joseph looked at his life, looked at what he wanted and went to his commander. "I don't want to stay here in Germany," he said. "I want to go to Vietnam." His commander obliged him.

Joseph was gung-ho to participate. He was from a warrior family, and he felt an internal drive to go to war and join the battle. When he arrived in Vietnam and connected with his unit, he had the impression that he would be going out on day runs to engage in combat and then would come back to camp each night to eat, drink, laugh and sleep before he headed out the next day again. Instead, his unit's mission was to engage the Vietcong in guerilla warfare, organizing resistance and generally creating chaos behind enemy lines. As you might imagine, this was not a video game experience. It was a four-dimensional immersion into hell. Joseph was immersed for most of the next year. He told me that his unit had a 500 percent casualty rate. This number floored me. It also explained the level of trauma and bonding that happens between people in life-and-death situations. He and his band of brothers were dependent on each other for survival and survival had no guarantees.

Joseph stated that the entire experience seemed random. One time he may have zigged and his friend zagged, and this his friend died in front of him. Through the experience, his understanding of the terribleness of war grew. Joseph said that to cope, he had to shut down and close off parts of himself just to survive. By the grace of God, the universe, sheer luck, or all of the above, he survived his time in Vietnam. He was shipped home at the end of his tour, but he was left with a lingering and haunting question: Why me? Why did I survive when all these other good men died? Why am I here? Why, why, why? This question haunted him. Often in the form of his fallen friends' ghostly faces following him.

Joseph described wrestling with the "why" and how the "why" brought him anger, guilt, shame and hurt. It reminded him of his fear. His sense of self was shattered, and it affected his family. Marriage and relationships are hard enough under the best of times. Joseph's marriage didn't survive his "why," and once his wife and children were gone, he was left with himself.

Joseph said to me, "I didn't even know I could have PTSD. I honestly thought it was only something women or those who are weak get."

But the ghosts were not leaving; the pain and memories were not going away. It didn't matter how hard he worked to shove those ghosts into the closet of his mind; they still came out and harried him. He saw how other veterans sank into the darkness, using alcohol and drugs to help numb their pain while being unwilling to talk about their experiences due to guilt and shame.

Joseph grew up in Nebraska on the Omaha Reservation. His history was steeped in a deep belief in community and facing fears. When he reached the point where he could no longer stand his overwhelming feelings, he turned to his roots and explored many different paths to help him heal his PTSD—storytelling, being witnessed, drumming and the sweat lodge. For many cultures, the sweat lodge is a way to re-purify a person's spirit and help him or her find the way back to his or her true self—one's core essence, if you will. The sweat lodge represents a place of spiritual sanctuary, a place to heal your mind, your body and your spiritual essence. For this reason, Joseph decided to participate in it.

On the day of the sweat, the fire master asked Joseph to pick up the sweat leader on his way to the lodge. On the drive there, the sweat leader asked Joseph, "What do you want to get from this experience today?" Joseph responded, "I want these ghosts to leave me alone." The sweat leader then asked, "Joseph, do you think it's possible you are the one holding onto them?" Joseph sat with that, through the sweat; it worked at his thinking. He had never thought about what he might be doing to continue to hold onto his pain. He recognized the choice in front of him; he could hold onto the pain, or he could let go of the ghosts. Then an interesting thing happened—he decided he was going to change his relationship to the PTSD. He made a clear decision that he was going to quit feeling guilty and instead honor the loss of his friends in war by living a full life that they would be proud of.

This was such a profound insight for Joseph that it changed his whole story. He became curious about how to bring the ghosts of his friends inside of himself so he might honor their gift to him. He stopped asking "Why?" and instead decided he could help them continue to live through his memory and he would share his life with them. He allowed himself to grieve them, love them and was courageous enough to bare their souls within his heart.

Joseph's second wife, Annette, told me that one of his enduring qualities that helped to guide him was his self-examination. Annette shared that when she would occasionally get angry at him, if she said something like, "You're being such a jerk." Joseph would take some time, leave the situation, explore and sit with it and then he would come back and say, "You're right, I was being a jerk," or "No, I had good reasons for what I said. I stand by my words." Annette added, "He is no one's pushover." It was that same self-examination that led Joseph away from the "why" of his survival and to the "what" of how to live his life in a way that honored those who sacrificed their lives and for whom he was grateful. In retrospect, he told me, "The war has been a powerful teacher in helping me become the man I am."

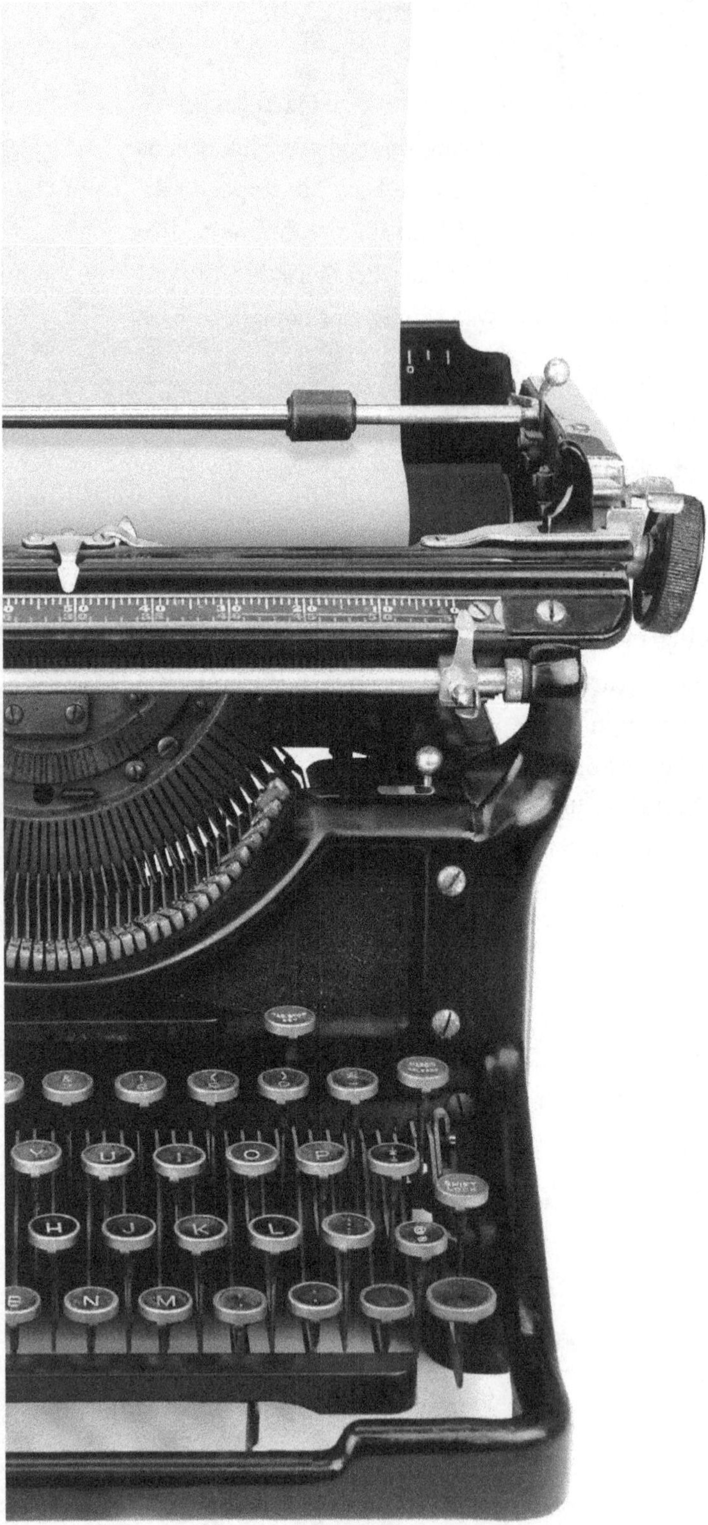
Y U I O P
H J K L
N M

3 6
DEVELOPING COURAGE

"Courage is the most important of all the virtues because without courage, you can't practice any other virtue consistently."

— *Maya Angelou*

In any endeavor of importance, you are going to be challenged by fear. You may feel it when you start a new job, or a new relationship. You will juggle fear in many ways and for many reasons in your life. The only sure thing is that when you confront it, you have an opportunity to get stronger. Know that if you want to do anything audacious, fear will probably show up. Be it going to school, getting married, moving, or starting over in life. All actions that take you out of your comfort zone will take your courage and your willingness to breathe through fear.

Something interesting happens each time you face your fears. Each time you push up against fear, breathe into it and move through it, the whole process gets a smidge easier. You build up your courage muscle. If you are a person who has spent your life pushing past your fears, you will still feel the fear. The fear may, in fact, elevate your senses and engage your courage muscle. The more you develop that muscle, the easier moving through fear becomes. If you are a person who has avoided facing or moving through whatever causes you fear, then you're going to need to pull up your Captain Courageous pants. You will need to collect your strengths, align with your values, create support systems—family, friends, maybe a coach, tools, grit—and a mindset of determination to help you push through to the other side. Still, it's not easy or pleasant, and yet it's the only way to freedom. And I encourage practice, practice, practice. Start small. There is no need to jump into the deep end first. Learn to swim in the part of the pool where you can touch the bottom with your feet. Then push yourself until your skill supports the leap. Whatever your big audacious dream, whatever rewrite your story needs. The only way to that dream is through the fear that stands between you and your goal.

Bears

I have taken many opportunities to push through fear. I learned to push myself outside my comfort zones by adventuring, exploring, doing things on my own, jumping out of airplanes and allowing myself to make mistakes and fail. At times, I was reckless, but I learned and continued pushing through my fear to give myself options and not be limited as I chose my path. It hasn't been an easy thing to push myself, and sometimes it happens by accident. I have been forced to make the courageous choice because the alternatives suck.

I love bears and on my bucket list was going to Alaska to experience being around bears. So Michael and I took off for parts north. I had found a fishing outfit that took people on fishing trips, but also took people to Brooks Lodge to see bears. Brooks Lodge is a pretty famous place where humans and grizzly bears, for a few short months, can mostly safely hang out around each other. Mainly, the bears are focused on eating a lot of salmon. July is the peak of the salmon run, so it also happens to be an excellent time to see bears up close in the wild and reduce your risk of being eaten.

I was in heaven. Every day we were out walking on bear trails, watching bears fish, hanging out with interesting people and having an amazing adventure. On one of our days photographing bears, I saw a group of individuals fly-fishing in the river below the falls where the salmon jump and bears congregate to snatch them out of the air. I said to myself, Self, I want to fly-fish down there close to the bears. Then I said it out loud, so Michael and I began to make our fishing plans. We had our fishing guide from the lodge, and we were outfitted up to the armpits so we could get into the water and spend a day fly-fishing. We started off in the area closer to Brooks Lodge that still has a lot of bears, but less of them than when you get closer to the falls. I even landed a ten-pound salmon, which I released because there was a bear on the shore watching me.

As the day progressed, I worked up my nerve to get into the water closer to the falls. On we went, getting to the falls and then stepping neatly off the observation area and into bear territory. I can only tell you that I have never seen grass that grows so high or thick. I found myself walking through the nearly six-foot grass on a bear path. I could see nothing, but every sense in my body was on fire with awareness. I don't know that I have ever been as intensely aware of my body, my surroundings, or my primal emotions as I was at that moment. Every metaphorical hair on my body was standing on end. Every level of awareness was engaged: physical, mental, emotional, spiritual and energetic.

When we came out of the tall grass to the river's edge, what was walking up the shore, directly toward us? A bear, of course. So we had two options: a) Go back into the tall grass where we couldn't see anything, or b) Go into the river. What a choice to make, and this was one of those moments when you had to choose quickly. We waded out into what had appeared to be a nice lazily moving river, but upon entering the water, we learned it had an uneven, rocky bottom with a swift and strong current. Crap! That had not been on my mind when I planned this adventure. I was standing there in my giant waders in this swift current and a bear about six feet away. My only thought was, Bears can run fifty yards in three seconds. That wasn't particularly helpful, but it was the only thought in my mind other than, What the heck had I been thinking? Am I a complete idiot? Crap, crap, crap! Maybe I can run faster than Michael and the guide? Then I decided I had chosen this experience. Whether or not I had fully appreciated the consequences at the time. I was acutely aware now that every cell in my body was firing at the same time. Then because I was willing to feel and hear the fear, I could use that awareness to create some space, breathe and choose my response.

And, thankfully, another voice showed up. It's okay. You're in it so breathe. Shift the fear and just be in this moment. Because running like a freaked-out, crazy redhead past the bear is not a good option. The second choice point, I could have gotten mad at Michael for letting me get us into this situation. Then my next awareness popped up: And you don't get to blame anyone else for your choice.

Because bears are interested in salmon in July at Brooks Lodge, the bear walked on. I was still pretty puckered up for a while, but I kept working on managing my thinking and breathing through my emotions. At one point, we were surrounded by four younger bears, all jumping through the water chasing salmon and I survived that too. When I relaxed a little, we did do some fishing. I had done it. I had stood up to my fear, not by pretending I wasn't afraid, but by acknowledging the fear to myself and then choosing to work through it so I could react differently. I also owned that I had created the situation. I wasn't going to bolt and run like my inner freaked-out, fear-based voice had recommended. Then, I did a little jiggy dance to celebrate.

Here's the deal: Developing awareness and courage in the moment is not only about noticing the emotional freak-out. It's about becoming more transparent with yourself and gaining perspective. It's about practicing the habits that will help you calm yourself down, breathing through the fear, recognizing that things are going to happen in your body and your brain and realizing that you are capable of standing firm through the experience. It's been a part of my awareness development program to gather enough tools to explore different parts of myself. I want to explore my interpretation of experiences from various perspectives and ultimately, have more directions from which to observe the situation.

Given enough practice, we can all change our reactions and responses to anything. This may sound like a simplification, and it is simple. It's just not always easy. So be willing to hold some compassion for yourself as you choose and develop your toolbox. Find the courage to stand in ownership of your choices and your life. Not all bears want to eat us, so how do we choose to stretch ourselves out of our comfort zone? How do we move out of our habitual stories and give ourselves permission to explore ourselves in new ways?

EXERCISE:

If you were to think about your fears, what would support you to breathe and push through them?

_____

_____

Set an intention for your own growth and the development of your courage. What steps would you set for yourself to help you as you move forward?

_____

_____

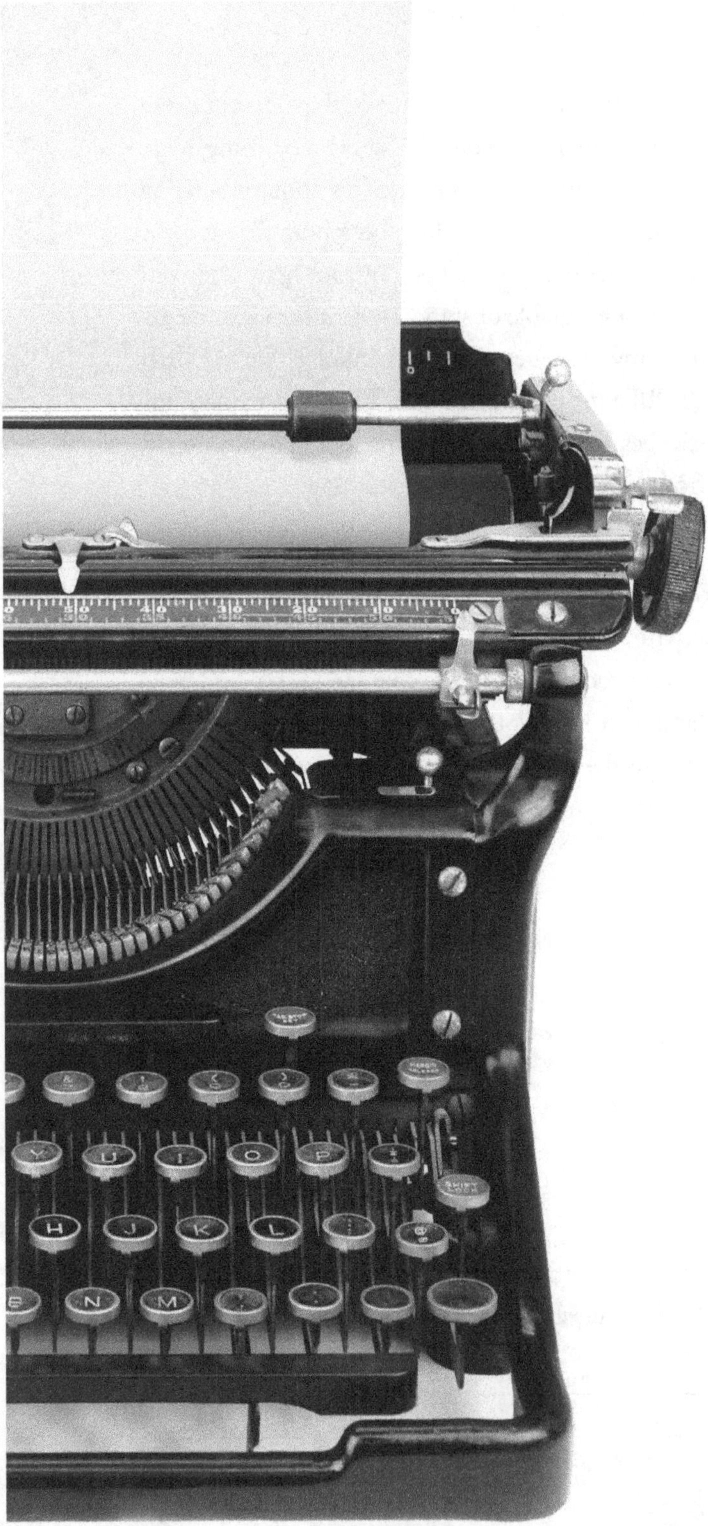

37
REINCARNATING PATTERNS

*"I love the idea of reincarnation, so just in case it doesn't exist,
I decided to be different people in the same lifetime."*

— *Nuno Roque*

I can't prove reincarnation, in the spiritual meaning of the word, is true. What I have seen through the years is that people reincarnate past problems into their present situations and relationships all the time. I love the quote usually attributed to Albert Einstein that says, "Insanity: Doing the same thing over and over again, expecting different results." I love it because it sums up the situation.

Let me give you an example. Let's say you have a bottle of cola. You want the cola to get cold, so you add some baking soda to the bottle. Is that going to get it cold? No, the cola is going to fizz up and spew everywhere. Now, you want it hot, so you add the baking soda. How does that work this time? What, not hot? Oh, it's bubbling and spewing all over the place. I see. I could go on all day like this. Adding baking soda is never going to do anything other than making the cola salty and frothing. It will spew all over you, like a child's science project gone wrong—which is perfect if what you wanted was a volcano. We do this in life—regularly employ tactics to situations that have poor or unexpected results. And, rather than do anything differently, we just keep doing the same thing over and over again. Hoping it will work and not drive us crazy. If you enjoy this, just draw a circle on your wall and bang your head against it. Oh, and try to stay in the circle, because that's the best you're going to get from the activity.

I have a client named Jennifer. She came to her coaching session wanting to discuss work. She hated her job. She hated waking up on Monday morning because all she felt was dread. She wanted to take a global look at her life from the 30,000-foot perspective. She came to the session feeling defeated and kept saying, "I'm in a funk, and I hate where my life is right now." I asked her whether there was anything she was feeling about her job now that felt familiar. She sat with that a while. "You know," she said, "I had this same feeling in my marriage." Well, that's interesting. "What comes up for you when you hear yourself say that?" I asked. "I seem to have gotten myself into a similar situation," she replied. "With my marriage, I felt powerless and as though I didn't matter. What I wanted didn't matter. What I had to offer, didn't matter. And I have a similar feeling in my job, like whatever I have to offer or give isn't good enough. I don't feel appreciated and I just want to run away."

And there it was: the "I'm not enough" voice. It showed up in her marriage and her job. I asked whether she wanted to explore the "I am not good enough" story. She did. And through the discussion, she was able to connect that story back to when she was a kid. When her mom had passed away, she lived with a dad who coped by being an alcoholic. She had worked hard to help him, and the family feel "okay." She tirelessly tried to make the family whole again. She understood, from her adult perspective, that as a kid she couldn't fix the situation. Yet, that kid part was still finding familiar situations and trying to be everything to everyone. It was exhausting Jennifer, and she was left feeling in a funk because she still wasn't "good enough" to fix it all.

That insight gave her the window into her pattern. As we explored, she noticed other areas that were also part of the same pattern. Places she was trying to be "good enough" to help her friends, her children and her boyfriend. Interestingly, she was less focused on being "good enough" at taking care of herself, her needs, her situations and her choices. Insight into the pattern allowed her to explore what she needed to pay attention to in her life. To be fair, it's not an either/or situation. If we don't recognize or notice the pattern that keeps showing up, what will it take to shift it? If we are reincarnating the pattern in other places in our life, what do we need to explore? What capacity do we have to help others if we can't help ourselves?

It seems that situations show up repeatedly for all of us. Or at least for all the people I have worked with or know. These repeated stories are, ultimately, a doorway into what is below the surface that we are still reincarnating. They offer the opportunity for us to heal ourselves. In Jennifer's case, it's the story or belief about not being "good enough." My guess is that until she is willing to explore that story to see whether it is serving her in any useful manner, she will continue to have that "not good enough" story get triggered in every difficult situation that trundles her way. The same is true for me and probably for you.

EXERCISE:

What patterns do you notice in your life that seem to reincarnate in present situations?

_____

_____

_____

_____

What is the story beneath each of those patterns?

_____

_____

_____

_____

What is at risk if you ignore the patterns?

_____

_____

_____

_____

What could you gain if you acknowledge the patterns and choose to let them go?

_____

_____

_____

_____

3 8
VULNERABILITY

"What happens when people open their hearts? They get better."

— *Haruki Murakami*

Vulnerability is a hard concept for most people. Most of us have a story that sounds like, "Vulnerability is a weakness." It makes sense that we view vulnerability that way because our dictionaries have definitions like: susceptible to hurt; or open to attack. The word's origin is vulnerary, which means: to promote the healing of wounds; or a remedy for wounds. Now that's an interesting difference.

Learning to be vulnerable was also a difficult concept in the Anger Management classes I taught. Men, especially, are often socialized to avoid appearing weak. Frankly, women are too, but they have a bit more latitude on this issue. I honestly do not like to feel or appear weak myself, so I get it. Who wants to be that kid on the beach getting sand kicked on him or her by some big bully? And what happens to those poor little kids who stop on the playground and start talking about their feelings? I mean, seriously, we aren't kind to that idea of vulnerability. Nor do we enjoy feeling it. We don't like it in ourselves, and we especially don't like it in others. When I met Michael, he told me that he didn't cry. He couldn't even remember the last time he had teared up. To be fair, he still doesn't cry. It's not a part of his sense of self.

Personally, I don't necessarily see all crying as being vulnerable. Crying can be a form of vulnerability if you are working to heal. Or, it can also be a manipulative ploy to get someone to feel sad for you. It can be an emotional and physical release. Like when we are sad or overly frustrated and cry; I once burst into tears in a staff meeting, because I was so angry. Vulnerability isn't necessarily about tears. At its core, it is about promoting healing from inside of ourselves or helping others to heal. We are a communicative species. We often heal ourselves emotionally by communicating honestly about something we are processing. Brené Brown talks about being vulnerable and sharing only with people who have earned the right to hear your story. With these few people, learning to be honest, open and authentic, in the service of healing is the point of vulnerability.

Since there are different types of vulnerability, how do we decide which one is appropriate in which situation? Let's look at two of them: the "Great Overshare" and "Authentic Vulnerability."

The Great Overshare is a form of pseudo-vulnerability that doesn't add up to much as far as growth or healing. It happens when you go too far in your sharing for the situation or for the people to whom you are talking. Several key indicators will signal that you have hit the overshare button. One is that when you walk away from the conversation, you don't know anything about the other person and you've been on audio output for more than five minutes. Five minutes is probably still too long to be sharing much of anything, without getting feedback from your conversational partner. Another indicator is that you may feel judged or your shame trigger gets tapped. Many of us have an internal regulator that starts to blink when we overshare. We find ourselves walking away from a conversation feeling uncomfortable. Feeling like we said too much and now we feel upset that we said anything at all. When we notice this uncomfortable feeling, we need to ask ourselves, "What is going on that I needed to share this story with these people? What was I hoping would happen from the sharing?" These questions help lead us to the vulnerability's root. What is going on? What do we need to get curious about in our overshare, so that we can heal?

Honestly, the overshare does feel vulnerable because we are sharing ourselves in a manner of speaking. If there is no sharing coming back to us, it can feel like an overwhelm to the other person. He or she may be smiling and nodding pleasantly, but I haven't met many people who only want to listen to someone's story—unless they are therapists and remember they get paid. Most people, at least in my experience, want to share a bit also if they are at all interested in the conversation. Dialogue is defined in part by the give and take of information and ideas. A one-sided conversation doesn't exist. A one-sided conversation is more often a lecture or an allocution. We need to take care when we are so absorbed by our story or ideas, that we share the metaphorical stage with others. I, for one, know the sirens' song of over sharing my deep thoughts or insights. Only, I don't call it a conversation…in this case, I call it a book.

What is important about vulnerability in StoryJacking? What is the benefit of being vulnerable?

Let's look at the other type of vulnerability. Authentic vulnerability that leads to healing is a very different kind of vulnerability. It's the vulnerability that is all about courage and facing fears. It's not about trying to get people on your side or manipulating them into feeling sorry for you. It's not about trying to get anyone to do anything for you at all. It's about being willing to look at what happened, fearlessly. Not getting lost in the victim story and exploring the underlying motivators in your part of any given situation. What is the pattern? What is going on with me? What is my thinking and what am I feeling? What do I need to do to move forward? Vulnerability equals taking personal responsibility, not just for your brilliance, but also for the rough edges that aren't helping you to heal or that aren't helping you to have authentic relationships.

Earlier, I mentioned that my parents divorced when I was nine. That experience colored my ideas about relationships. My negative beliefs cemented as I watched my parents' subsequent painful relationships. I created a story about love that sounded like, "You can't trust people because they lie or they leave you. I won't be vulnerable. I don't want to hurt like it hurts when I get rejected. People won't like the real me. They will try to change me because I am unlovable as I am. And, I won't have a relationship because I don't want someone to change me."

Now, this compounded story affected what I was looking for in a partner when I was older and decided I did want a boyfriend. With these underlying beliefs as my foundation, I found myself unconsciously attracted to unavailable men. If he was still in love with his last girlfriend, wow, I was attracted to him. If his focus was his career, color me infatuated. I could pick out the married guys at 100 paces. If you were a sweet, available man, who was interested in exploring a relationship with me, forget it. I couldn't find one thing attractive about you, other than as a friend. I had a story that said what I wanted didn't exist. So I embraced that I would never find real love and had to keep myself safe. I built a wall around my emotional self and wouldn't let men close to my heart. I had great friendships with men I wasn't interested in intimately. And I had great relationships with my girlfriends. I could and would be vulnerable to the extent that one is with friends. But to take a relationship that might lead to honest and open couple intimacy—no way, not safe. I wasn't going there. In hindsight, my choice of unavailable men was my way of staying safe. If he was in love with his career, or last girlfriend, or whatever the complication was, I could be in a relationship. I had all the drama of never knowing where we stood and never needing to be vulnerable myself. It was a win-win, right up until it wasn't. At some point, I was lonely and tired of my reincarnated pattern of unhealthy choices.

I remember sitting in the Frontier restaurant in Albuquerque, New Mexico with a college girlfriend and crying (the release and feeling sorry for myself sort of tears). She listened for a while and then asked me, "If you don't like this situation, why are you still choosing it?"

What? It was the first time I consciously got that I was choosing these unavailable relationships. And, big aha here, I didn't have to. That was liberating and terrifying all at the same time. I mean I had spent twenty-five years developing an attraction to the unavailable, all to keep myself safe. How was I going to undo that and start finding sweet, lovely, available men attractive? There wasn't a switch I could just flip from "unavailable guy" to "nice guy," was there? Well, yes, there was a switch. Only it wasn't an instant switch. I had to start looking at my situation with some discernment. What feelings indicated I was interested in someone? Once I started getting curious about my attractions, I began to look a little deeper into whom I was feeling attracted. And, I kid you not, for the next two years, each time I felt attracted to someone, he was, you guessed it, unavailable on some level. I was knocking my head against the wall, over and over, trying to make a healthy relationship pop out. It wasn't working. I finally decided I was going to quit dating and deal with my crap. I was going into my psyche, my stories and cleaning out some baggage. As with us all, it's an inside-out life for me too.

I joined an empowerment and growth group in graduate school. Ironically, it was run by a man, and I was the only female with five guys in the group. Weird, right? Apparently, the universe had decided I was going to deal with all my man issues. In the group, I learned a lot more about men. I developed compassion for their struggles and saw their deep emotions. I also worked on my fears, choices and wall building. I would go to a party, meet a guy and then walk away because I knew I was still attracted to the unavailable.

I didn't date at all through graduate school. Instead, I took the time to read, write and work on what was below the surface of my stuff. I journaled, owned my crap, worked on being honest and authentic about who I was. I got curious about other people, and I asked a lot of questions, especially to those who had what looked like healthy relationships. I played through what I wanted in my head. I wrote down lists of what I was looking for in a significant other. I boiled it down and kept working on myself. I held myself accountable for my fears and for continuing to grow into the sort of person I wanted to be with, in a relationship. When I got out of school and moved home, I started dating. I would like to say that all my work paid off immediately and I met the man of my dreams, but no. I dated and dated and dated for the next two years. I went out for coffee or dinner, met for drinks or a movie with about 180 different men. I had conversation after conversation after conversation. It was exhausting. I did, however, develop a clear insight into the type of person I didn't want to be with, in a relationship. Because of that, I clarified what I was looking for in a partner. I joke that when I met Michael, he was lucky 181. In all sincerity, I was the lucky one. I had put in the work, yes. I also recognized he was an amazing human being. I continued to face my fears, and I didn't run away.

This is what the healing kind of vulnerability did for me. It healed a wound I didn't consciously know I had. I had been in total protective mode. Vulnerability asked me, to be honest with myself and then be strong enough to work through the bits of myself that were not helpful. Vulnerability helped me develop into what I said I wanted: a healthy relationship. Vulnerability also helped me not mess up my relationship with Michael. When I felt scared or overwhelmed, I just told him, "I'm feeling scared or overwhelmed. It's not you. It's my issue. I just need to breathe. I am not going anywhere, but I have to breathe through my anxiety right now." Because I had chosen a person who was emotionally healthy, he was chill and let me do my thing. He didn't personalize my process. Instead, he supported me in taking care of myself. And, this bears repeating, I didn't run away.

At times, I desperately wanted to run because being intimate and vulnerable doesn't always feel good. It can feel overwhelming and scary until you get used to it. But here's a funny thing: If anywhere along the journey, Michael had been a jerk or not worthy of trust, all my work on myself would have helped me to opt out and move on. The vulnerability made me smarter and stronger. If I had gone guarded in the relationship, it wouldn't have lasted anyway. I would eventually have been reactive and freaked out. Probably blaming Michael the entire time for not making me feel better. We would have parted ways long before I ever got the chance to experience the relationship we have built together. I didn't know it when I started my intimacy work, but I didn't have anything to lose by being vulnerable. I only had everything to gain.

EXERCISE:

What words do you associate with vulnerability?

_____

_____

In what ways do these words support or hinder you?

_____

_____

What could you be exploring below the surface to shift your ideas around vulnerability and healing?

_____

_____

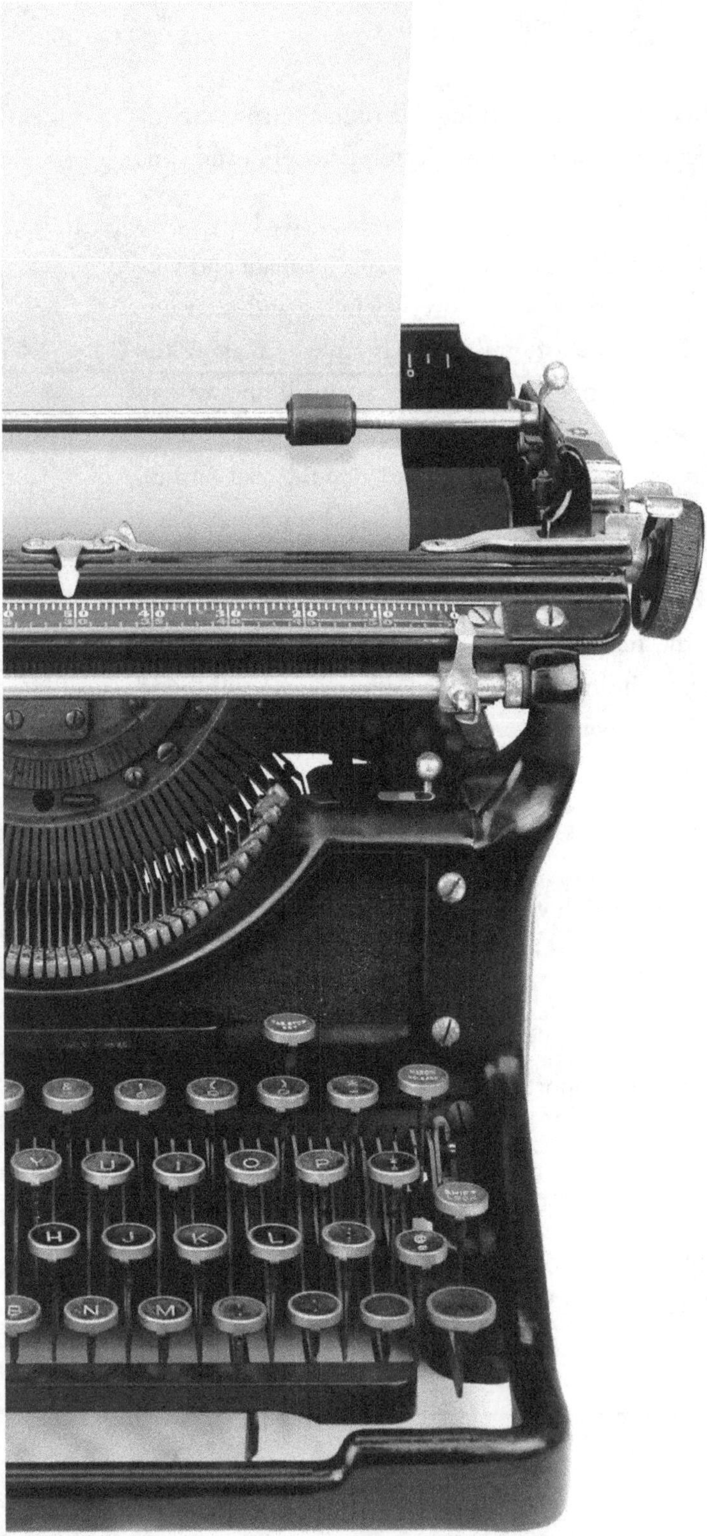

39
VISUALIZING THE GOAL

"When it is obvious that the goals cannot be reached, don't adjust the goals, adjust the action steps."

— *Confucius*

Now that you have a better idea of who you are and what your strengths, values and essences are, what now?

Tony Robbins says, "Setting goals is the first step in turning the invisible into the visible." Our ability to visualize and emotionally connect to our dreams is pivotal to our success. The goal of living a life filled with people we enjoy, enjoying our days, feeling good enough, loving ourselves and giving back to others. These ideas are the manifestations of big, bold, audacious dreams.

I didn't know what life would hand me. So, when I was dating, I developed a clear vision of the type of man I wanted in a relationship. Sure, there were some superficial things I was looking for like "tall, dark and handsome." The real meat of what I valued though were the things that would foster a healthy relationship. I wanted someone emotionally robust enough to work through disagreements respectfully. I wanted someone who loved to laugh and looked at the world as a playground. I wanted someone who was responsible, curious and most importantly, wanted to be in a relationship with me. I set the vision firmly in my head of a relationship, and I fleshed it out with my essential values. I visualized myself having respectful disagreements, or traveling, or laughing with this person. Over time, as I kept dating, I garnered clarity about different people—were they disrespectful to the waitress, or kind and friendly? All these data points helped as I honed in, getting closer to the image I had set.

When I met Michael, I didn't instantly know he was "the one," but I did immediately know I liked him as a person. I could tell after our first conversation, as we walked through a bookstore discussing books and ideas, then through coffee and dessert, discussing dreams and directions, that I honestly liked him as a human being. So much so that on my way home I called him. I wanted to tell him that I didn't know where all this might lead, but that I wanted to be friends and see what might show up. Nineteen years later, we are still friends, and that is cool. And I owe it to getting clear about what I wanted in a relationship and then working hard to practice being the kind of person I would want to be with, in a relationship. I wanted, to be honest, open and allowing that the other person didn't have to see me as perfect or need to save me. Without the vision or goal, and the personal work, if I had met Michael and we'd created the relationship that we have, it would have been like winning the lottery. It would have been a 1 in 718,000,000,000,000 chance. Simply put, highly unlikely.

Goals are the markers that we use to navigate the course. They give us waypoints in life. I graduated from school here. I had a baby there. I got my favorite job on this date. But each of these waypoints, if we are going to take more than accident and chance as our compass, require acknowledgment of the goal.

In my work with clients, one of the first conversations we have is getting clarity about the goal. We develop an idea about how you will know you've gotten what you wanted. We practice being transparent with each other about what are we agreeing to explore together. We not only share a vision of where you want to go, and we develop our attunement to the co-creative process. In each area of your life, be it money, intimacy, family life, creativity, social community, health, spirituality or career, you need to visualize what you want in your life. If certain areas of your life are working well, how did you support that outcome? It's an opportunity to put on your Sherlock Holmes hat and notice what worked and what didn't. What choices did you make? What actions did you take? What thinking did you challenge? What helped you to create this success? Let's take some time to think about those questions now.

Exercise:

Go back and look at your life wheel. What area of your life do you want to focus on?

_____

_____

_____

_____

What would you like to see shift in this area of your life?

_____

_____

_____

_____

Write out a clear goal:

_____

_____

_____

_____

What will be different in your life when you achieve the goal?

_____

_____

_____

_____

What, right now, is between you and achieving this goal?

_____

_____

_____

What would be one or two first steps toward your goal?

_____

_____

_____

_____

40

YOU ARE ALWAYS AT CHOICE

"Until a person can say deeply and honestly, "I am what I am today because of the choices I made yesterday," that person cannot say, "I choose otherwise."

— *Stephen R. Covey*

You are always at choice. There is, in fact, no time that you are not making at choice about something. You may be choosing "for" something or "against" something. And even the act of not choosing is a still a choice.

Let's look at how the same premise works in your daily life. What are the things to choose consciously? What are the things you reject consciously? And then what are all the choices you abdicate by either being unconscious that you have a choice or because on some level you believe that by not consciously choosing, you aren't, in fact, choosing at all? I will repeat this again: You are always at choice.

Some things might not matter to you, like which restaurant you and your family are going to eat at tonight. Maybe the choices are all healthy, and you're fine with any of them, so let someone else decide. Or they are all terrible choices, but you don't want to rock the boat. You figure you'll find something to swallow when you get there, so you give your choice to someone else who is more definite about what he wants. That's all fine. All those choices are conscious. It's when you are making an unconscious choice or abdicating your choice because you don't think you have one. That's when you may start spinning or wallowing over the consequences. Maybe no one made the decision you wanted, or there are unintended consequences you had not considered and now dislike. That's an interesting place to start to look.

Are you a bird person? I will just say that I am. I love those beautiful winged creatures. They make me happy. I also love coffee. In fact, I am a bit addicted to my morning brew, hot and creamy, there to wake me up. Do you love coffee too? I recently read an article by Gustave Axelson titled *In Colombia, Shade-Grown Coffee Sustains Songbirds and People Alike.* The article discusses how just by choosing shade-grown coffee, grown with the idea of a sustainable ecology, the number of songbirds in the region increased. Now, you may or may not care about coffee or songbirds. The point is that even the choice you make about something as seemingly minor as your morning breakfast beverage has consequences of which you might not be aware. If there are issues you are passionate about—human rights, educating children, community health—then ask yourself, "What choices am I making that put me in direct conflict with what I say is important to me?"

Choices are everywhere—whom you vote for, where you live, whom to do business with, whom you marry or divorce, whether to have kids or not, whether to get a cat or dog. The list is endless. Choices are every moment-by-moment decision you make, and each choice you make takes you to your next choice point. The choices you make are linked inextricably to your consequences. *There can be no action that doesn't have a corresponding reaction.* (That's Newton's third Law of Motion and, oh yeah, a super-secret of the Universe.) Every choice or decision you make, good, bad or indifferent, will lead you in the direction that the choice laid open for you. What matters most is that you begin to recognize where you have power. In case you need a quick reminder, it's not in what everyone else is or isn't doing, the external locus of control. It's instead, your internal locus, what you are or are not doing or choosing.

It's the same with all your choices. The stories you tell yourself about your life are choices, too. When you see yourself as a victim, the stories that you choose to press "play/rewind/repeat," become the stories of your life. These stories determine your focus and your mindset. Your focus and mindset then define your limits as well as your opportunities. The choices you make and the stories you choose make all the difference in the outcome. They will create the path for all your future options.

When I was in college, I was fascinated by history. I loved art history, world history, and human history, the whole kit and kaboodle. I took courses in the Anthropology Department at the University of New Mexico, and I ended up in a class with Professor Jane Lancaster. I loved her class. Her lectures lit me up and had my brain popping with all sorts of ideas. Most college courses require writing, and this one was no exception. Quick aside, I have struggled with dyslexia my whole life. I was lucky that my mom read to me every night, so I have a love of stories and language, but spelling and grammar—forget it. I want to point out that this was in the 1980s, before spell check and Grammarly, and I didn't yet realize the brilliance of having an editor.

Professor Lancaster assigned an essay paper. I worked tirelessly, and it was the best piece I had ever written. I was on fire with excitement, and when I turned it in, I had a big smile plastered on my brain. When I returned to class the next week, Professor Lancaster handed back the graded papers. Instead of the A+ and the "Tour de Force" I was expecting, I had a C. My stomach dropped. My heart clenched. My brain fogged over. The internal meltdown I was having was epic. I sat through the remainder of the class in a coma. I left class and, when I could finally breathe again, I reread my paper. I didn't understand the C. I was in a daze. I could have left it there. It would have been easy to shrug this off as a "crap situation," a mean professor, an indicator that I sucked, you know the drill. Instead, I called her and asked for an appointment. When I came in, I had tears in my throat, my voice was wobbly, and I asked, "Why did you give me a C? I worked so hard on this paper."

I will never forget her response. "You have great ideas. You clearly understand the theories, and your insight and connections are well-argued." As she spoke, my confusion didn't abate, but my brain started to listen. "Since you've asked, your writing skills don't match your thinking skills. I would recommend that you work on those. You will not be as successful in sharing your perspective if you do not learn to write more clearly."

I sat there in my moment of choice. I didn't know what to say or how to feel. Knowing me as I do, I probably asked whether I could rewrite and resubmit. Honestly, I don't remember. I am sure I thanked her as I left her office. I was probably fighting back tears, with a look on my face that spoke volumes about my shame. I know I sat with this conversation about my writing for days. There were many stories I could have chosen. I could have followed the rabbit hole of anger, self-pity, or denial. They were all available, and I tried on each one. I thought, whatever I decided to do, I am going to be 100 percent responsible for my choice and the consequences that came from it. What I chose to take away from this experience was gratitude. I was so incredibly appreciative that Professor Lancaster would have bothered to share a hard truth with me—some undergrad in one of her basic classes. She challenged me to improve. It was a gift, this truth, and I had an opportunity either to shrink in or to expand out. I decided to grow. I took writing classes. I got friends to edit all my writing. I read my work out loud, and I kept working at the skill.

It became a challenge that I wanted to work through. I was not going to be limited by my learning disability, and I was not going to give up on myself.

In graduate school, I again wrote a paper that made me feel proud. I turned it in, and when I saw the A+ and the, seriously, no joke, "Tour de Force" written at the top, I beamed and thanked Professor Lancaster in my head.

To StoryJack yourself, you will want to come to terms with having 100 percent personal responsibility for every choice you choose or don't choose. This is the same truth for all of us. You are the culmination of every choice, conscious or unconscious, as well as every non-choice, conscious or unconscious, you have ever made. A clarity of vision and having an audacious juicy goal to move toward will help you to align your choices in the direction you want to take your story. Be it getting an education, learning a trade, choosing a job, staying in a job that makes you unhappy, selecting a partner who doesn't share your "deal breaker" values, or even eating the cupcake when the swan apples were right there, looking so lovely. You attach meaning, belief, and stories to all your choices. Ask yourself, "What am I about to say, think, or do and will it take me one step closer to my goal, or one step farther away?" And since each choice will affect you, I invite you to get conscious so you can choose wisely. Your tomorrow self will thank you.

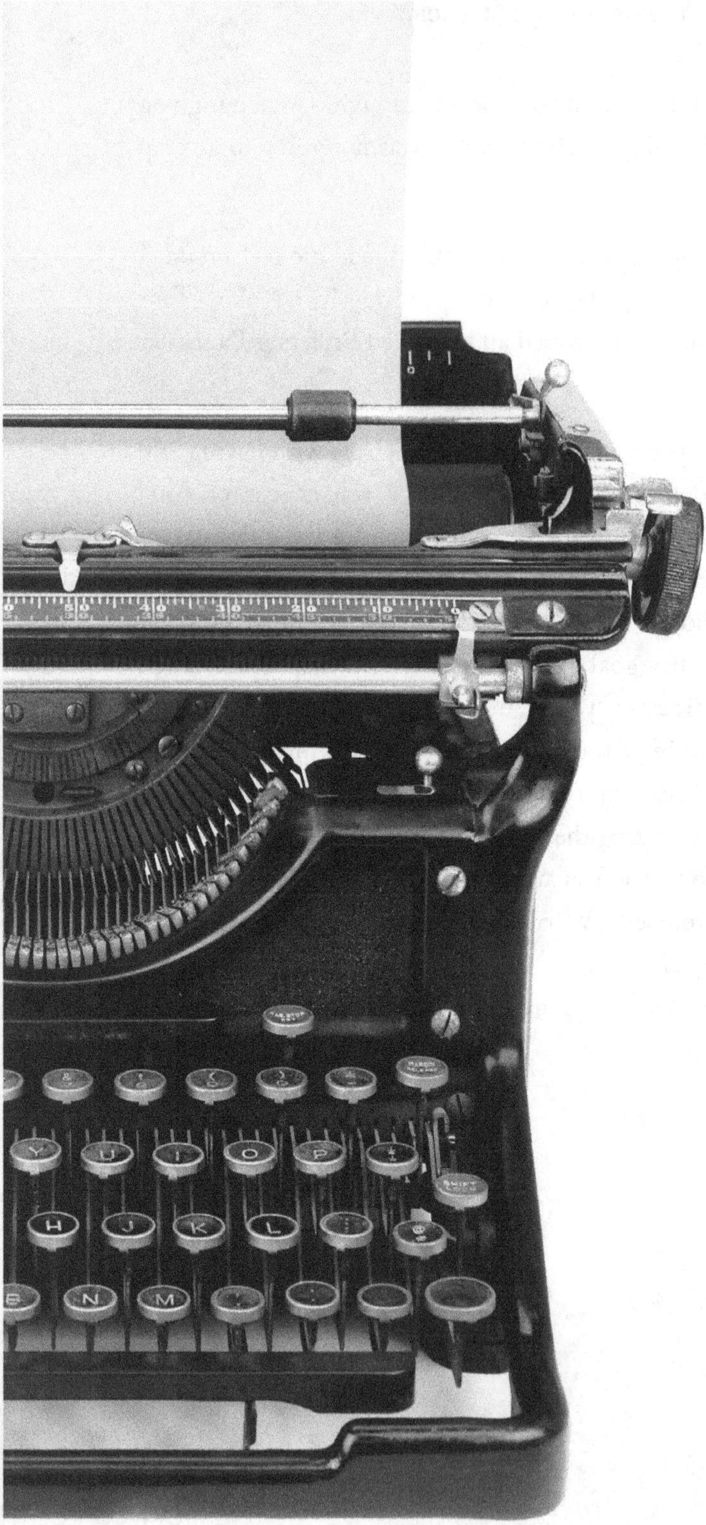
50 40 30 20 10
Y U I O P
H J K L
N M

4 1

HABITS ARE
HARD-WIRED STORIES

"We are what we repeatedly do. Excellence, then, is not an act, but a habit."

— *William Durant*

When we repeat a story often enough, it becomes hardwired. When you tell yourself "Nobody understands me," long enough, there isn't much anyone can say that will remove that thought. The story of uniqueness combined with loneliness in the idea that no one will understand you is a powerful combo. It's a tragedy for sure. You get to be the victim in an unfriendly world where no one can understand you, and that epic loneliness gives you what? Permission to wallow? Maybe never follow your dreams because no one cares? I don't know, but if this is a thought in someone's head, if this is the story that she tells herself for years, I can promise you it gets firmly lodged and is terrifically difficult to challenge. I know because I have worked with clients who are very attached to this type of story and it sometimes took years of moving the pry bar back and forth to break them out of that belief. It was exhausting for them, and it was exhausting for me.

Have you heard the popular wisdom that it takes twenty-one days to change a habit? Really? I'm skeptical it can be done that quickly. From experience, I know that if I am trying to start a new exercise habit, I can be doggedly committed. I can work out four times a week for three months. Hell, let's say six months! And the first day I sleep in and don't exercise, I may have to start all over again at what feels like the beginning. I can't answer for you, but for me, it's a mystery why we think we can create a new habit in three weeks and then believe that it will stick for the rest of our life. Come on. How's that working for you?

What I do know is we can lay the foundation for a new habit in about twenty-one-plus days. We can establish a new neural network, and we can move forward with the new habit. But, seriously, if you want a new habit to be hardwired, it must be repeated for a lot longer than twenty-one days. And, there is an essential ingredient that you will need to make a new habit stick, which I will discuss further in a moment.

True story: People would come to my anger management group and ask, "How long do I have to come to this class to manage my anger?" My typical response was, "I don't know. It depends on how hard you try, how willing you are to call yourself on your shit and how courageous you will be in the face of your triggers. But what I can promise you is this: You took twenty, thirty, forty years to create your unique flavor of anger and I don't have a magic wand. So, let's just say it's going to take some time." This usually wasn't the answer they wanted. They were looking for that magical Anger Management Class where they would take six or twelve classes, then receive a piece of paper they could wave around and proudly proclaim, "I did it, see! You can't tell me about my anger because I took the class!" The average person in my anger management group stayed for over a year. By teaching the class, I took Anger Management once a week for seven years, and twice a week when I taught it at the confinement facility on base. Is my anger management perfect? No, I can still default to being pissed off and unreasonable sometimes. I am much better at catching myself now. I have clarity around my triggers, I can reason with myself and I can engage a suitcase full of tools. And I still get mad.

One day, I saw a bumper sticker that made me chuckle that said: "The difference between a rut and a grave is the depth." Sometimes, this is the whole truth. The deeper the habit, the harder it's going to be to jump out of it. All patterns can change, but it will require your full commitment. Do you find yourself asking, "Why do people always treat me like XYZ?" or "Why do I always fall in love with this sort of person?" or "Why does this pattern keep showing up?" If so, you may be hardwired from years of practice. The good news is that we can adjust our wiring and change our habits, even our habits of thinking.

TINY HABITS

I always find it curious how people or ideas show up in our lives. A while back, an old college friend of mine, Brad, came to Seattle on vacation with his parents and kids. We decided on a day to get together, and he and his family hopped the ferry and came to Bainbridge Island. I had the luxury of spending an afternoon exploring the island with his lovely family. We caught up on life, talked a lot about the island's fascinating history and had a beautiful, relaxing day. At one point, while walking through the Bloedel Reserve and discussing my book, Brad mentioned Dr. B.J. Fogg. I had never heard of Dr. Fogg, but Brad was sure I would be interested in his work. After Brad had left, I looked up Dr. Fogg and found a couple of TED talks he had done. The first was about Tiny Habits, which I loved for its sheer simplicity and a slight twist on an old idea—making habits stick.

Let's say you want to develop a new habit. We all know how hard that is. You look for some small step that would take you toward the new habit. Dr. Fogg talks about wanting to do more pushups. Next, you look for something that you do every day, naturally. In Dr. Fogg's example, he discusses going to the bathroom. Then you link the two. So every time you go to the bathroom, you do a pushup. I decided to try this one. Every time I went to the bathroom, I did a pushup. I started with one each time. I also, for full disclosure, am doing knee pushups, not full pushups. But any pushup would be one more than the "none" I was doing when I started. Over the next week, I went from zero pushups of any type to steadily increasing my pushups until I was doing about fifty a day. In one week! Anyone reading this who knows me will know that is amazing.

The tiny habit doesn't end with the linkage. In operant conditioning, we need a little reward after we do the behavior. And this is where tiny habits bloom into utter genius. You look in the mirror, look yourself in the eye, raise your fists in the air and shout, "Yea!" or "Awesome!" This reaction gives you a little happy hit of neural chemistry and helps to lock in the new behavior. Hence, I am still doing pushups weeks later.

My mom has medication that she must take every morning and evening. Her medication keeps her healthy and out of the hospital. Obviously, I don't want her in the hospital, so helping her to remember to take her meds is high on my list of things that must happen. The pattern that emerged was that whenever I check her meds, and she hasn't taken them on time or has forgotten to take them, I get frustrated and worried, and out of that, upset. Apparently, I become snappish and have a "tone." My mom then starts feeling resistant, micromanaged and guilty. All these negative emotions between the two of us seem to increase the likelihood of more negativity evolving in our morning interactions.

After I discovered how well tiny habits work, I told my mom about them, and we worked out a plan. She wrote down a list of her medication, and she wrote down times linked to something she was already doing, like brushing her teeth when she wakes up and goes to bed. We then linked her taking her morning and evening meds to brushing her teeth. After she finished taking the meds, she looked in the mirror and said, "Yea!" with a big smile and feeling like she did well. She and I chatted about it for a couple of weeks, reinforcing the "Yea!" each morning. We still do, just not every morning, but the habit is still going. I know the linkage worked because I fill up my mom's meds every couple of weeks and check on them regularly. I have found that she is doing better on her own. She has only missed taking them occasionally, which is mind-blowing because we were constantly having the argument in the months leading up to the tiny habit.

Over the years, I have talked to clients about increasing mindfulness. Instead of trying to sit down and quiet your mind for thirty minutes, which is almost impossible to do if you've never meditated. Each time you go to the bathroom or stop at a stoplight, or whatever, focus on your breathing for 1-3 minutes. Turn your attention inward. Quiet your mind for 1-2 minutes. Then add the missing ingredient—the little celebration at the end.

- Think of some habit you want to create—maybe getting better at flossing or doing more strength-building. What is that habit?

- Think about some tiny habit that might lead to a bigger habit. Remember, think tiny, like flossing one tooth or doing one pushup. What is that one tiny thing you could do?

- Is there some behavior you already do regularly without thinking about it? Heating up your coffee in the microwave, going to the bathroom, brushing your teeth, getting out of bed. Notice your regularly occurring habits. What new habit do you want to link to an old one?

EXERCISE:

Now, link the two behaviors. Example: After I brush my teeth, I do a pushup and then a quick full body celebration: Awesome! Remember the celebration piece; the celebration helps to lock in the new habit.

When I _____

Then I _____

Awesome!

4 2
CREATING BOUNDARIES

"No one can make you feel inferior without your consent."

— *Eleanor Roosevelt*

Have you ever had to say "No" to someone? Did you avoid saying "No" until you were so annoyed that you ended up either shutting out the person or screaming? Most people struggle with creating healthy boundaries. Some are so good at boundaries that they have built a moat around the stone wall they have to keep safe. And, that's not a healthy boundary any more than being a doormat is a healthy option. Boundaries are the lines in the sand that we create to clarify what we are or are not willing to do, or become. When I look back on my first love, what he needed was someone to adore him, to help heal his broken heart. I did that for about two years. Then I realized, if any other man in the world had asked me to love him unconditionally, even though he would never love me back, I would have said, "No." So why was I stepping over my healthy boundary to love this particular man? Because of love, hopefulness and wanting to believe in his words over his actions? At some point, my healthy brain re-engaged, and I started creating healthy boundaries.

To be clear, for the person on the receiving end of your boundary, it can feel like an ultimatum. You won't always get a reaction like, "Gee, I never looked at it from your side. Of course, I'll respect your boundary." Often, you will find yourself juggling emotional blackmail, noticing the plot twist and having to StoryJack your perspective. Repeat after me, "I would rather be healthy than angry. I would rather take care of my boundaries and not walk all over them."

What happens when you let people step all over your boundaries? You might feel used, you might have thrown yourself full tilt into the victim role, and you may be angry or resentful. Noticing your emotions is key. Negative emotions are often the doorways into understanding a boundary breach. I have come to believe that my level of irritation in a situation is equal to the degree that I have allowed a boundary to be crossed.

Another of the super-secrets of the universe is: *Anyone can ask you for anything, but you don't have to agree to the request.* Seriously. I could ask you for a million dollars right now, "Will you please give me a million dollars?" And you have the right to say, "No." You don't have to be a jerk about it. You can say, "No" nicely. Let's say you have a friend, Jane, who asks you to babysit her little girl, Emily. Jane says she is going to be gone for the next four hours because she is going out on a date, going for an interview, whatever. You say, "Yes, I am happy to watch Emily; she's a great kid." Jane calls four hours later and says she is going to be a bit longer; is it still okay? You say, "Okay, how much longer?" She says another two hours. She can ask for anything, but you also have the right to say "No." At this point you need to determine a) "Am I okay with another two hours?" or b) "Am I going to be annoyed?" There is no right or wrong choice, but you do need to acknowledge what your limit is.

So, what is a healthy boundary? As with most things, it's easy to think it's the same for everyone, when, in fact, a healthy boundary could be completely different for two different people. Let's say I am the sort of person who is not good at saying "No," so I find myself drowning under agreements that I make to keep everyone happy with me. I say, "Yes, sure I will keep Emily for another two hours," but I am super-annoyed. If by saying "Yes," I am now short-tempered with poor Emily, I need to examine my behavior. Emily is just a little kid, and I am the one who stepped over my boundary, not her. Finding my "No" is probably a good place for me to explore. On the other hand, if I am a person who says "No" so often that most of my conversations sound like, "No, no, no, no, no," then maybe a healthy boundary is about finding a way to say, "Yes." Of course, because all this is a spectrum, perhaps I say to Jane, "I can keep Emily for one more hour. I have errands to run" (or "people are coming over," or "I need a nap").

We often think we need boundaries to protect us from other people. Maybe we need a wall around ourselves, so we don't get hurt or asked to do too much. What if a healthy boundary was flexible? What if it ebbed and flowed as needed? What if it tied directly to taking care of ourselves and being honest in our dealings and relationships? What if it didn't have anything to do with anyone other than ourselves? What then? What would a healthy boundary look like then?

A healthy boundary is a limit that supports your emotional balance. It may not feel comfortable to set the limit, but when you do, you feel relief. When you don't set a boundary, you might feel irritated, angry, used or unappreciated (insert negative emotion here). A healthy boundary has a realistic expectation attached to it. Conversely, a problematic boundary has an unrealistic expectation. Such as, "If I help with your request, then you will stop asking me forever." If my mom isn't good at remembering appointments, then getting upset when she forgets, is silly on my part. In my family, a healthy limit would look like: Mom forgot to call for her ride yesterday. When she remembered her appointment, it was too late to get the ACCESS bus to come pick her up. I look up, and my mom is standing in the office doorway. She says to me, "I have PT today at three. I forgot to call for my ride yesterday." Her expectation is that I am going stop what I am doing and give her a lift. I was all right with this expectation occasionally until it became a regular pattern. I began feeling annoyed. I had to stop what I was doing, maybe rearrange my schedule and take her to her appointment. Then wait for her and then bring her home. A realistic expectation on my part became, my mom is going to continue with this behavior unless I clarify my limits. So I sat down and explained my boundary. I set the limit to save my sanity and my relationship with my mom. "Mom," I said, "I love you. I am happy to help when I am able. Please consider that I cannot be your backup each time you forget to call the ACCESS van. Next time this happens, you are going to need to call a taxi." She agreed, and I took her to her appointment. The following week, I looked up from my computer and who was standing in my doorway? Yep, my mom. "What's up?" I asked. She looked sheepishly at me. "I need a ride. I forgot to call the ACCESS van yesterday." "Hmm, well that's unfortunate. I am sorry. I'm busy and can't help you today. You'll need to call a taxi." Then I had to breathe through all the voices in my head saying I was a "bad daughter," "overreacting witch, just give her the ride." I managed to keep my mouth shut as she called a taxi and experienced the consequences of not calling for her ride the day before.

This situation happens all the time in relationships. We teach people how to treat us by what we agree to do for them. If we don't like what we have passively agreed to do, because it was scary to rock the boat, or make someone mad at us, or deal with the voices in our head, then we may need to renegotiate the agreement. "I love you Mom, but I'm not a taxi." By setting the boundary, being kind and forthright with my mom, then holding myself accountable to what I stated I needed, I discovered

I wasn't angry. My mom was okay, the $20 cab fare was an excellent consequence, and she hasn't assumed since then that I am going to drop everything to save her. That said, later in the week when we were looking at her schedule, there was a place where I could help her. I chose that, consciously and happily, picking her up and taking her to another appointment. See, flexible.

Ask yourself, "In which of my relationships do I have strong negative feelings when someone asks something of me?" That's where to look. And, again, people aren't necessarily going to like your boundaries. A client of mine, Jessica, has a son who is unhappy in his life right now. He has all sorts of reasons for his anger. He is angry because of his parent's divorce, a physical injury and life not turning out like the brochure in his head. Jessica has been struggling with guilt over playing the victim in her life and modeling this behavior for him. Her guilt has led her to be supportive of some pretty poor behavior on his part. As we talked, she said, "My head knows what I need to do, and my heart feels guilty. Why couldn't I have been a better mom when he was little? I did the best I could at the time, but I know more now. I wish I could have been the Mom I am today when he was little."

The more we talked, the more clarity Jessica had that her guilt was carrying her over her line in the sand. She was stepping all over her values and her boundaries. She was doing this with her son, partly because she felt guilty, and partly because she feared he would stop talking to her and possibly shut her out of his life. He was making poor choices, drinking, smoking pot, failing his classes and generally wallowing and spinning in his self-pity. When she asked him what he wanted, he told her, "I want to be happy." Remember, happiness doesn't come from outside of us, it's an inside job. The more she talked about it, the more she realized she was going to have to help him to look inside himself. Support him to notice his internal locus of control. Recognize that he's playing the donut and not the bicycle tire.

What applies to Jessica's son is the same for everyone else. He has control over what he says, thinks and does. If he wants to be happy, then what is he willing to do to make it happen? Jessica took a deep breath and got real with herself. She knew the mom she is now wasn't willing to look back in five or ten years and wish that her "today self" had been the better parent. She was going to have to set some boundaries, even if he didn't like them. She was going to set them with love. She was going to be flexible so she could continue to offer healthy support. What she wasn't going to do was shrink back from her boundaries and limits.

Jessica knew she couldn't start throwing out threats because if she set a line that she wouldn't hold herself to, then it was an empty threat. She loves her son, and she wants to be able to stay in the conversation with him, so no ugly threats. Only authentic love and healthy boundaries were on the menu. When she started looking at her real line in the sand, she realized she was unwilling to watch him spiral and wallow without being open, honest and loving. She decided to be direct and clear about what she was seeing and what the word "support" meant to her. She decided that she wouldn't pay for him to sit and spin. She could help him with school, she could support him in recovery, but she wasn't going to support—financially or otherwise—his addiction and numbing out with pot, alcohol, or whatever he was using. She would not help him continue feeling sorry for himself. When I asked her, "How will your 'tomorrow self' feel if you continue to beat yourself up for the past, versus be the mom you can be and stand for your truth?" She replied, "I need to think about this. I am fairly sure my tomorrow self would not be happy if I don't set boundaries today."

Was this process easy? No. None of us have the power to make anyone feel different. We don't have the ability to make someone like our boundaries. By the time a baby is six months old, it knows what it likes and what it doesn't. Just try feeding a baby whirled peas. If the baby doesn't like peas, they spit them at you. Babies know. For a while, parents can make their kids eat the peas, but they cannot make them like the peas. The kid is the only one who can ever make that change. So, no, it's not easy to find the healthy boundary. Add to that holding yourself accountable, without spiraling into the drama swirl yourself. With practice and support, you can set healthy boundaries and maybe even discover a bit more happiness yourself.

EXERCISE:

What is one situation where you need a healthier boundary?

_____

_____

_____

_____

How are you stepping over your own line in the sand?

_____

_____

_____

_____

What is one way you can share your expectation or limits to honor your boundary?

_____

_____

_____

_____

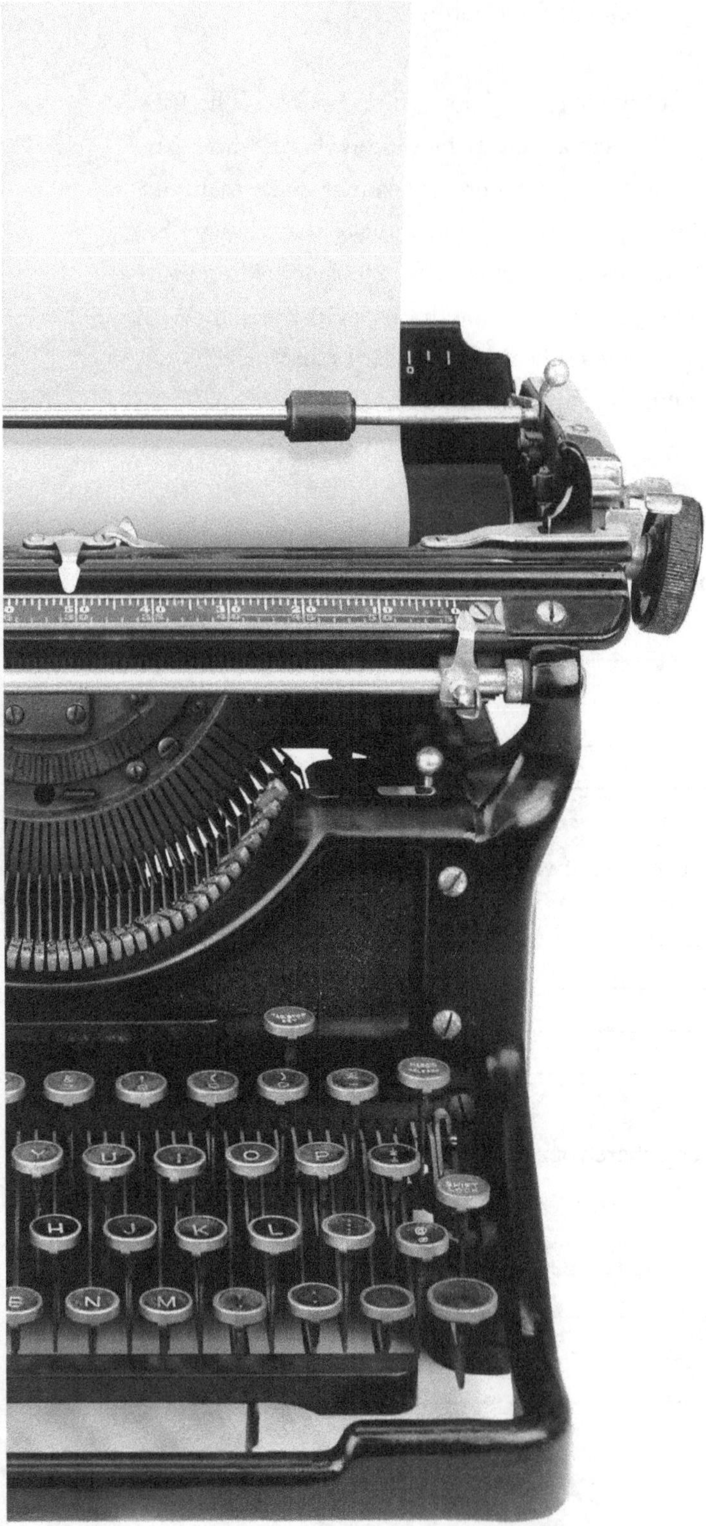

43
FAIRY TALES AND GROWING UP

"It takes courage to grow up and become who you really are."

— *E.E. Cummings*

One of our prevalent life stories is the one about Prince Charming and the Perfect Princess. We all know it because it's a story we've heard since we were born. We've watched the story play out in books, movies, and songs, yet we rarely see it work in life. Even so, we've all bought into the fairy tale because at different times we have tried to save someone or wished with all our might that someone would come along on a white steed and save us. I know I am guilty of this wishful thinking. In my twenties, I was ambitiously looking for Mr. Right to come and save me from whatever I needed saving from. I wanted to be Sleeping Beauty, awakened into a comfortable life.

The fantasy of Prince Charming is a little like thinking about what you will do when you win the lottery. It's a great tool to distract us and perfect if we're avoiding our life. I might even make the argument that the lottery fantasy is the same story with the character of Cash instead of Charming. These are hard stories to live with because we sit around waiting to be a hero in someone else's story, or we sit around as a victim, waiting to be swept away from all our troubles. Unfortunately, when we are sitting around, we aren't doing anything to change our life. At least not in any of the meaningful ways we might if we were taking action.

That last bit—the need to take action—is key to why you need to let go of the Sleeping Beauty/Prince Charming myth to grow.

If you're hanging onto this myth, ask yourself:

- What about being asleep through your life makes you worth saving?
- What do you learn about taking care of yourself if you are waiting for some magical solution to show up?
- Have you ever met anyone who could perfectly take care of you, past the point where he or she started to bug you?
- At what point are you taking care of your baggage if your focus is on fixing someone else's?
- How will you grow up if you choose to hold onto a fairy tale?

I like fairy tales. I love to read them and watch them at the movies. I just don't want to pretend that I am waiting for the fairy tale to show up and save me from my life. I don't want to wait for Prince Charming, the lottery, the perfect mentor, the perfect body, or the perfect job. I want to go out and find what makes me happy and grow it from the inside. It's time to wake up.

I've always wondered about the end of the fairy tale—the "and they all lived happily ever after" part. *Not only is there no such thing as "happily ever after," but it is an ending to a story that continues on the next page.* Our degree of attachment to this fantasy gets us into some serious trouble.

What if life is filled with the usual ups and downs? What does that mean about my value, my abilities and me? If I never meet Prince Charming, am I lost? Or what if I don't get the happily ever after even after I meet Prince Charming? What then?

Maybe I did find my Prince Charming. FYI, he has a few bad habits: He doesn't always listen to me the way I want. He doesn't always clean up after himself, no matter what he tells you. He disagrees with some of my genius ideas. He needs me to take care of him sometimes, and sometimes he just needs me to be quiet. Happily ever after has taken a heroic amount of work and willingness on both our parts to find a middle path. In fact, finding the right partner in life took a lot of courage and an astronomical amount of self-realization, self-improvement and some genuinely honest and painful conversations with myself. I won't even go into the painful conversations with my partner about my "not so princess-like" qualities. I have had to take a good look in the mirror so I could address my crap. I am happy. In fact, I may have found what amounts to an authentic happily ever after. But I am not happy because I sat around waiting for someone to come and save me from my past, my problems, or myself. I am, in all truthfulness, satisfied with my life because it didn't just magically show up. I have worked on my thoughts, beliefs, attitudes and actions. I have learned to take ownership of my crap. These tools will stay with me, and I will continue to collect more through the rest of my life. My ability to learn and grow will add to my happily ever after in real and tangible ways—in part because life continues to give me daily opportunities.

Learning to take care of yourself means you are willing to take your own leaps. You get to run with your equals. Learn to trust yourself and learn that you don't require someone else's help or need anyone's permission to feel empowered. You don't need to be saved. Your self-care is dependent only on you. And, your empowerment can't be taken away. You get to make choices, make mistakes, learn, grow and kick ass for the rest of your life. And, magically, you will find friends and partners to share all this with as you continue to "own yourself." You get to keep these brilliant gems of experiences and learning the rest of your life because they're yours. And the lovely people you invite into your life, you get to keep them too. Because you're showing up authentically, and you're not wearing people out with your need to save them or be saved by them. Often they decide they just might like to stay a while.

I don't want to sleep through my life, even though dreaming is great. I want to wake up. To consciously dream in full color, the vision of my life. I want to be aware so that I can choose, pivot and proceed. Happiness is a direct result of my willingness to grow myself into a person with whom I would enjoy being with, in a relationship. I want to be a woman who owns her good qualities and her "in need of improvement" qualities too. I want to be a person who listens even when she disagrees. And I want to kill the fairy tale, so I can choose to wake up and get on with my life, finding my happiness along the way.

EXERCISE:

What resonated for you in this section?

_____

_____

_____

_____

Looking inside yourself, what is the fairy tale you tell yourself?

_____

_____

_____

What is the StoryJack you are willing to explore?

_____

_____

_____

_____

_____

SECTION IV
You Are Creative

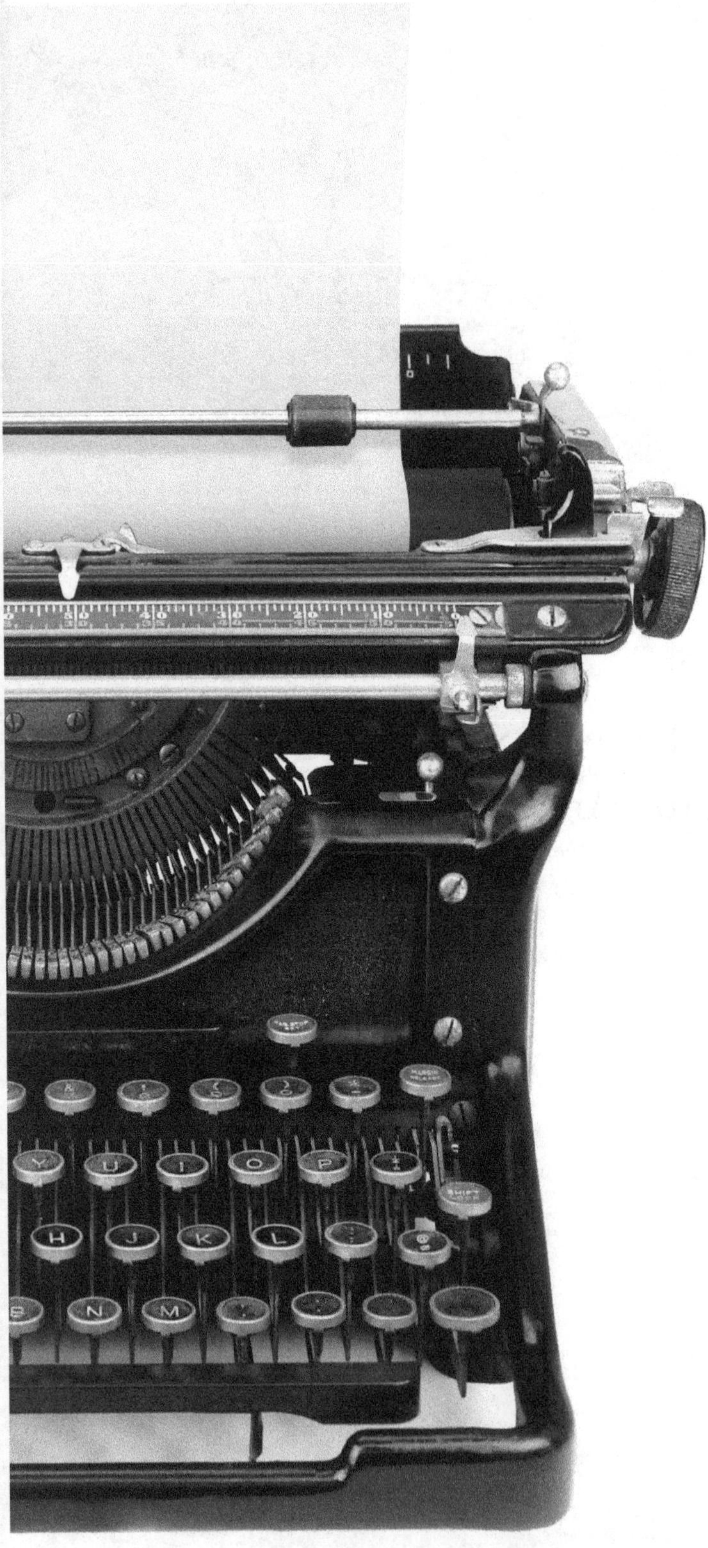
Y
U
I
O
P
H
J
K
L
N
M

44
EXPLORING YOUR CREATIVITY

"A musician must make music, an artist must paint, a poet must write,
if he is to be ultimately at peace with himself."

— *Abraham Maslow*

This section of the book is the shortest, in part because how you use the tools is a unique and individual decision. Creativity is all about your digging into what lights you up, getting out of your own way, practicing your craft, believing in yourself, using the tools that will support you in your exploration and then getting busy. For me, it's getting outside of my head and exploring my life, my experience and my future from different perspectives. Maybe you use the tools in the book as is. Or, perhaps you innovate and use them in new and unexpected ways because you realize that no one can tell you how to be your most creative self. Or possibly you explore your life and what you want, in ways that don't show up in traditional ideas of how you are supposed to explore your life. Maybe you're a rule breaker, forging a new path.

There are as many ways to be creative as there are people on the planet. All that is required is your willingness to allow yourself to connect with your creativity. There is no wrong way to explore what brings joy and light into your life, and into the lives of others.

When I think about creativity, in a big picture way, it comes down to what way are you going to challenge yourself to play with the tools? Start with taking notice of all the ways you are already creative. Look for the types of creativity that sync to your spirit. Acknowledge that there is no perfect way to be. Accept that you are perfect and messy and muddling through like everyone else you meet. Allow your inner self to shine through. Maybe your creativity takes the stage as innovative thinking or dressing in a creative manner that expresses you authentically. Maybe you do art, write poetry, paint motorcycles, or write computer code. You are a creative being. Just accept it and then look at what you want to bring into your life. Look at your strengths, look at your spirit's essence and use all the tools at your disposal to create new neural networks and new habits to get you where you want to go. The tools you choose can come from anywhere. They only require your conscious awareness as you pick the ones that will help you to explore in unique ways what you want for yourself and your life. That's what it means to be a StoryJacker. That's what I think of when I envision you being creative. I am in the business of belief, and I believe you can be an innovator, a provocateur and a creative force in your life.

There are absolutely no limits to how you get to play with the tools. There are no limits on how you can look at your reality and then innovate the hell out of it. You don't have the same choices or options that I have; we have each walked perhaps similar but still unique paths. Even so, in this moment, when you read these words, you and I are connecting. Across all time and space, a quantum thing is happening. And I need you to hear me. The moment in which you find yourself—right now, right here—there are opportunities all around you. I don't know what they are, but there is an intersection between what you love to do, what gives your life purpose and your skill set. It's an intersection that you need to explore. Maybe you're the next cat door innovator, or motorcycle builder, or master at painting cars, building furniture, designing communities, or teaching kids. I don't know where your light will shine the brightest, but it's inside of you, sitting there waiting for you to claim it for yourself. It's your birthright, and the adventure of discovery will bring to you every obstacle you will need to overcome so you can become strong enough to own it.

For me, the intersection lies in becoming the Untethered Coach. I have transformed myself by way of my adventure, and my journey has ultimately changed my business model. I started to build my private practice in 2004, but when Michael retired from the Air Force in 2005, I decided to take the leap and stop working for the Air Force. We settled down, had a home in Albuquerque, had great friends (still do) and we were committed to staying put, so it felt like the right time to transition into private practice. I began the process of developing my network. I took a lot of training. I went out and taught. I spoke to different organizations in the community, and I became well-known as an expert on Relationship Issues, PTSD and Complex Trauma. I had a full practice, and I loved my clients. My mother, a Clinical Psychologist and I purchased an office space together, and we found other therapists to rent space. It was wonderful. The best of being an entrepreneur and having other people around. I loved my life. Yet, there were changes in insurance reimbursements that were impacting my ability to stay in private practice. My expenses continued to climb, and my reimbursement payments continued to fall. It was not a sustainable model.

At times, when Michael and I chatted and dreamed in the evenings, I talked about moving to the Pacific Northwest. Possibly to start over. I wasn't serious, as in I was looking for a new job. However, I was serious in the sense that I knew I wanted to get out and explore other places to live and other ways of being in the world. Then an opportunity showed up for Michael's career that required we move to the Seattle area. It was another chance to leap into the unknown, and that was simply too good to pass up. It was a moment when my life and my dreams intersected. It was terrifying. Michael had to move to Seattle right away. He was gone by December 2012. I spent the better part of the next year selling my office, moving my mom in with me, closing my practice, selling my house and then finally packing up her life, my and Michael's life, our pets. We loaded up a truck full of belongings and moved to Bainbridge Island. I arrived at the tail end of September 2013. After the first two months, I realized I wasn't on an extended vacation. I was going to have to figure out what to do with myself. It was like ripping the Band-Aid off my comfortable life and taking the first four layers of skin with it. I had no network. I had only my friends in New Mexico. I had no job, and I wasn't sure I wanted to continue being a therapist.

Unknowingly, I had thrown myself into a colossal transformation without being fully conscious of just where I had leapt. There was the reality that my business no longer supported me. I was no longer taking insurance, and most of my clients wanted an "in person" coach or therapist. Frankly, after twenty-plus years of trauma, I was exhausted. It took me the better part of the next year to decide what to do. In the end, I decided to move fully into being a coach. I also decided I was never going to set myself up to build a business and then lose that business because I moved. And, the Untethered Coach was born. I took every tool I had in by toolbox to keep myself moving forward. I had to breathe through levels of fear and anxiety I had never experienced before. I am normally an introverted person who likes to have a close group of friends to hang out with and laugh. But all my friends were busy living their lives in New Mexico. Apparently, I had to leave my house and, like any new kid at school, start meeting people.

I had to get creative and innovate myself, build a new network, find a new purpose, create new goals and pick up my pen to rewrite my story. It hasn't been easy, but I will say that it has been a real adventure. I wouldn't change a thing.

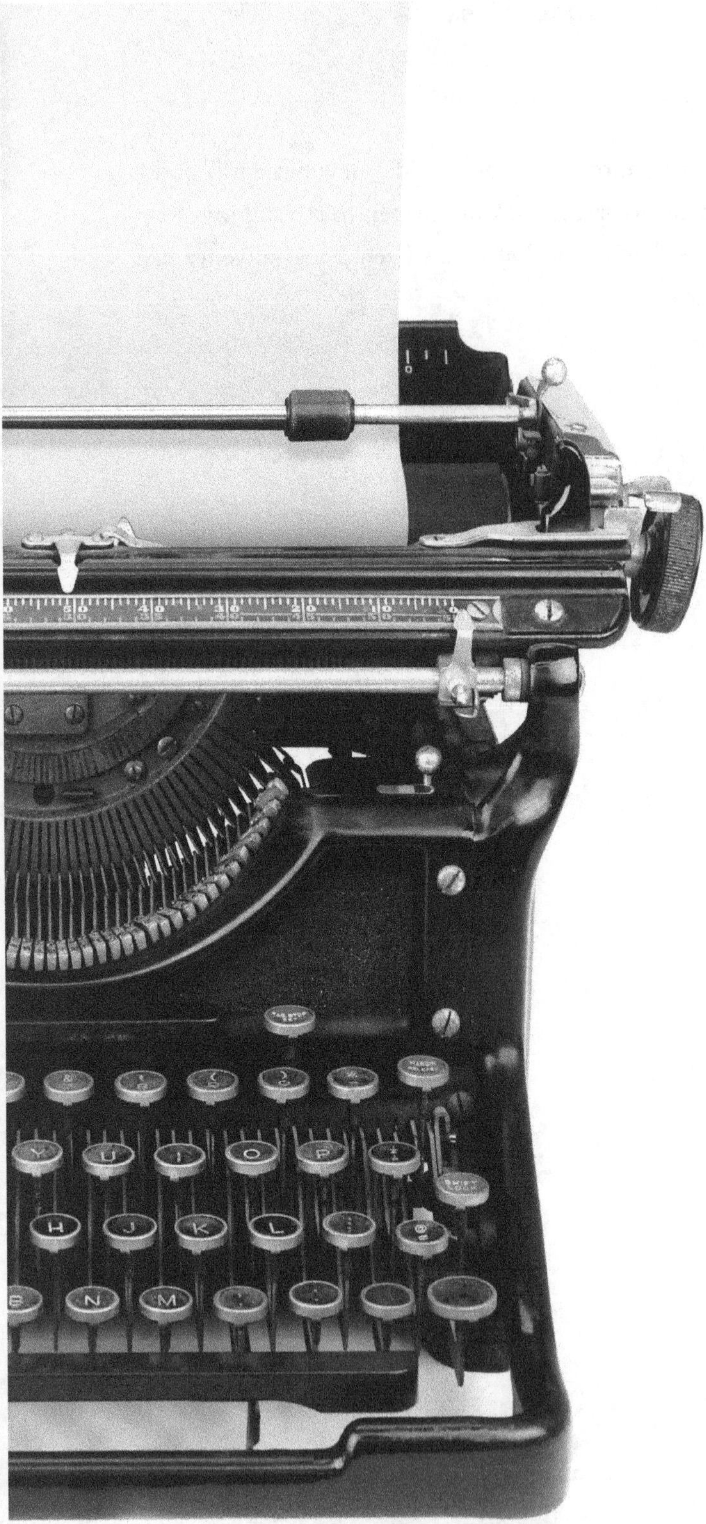

45
PLOT TWIST

"Plot is no more than footprints left in the snow after your characters have run by on their way to incredible destinations."

— *Ray Bradbury*

The plot of any good story requires more than a straight line from beginning to end. Stories need twists and turns along the way. Otherwise, something is probably wrong with the story, and maybe it's terribly boring. A plot twist is a profound shift or an unexpected change of direction in the outcome of a story. When we watch a movie, or read a novel, we love all the twists and turns that happen. It forces our characters to pivot, adapt, rethink and adjust as they move through the storyline. Plot twist's keep you and I interested. And if done well, it can surprise and delight us, as it unexpectedly shifts the outcome. Even if the plot twist's hard for our hero or heroine, it's critical to any adventure that plans to hold our attention.

Many people dislike the difficult plot twist when it shows up in their life. We want only positive, lucrative, or happy events to occur. We gnash our teeth over the twists in our storylines that require our creative flexibility to see our way through. Yet, how would we ever actually grow as insightful, courageous, or compassionate people if we lived in a bubble of perfection? I once had a client whose wife had caught him having an affair. Filled with shame and regret, he said, "You probably think I am a terrible person for what I did and where I am at in my life right now." I responded, "I have never met an interesting person who hasn't had to overcome some pile of crap they had landed in, whether by accident or by choice. In all honesty, I find you much more interesting because you are owning it and working through it, rather than pretending to be perfect, blaming your wife, or running away."

I am a great believer in the power of a plot twist to strengthen us. In this client's case, it took time, but he was able to heal his marriage. I recently heard from him; he is still happily married to his wife, and he told me, "You helped me through some rough patches in my life. Thank you." Who would have known that getting caught cheating would have been the plot twist to recovering the passion and joy in a marriage? It doesn't always happen that way, but that has more to do with the people involved than the situation. You have an extraordinary capacity to grow and change from even the most outrageous situations. I know I've had a few thousand plot twists of my own. I think I can speak to this from personal experience. So can you.

It's clear that none of us gets through our life, long or short, without a plot twist or two—or a thousand. My mom lost 75 percent of her vision due to a brain tumor at age sixty-five. She lost her ability to drive, to live on her own, her depth perception and her confidence. Plot twist. We didn't see it coming, no pun intended and she has had to find a way to move forward or sit and wallow in the unfairness of it all.

When Michael and I were planning our move to the Seattle area, we never expected that we were going to need to bring my mom with us. I didn't have it in my career plan to be her primary caregiver, taxi driver, personal assistant, or financial planner. Plot twist. Or, that my mother-in-law, Judie, would need to move in with us. I didn't see it coming that she would get diagnosed with end-stage pancreatic cancer; and that we would spend the next nine months with hospice, as she died at home. Michael and I took care of her to the end. Plot twist. None of us, not my mom, not Judie, not Michael, nor I expected any of these things to happen. And yet, they did, and we all had to adjust to the unexpected radical change in our expectations of how our lives were going to flow. What you do with your plot twists will define you. You will be called upon to figure out how to change your mindset, gather your strengths, find your bravery, and locate your tools. It's helpful to be ready to shift with the moving target you call reality.

Plot twists can be major, as above, or minor daily situations. My mom's depth perception makes it hard for her to do art the way she used to do it when her vision was normal. Having one eye to see out of will do that to you. We were recently chatting because she had slid into a funk. The reason was she can't do art in same the way she used to do art. We talked about how she was going to have to adjust to this plot twist in her artist story. She said, "I guess I am going to have to push through my plot twist, keep practicing and learn a new way of being an artist."

It is an opportunity for her to surrender into a new way of being an artist, being mindful of her actions, slowing down and allowing a new way of being to emerge. She is going to have to shift her relationship to her idea of herself as one kind of artist, practice with her new circumstances and find new ways to create a new story about herself as an artist. She must shift her method of creating.

For me, the daily plot twist might be that I had an expectation that my day was going to roll a certain way and then it went off the rails with phone calls, client needs, meetings, a long line at the post office, or whatever. I had to improvise to keep my head above water, paddling like a mad dog to fit it all in. Each challenge is just a place where my story unexpectedly changes direction. I can decide to StoryJack my internal narrative and challenge my negative self-talk. Any of these situations could have gone belly up in a multitude of ways, but I choose to see each one as a challenge that I could overcome. It's what I encourage you to do too. Look for the places to flip any plot twist that shows up in your life. You too can become a solution-focused StoryJacker.

If you are not feeling happy, then what part are you playing in the story you are telling yourself? I created this image to provide a visual of how a plot twist can turn us upside down and how it's within your locus of control to

Contentment
Forgiveness = Freedom
Happy

Ways of seeing yourself:

Whole	Capable
Creative	Resourceful
Evolving	Curious
Joyful	Connected

Other Indicators:

Hero Story
Clearly Communicated Expectations
Healthy Boundaries
Internal Locus of Control
Personal Responsibility
Learns from Mistakes & Failures
Grateful
Principled
Courageous
Appreciative
Compassionate to Self & Others
Empowered Sense of Self
Future-Oriented
Flexible Mindset
Thinks in Full Color

StoryJacking®

StoryJacking®

unForgiving = Suffering
DisContentment

unHappy

Ways of seeing yourself:

Lost	Inadequate
Confused	Inept
Stuck	Shut Down
Tragic	Disconnected

Other Indicators:

Victim Story
Uninvolved &
Unrealistic Expectations
Unhealthy Boundaries
External Locus of Control
Blame
Focus on Perfection
Bitterness
Fearful
Regret
Judges Self & Others
Disempowered Sense of Self
Past-Oriented
Holding Grudges
Fixed Mindset
Thinks in Black & White

choose to right-side up yourself.

What indicators do you recognize?

If you choose to see your shifting circumstances as plot twists, it can give you the space you need to gain a perspective that invites you to look for solutions versus feeling overwhelmed and stuck. How you define yourself because of the changes in your storyline tends to bring the other indicators to play. If you decide on the awful, terrible, horrible story, you may feel stuck, fearful, angry and disconnected—or unhappy to say the least.

You have a choice. If you opt for the flip side, you are choosing to empower yourself, get curious and envision a new way of being. Because of, or in spite of, the plot twist you might just find the silver lining on any dark cloud that drifts through your story.

EXERCISE:

What plot twists are happening in your life at this time?

_____

_____

_____

_____

_____

_____

What is one way you are willing to turn your story upside down?

_____

_____

_____

_____

_____

_____

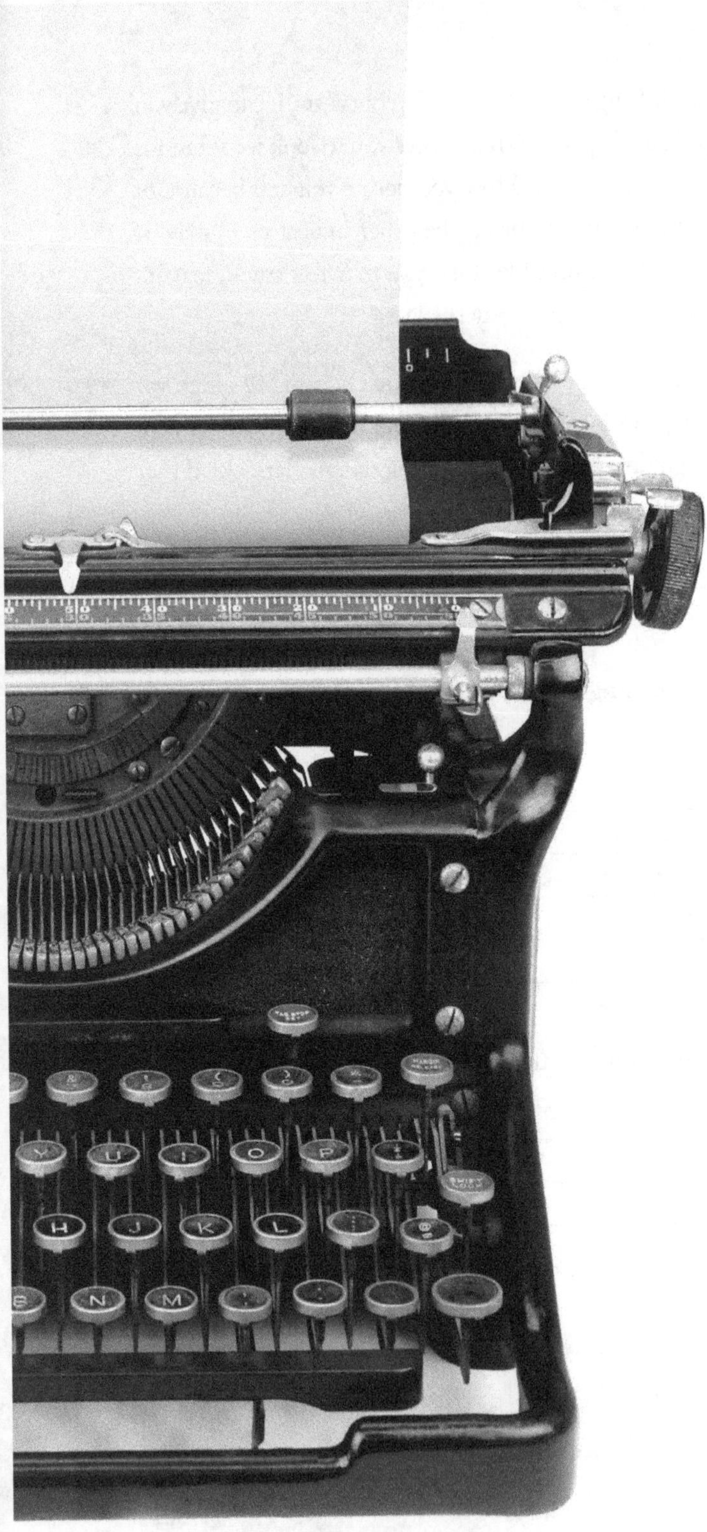
Y U I O P
H J K L
N M

46

GETTING OUT OF
YOUR OWN WAY

*"We must be willing to let go of the life we planned so as to
have the life that is waiting for us."*

—Joseph Campbell

The hardest thing that you will ever do is get out of your own way.
Allowing yourself to explore who you truly are, and deciding who you
truly want to become. You stop yourself more often than anyone else on
the planet with the stories that you tell yourself. Press the pause button
on the limits and explore what is possible. It is the greatest gift you will
ever give yourself.

A good friend of mine invited me to a Soul Collage evening at her house
recently. I had never done Soul Collage, and truthfully, I had been waf-
fling about going. She sent me a text the day before and said, I saved you
a spot. It seemed clear that the universe wanted me to go and I thought
something different would be good for me. Getting out of my own way

involved getting out of my head and playing from another perspective with my intentions. I wanted to capture my intentions on the Soul Collage cards. Seena Frost founded this process in her book Soul Collage Evolving. The ideas is for you to create cards in a collage process. The cards come directly from your psyche as you pick and choose images that resonate with you. The cards speak only the language of imagery, and only you can create a card that is meaningful. Each card is a representation of your exploration of a feeling, an idea or an intention. They bypass words and connect directly to your internal narratives, giving you access to new ways of exploring your inner life. As you set an intention, you choose images that speak to you, and you get to play with how you will put the images together in a collage that speaks to your heart, mind and soul. Imagery gets you out of your logic brain and opens new ways of exploring your inner landscape. Because sometimes there are no words that will help you explore yourself, but you still need to find a new way to move forward.

Maybe it's Soul Collage for you, perhaps a vision board, or painting, writing, journaling, possibly it's getting out into nature more or dancing at home to music that makes you happy. Whatever it is, do it. All of these actions will help you to move forward. They also contribute to reducing stress and fill your life with joy and meaning.

Some of these ideas may feel odd and out of your spectrum of normal. I will tell you what I have told hundreds of people: "If you came here for normal, I can't help you." Normal isn't working for most of us. In marriage, normal means unhappy or divorced. In your career, it means unhappy and bored. In life, it may mean coloring within the lines. I only work with people ready to be extraordinary. What will it take for you to embrace your extraordinary self? What do you need to explore your brilliance? I promise it will not come from the ordinary. Your brilliance will require of you the willingness to step into the unknown space inside of you and mine your nuggets of gold.

EXERCISE:

In thinking about your own intention for your life, what lights you up?

_____

_____

_____

_____

_____

What are your next steps?

_____

_____

_____

_____

_____

What is your why and how will you hold yourself accountable to your dream?

_____

_____

_____

_____

_____

These are all questions that anyone working toward waking up to life is going to ask. You are in good company.

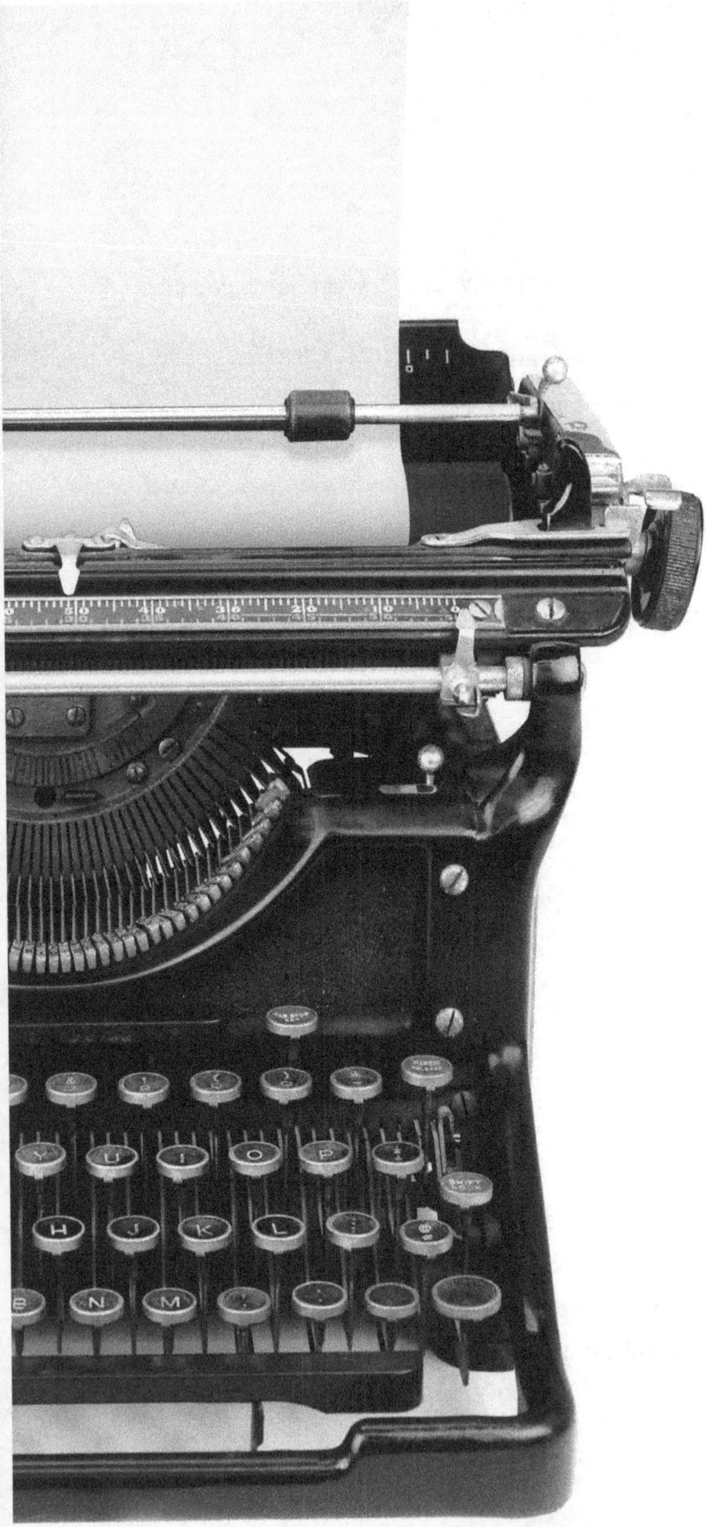

47
REWRITING THE STORY

"My goodness! My gracious!"
they shouted. "MY WORD!
It's something brand new!
IT'S AN ELEPHANT-BIRD!!"

— *Dr. Seuss*

When this book began, I invited you to think about two exercises: Life as a Pie and Authentic Core Essence. Let's run through them again, now that you are almost to the book's end. What thoughts, ideas or beliefs, have shifted for you? How do you see yourself now? What do you need to support your StoryJack? What resonates for you, when you look at your life, envision your goals and align them with your essence? These questions ask you to look inside yourself for the knowledge that comes from being self-aware. They are the foundation upon which to build the life you were born to live.

You are creative. You are a direct descendant of the most creative species on the planet. Your ancestors were masters of carving out an existence in a wild world. Your people transformed every aspect of the planet, and through their creativity and innovation, they created the world you now know. The people you came from were creative dreamers, wild imaginers and seekers of the universe's truth. You have creativity sewn and threaded through every molecule of your mind, body and soul. So how will you use your creativity to play with your insights and awareness and bring your essence into alignment with the story of how your life will grow?

Well, let me ask you this, how do you imagine a book gets written? You bang it out one time through, laying words to the page? Or do you think that the best books are edited, reorganized and rewritten where the story runs a little long or is too vague and needs some filling out? You are the best thing you will ever create. You owe it to yourself, to your children, to everyone who loves you or will love you in the future, to do the rewrite on the aspects of your life that you need to revise or edit.

There are many tools at your disposal; this book gave you only a few. You are a tool user, and I encourage you to seek out all the tools you might need. Fill up that toolbox you have so you can make the changes to your attitude and your beliefs. Challenge any part of you that tells you that you aren't good enough, capable enough, or worthy enough to have a wonderful life. I call bullshit on all the snapshot stories you have that might, in any way, keep you stuck or playing small.

You have one life you can be certain of, and it is this one. At some point, when you are bored with drama and playing the roles of victim, persecutor, or rescuer, you will come to the place in the road where it divides. I hope you will choose the path that takes you home to your soul. The road where you will get to know your essence and embrace your brilliance. If you still don't see that possibility, then I will hold that vision for you until you're ready to take it back and keep it for yourself.

Keep yourself open to possibilities. There is no need to hold yourself back. You can't know what will show up to help you once you toss yourself into the adventure. Creativity is the pathway, and it will come to you in a myriad of expressions based on your talents, interests and how you want to show up in the world. Honestly, your creativity could arrive as anything. I have seen people who bring their brilliance into the world as welders, plumbers, or mechanics. It shows up just as often in those roles, as in roles of being an artist, actor, photographer, writer, or musician. I see people who are moved to serve the greater good; they bring their passion to life as teachers, counselors, doctors, bankers, coaches and farmers. Any profession you can imagine has an avenue to explore. I love what I do, but I could bring my essence into the world as a greeter at Walmart. There are no limits on bringing yourself, fully alive and aware, into your family, your community, or the bigger world. The only thing that can stop you is you. Life is an inside job.

How you honor your journey is yours to discover. Rewriting some chapters of your life will liberate all manner of new endings. StoryJacking will require your absolute commitment. There are no fast tracks or magic wands that will take you where you truly want to go. There is a difference between being asleep and dreaming. In the movie Joe Versus the Volcano, Meg Ryan's character says something that stuck with me. "My father says that 95 percent of the people are asleep and the remaining 5 percent are walking around in a total state of amazement." You can't have a fleeting idea and then fall back to sleep. If you want to StoryJack your life, your relationships, your career, or your situation, you are going to have to wake up, dream big and grab hold of the life you want. You will also be making the necessary rewrites along the way to take you where you want to go.

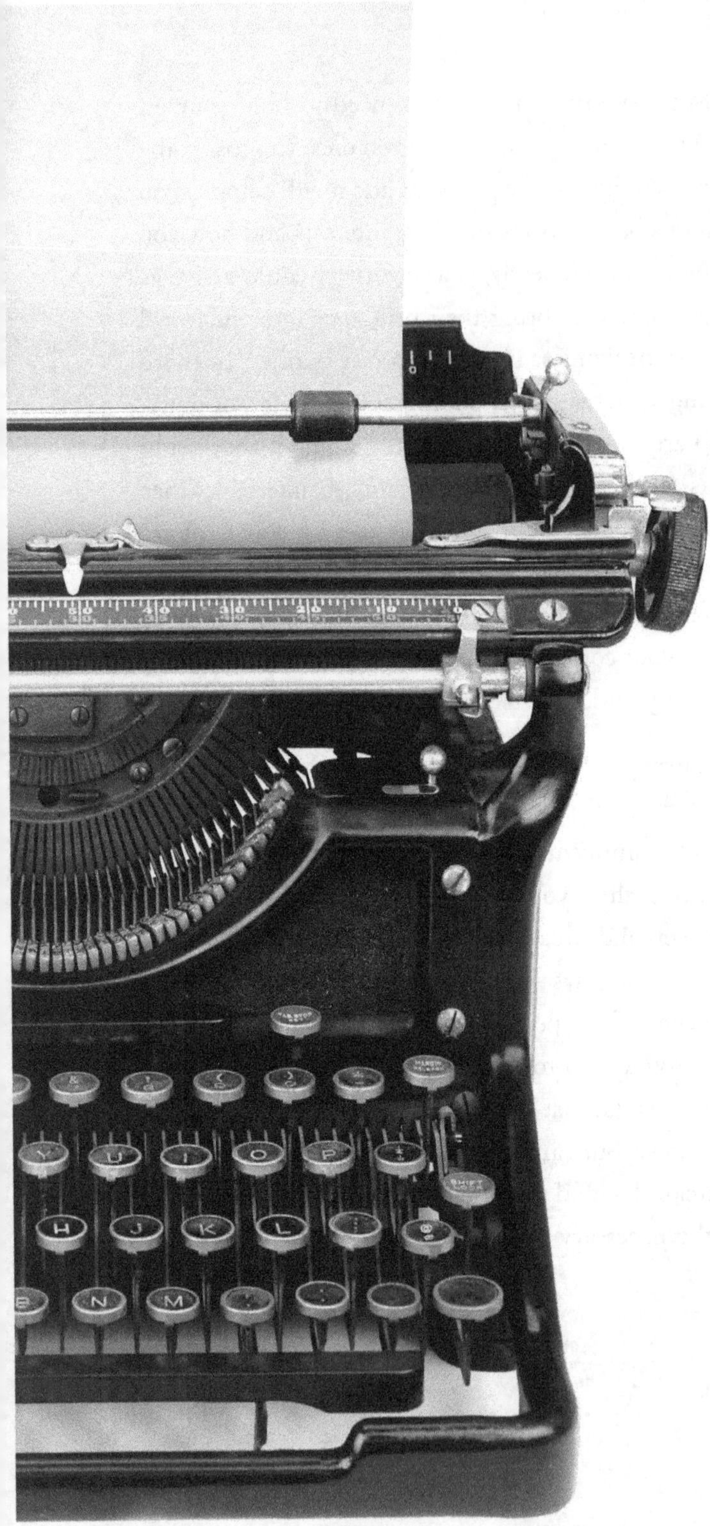

A Final Note

YOU CAN DO THIS!

"You said people come here to change the story of their lives. Well, I imagined
a story where I didn't have to be the damsel."

— *Dolores Abernathy, Westworld*

Last words: You were born a perfect, unique and naked baby. You were
born pure spirit and a light into a world that was and still is, wildly beyond your control. Through the next twenty years, as you trundled along
your life journey, you were given rules. Your values were hammered into
you, your beliefs of right and wrong/good and bad were developed. Every experience you've had and every bias you've gathered have helped
you define "I like this" or "That's wrong." You developed your expectations about how the world is supposed to work. You came to understand
the limitations or advantages you have, and you donned all manner of
outfits of identity, one layer at a time. If you look at yourself in the
mirror with open-eyed honesty, you will notice that you are like the
kid with 1,000 layers of coats trying to stay safe and warm. A big poofy
butterball of all these layers of concepts, beliefs and ideas. Some of your

layers have pockets that carry your strengths, and your diamonds have been wrapped up with your lumps of coal. Your courage, creativity, curiosity and your inner knowing are all diamonds you will need to unearth if you want to rewrite your life story's ending. Find these jewels, shine them, encourage them and set them firmly in your heart. Take the opportunity to do some closet cleaning, gathering up the limits you've placed upon yourself. Put them in a bag and leave them on the curb.

I have shared a few super-secrets of the universe with you throughout this book. Here is the most important one: *The only way to StoryJack your life is to face your fears with honesty and open-minded determination. The only thing between you and the new ending to your adventure, are the fears you hold onto and the fears you get curious about and transform.* Fear is the mind-killer. Fear that there is not enough to go around. Fear that you are not good enough, capable enough, or worthy enough. Fear that you won't be able to take care of yourself. All these fears can lead you to accept relationships or jobs that sap your spirit and sadden your soul.

This super-secret is expressed eloquently in Frank Herbert's novel *Dune*. The hero, Paul Atreides, uses the following litany or prayer to confront his fear so he may stay true to his path: "I must not fear. Fear is the mind-killer. Fear is the little-death that brings total obliteration. I will face my fear. I will permit it to pass over me and through me. And when it has gone past I will turn the inner eye to see its path. Where the fear has gone there will be nothing. Only I will remain." This super-secret shows up in every great novel you read or movie you love, like *Star Wars*, *Huckleberry Finn*, *Red Rising*, *The Incredibles*, or *The Hunger Games*. The hero must make significant changes in his or her life and in the lives around him or her. All heroes must face their fears. This super-secret also shows up in every great autobiography or true life story you love where the author writes about how she overcame her obstacles to become successful. It even shows up in self-help books like this one where you are the hero in your own story, learning to overcome your obstacles. Having a crappy childhood, or a disability, or living in a difficult situation doesn't make you special. What makes you special is your willingness to confront your fears and change your world.

StoryJacking is simple, but not easy. It will ask you to check out any rigid ideas and general unwillingness to get curious and to make changes. You must start peeling back the layers of all those outfits of shame, anger, bitterness and blame and reach down deep to find your true self, pull yourself out of the layers and encourage yourself to get to know and then grow that self. What I know for certain is that you will never change your story or your situation without confronting the thinking and beliefs that got you into the story in the first place.

We recapture our creativity when we operate from a learning mind. When we open our minds and our perspectives allowing ourselves the space to explore what we want for our lives. And when we allow ourselves to be in a growth mindset for the rest of the time that we have allotted to our life adventure.

In a class I took, a friend mentioned the classic nursery rhyme, "Row, row, row your boat." She said that she thought it might hold the simple truths to life. I hadn't thought about the rhyme in years, and as I heard it again, it got me curious.

> *Row, row, row your boat*
> *Gently down the stream.*
> *Merrily, merrily, merrily, merrily*
> *Life is but a dream.*

Because I was thinking so much about the rhyme, I brought it up to my friend Michele. We talked about how as children we may have understood the deeper meaning inherent in the song. As children, we often parrot the words of the adults around us, conforming to their ideas instead of forming our own ideas. What would happen if you let yourself play with the rhyme and see the truth it offers? What if you allow yourself to recapture your childlike wonder? Rediscover your voice?

Yes, you will have to row your boat, there is no getting out of it; you will row, row, row. You and only you can do the work of your life. If you find ways to go with the flow and find your passions and your purpose, it will be a much easier journey. Be joyful, be grateful, be gracious, be loving, be compassionate and kind. Merrily, merrily, merrily, merrily, row your boat; it's yours, and it's your transportation to the larger life you are moving toward.

And, always remember, this life can be a dream. You are a beautiful spirit having a human experience. Wake up and empower yourself to create the dream of your life. One that imagines a better place, for you, for those you love and ultimately for the entire world. This dream needs you to know yourself, make audacious goals, be willing to take risks, seek help, laugh, love and play with purpose and passion.

Here is the final super-secret of the universe in the book: *As you focus on your stories, your growth, and development, your side of the street, if you will, you will impact the world around you in ways you could never do if you were trying to force ideas on someone else.*

You have everything you need inside of you. You can ask for support, you can develop your toolbox and you can get curious. Never forget you have the greatest capacity to change of any species on this planet. You so have this: You are a StoryJacker.

Let's build a fire, and you tell me a story....

REFERENCES:

I have quoted directly from some books and others are books that shifted the ways that I thought about myself, my clients and the world. Each book listed touched me in some way and wove through the fibers of my experiences. I share each of them regardless of whether showed up in my book directly or indirectly.

Amen, D. G. (2000). *Change your brain, change your life: The breakthrough program for conquering anxiety, depression, obsessiveness, anger and impulsiveness*. New York: Times Books.

Axelson, C. (2016, October 11). In Colombia, Shade-Grown Coffee Sustains Songbirds and People Alike. *Living Bird Magazine*, (Autumn Issue). doi:The Cornell Lab of Ornithology

Bach, R. (1970). *Jonathon Livingston Seagull: A story*. New York: Munson Books.

Becker, G. D. (1999). *The gift of fear: Survival signals that protect us from violence*. New York: Dell.

Boser, U. (2014). *The leap: The science of trust and why it matters*. New Harvest.

Brach, T. (2003). *Radical acceptance: Embracing your life with the heart of a Buddha*. New York: Bantam Books.

Bradshaw, J. (1988). *Healing the shame that binds you*. HCI

Breuning, L. G. (2012). *Meet your happy chemicals*. Oakland, CA: System Integrity Press.

Bridge, D. J., & Voss, J. L. (2014). Active retrieval facilitates across-episode binding by modulating the content of memory. *Neuropsychologia*, 63, 154-164. doi: 10.1016/j.neuropsychologia.2014.08.024

Brooks, D. (2012). *The social animal: The hidden sources of love, character and achievement*. New York: Random House Trade Paperbacks.

Brown, B. (2012). *Daring greatly: How the courage to be vulnerable transforms the way we live, love, parent and lead*. Avery.

Bryson, B. (2004). *A short history of nearly everything*. London: Black Swan.

Cameron, J. (1992). *The artist's way: A spiritual path to higher creativity*. Los Angeles, CA: Jeremy P. Tarcher/Perigee.

Campbell, J. (1972). *The hero with a thousand faces*. Princeton, NJ: Princeton University Press.

Card, O. S., & Card, O. S. (1988). *Treason*. New York: St. Martin's Press.

Carroll, L., & Frank, J. (1955). *Alice in Wonderland.* New York: Random House.

Coelho, P., & Clarke, A. (2002). *The alchemist.* San Francisco: Harper San Francisco.

Covey, S. R. (2004). *The 7 Habits of Highly Effective People: Powerful lessons in personal change.* Free Press.

Crum, A. J., & Langer, E. J. (2007). Mind-Set Matters: Exercise and the Placebo Effect. *Psychological Science, 18*(2), 165-171. doi:10.1111/j.1467-9280.2007.01867.x

Dehaene, S. (2014). *Consciousness and the brain: Deciphering how the brain codes our thoughts.* Penguin Books.

Doidge, N. (2007). *The brain that changes itself: Stories of personal triumph from the frontiers of brain science.* New York: Viking.

Dweck, C. S. (2006). *Mindset: The new psychology of success.* New York: Random House.

Dyak, M. (1999). *The voice dialogue facilitator's handbook.* Seattle, WA: L.I.F.E. Energy Press.

Dyer, W. W. (2004). *The power of intention: Learning to co-create your world your way.* Carlsbad, CA: Hay House.

Emerald, D. (2016). *The Power of Ted The Empowerment Dynamic; 10th Anniversary Edition.* Polaris Pub.

Frankl, V. E. (1985). *Man's search for meaning.* New York: Washington Square Press/Pocket Books.

Gawande, A. (2014). *Being mortal: Medicine and what matters in the end* (1st ed.). Metropolitan Books.

Gilbert, E. (2016). *Big magic creative living beyond fear.* S.l.: Riverhead Books.

Gibson, K., Lathrop, D. and Stern, E.M. (1991). *Carl Jung and Soul Psychology.* (1987). doi:10.4324/9781315804231

Gladwell, M. (2005). *Blink: The power of thinking without thinking.* New York: Little, Brown.

Goleman, D. (1995). *Emotional intelligence.* New York: Bantam Books.

Goleman, D. (2006). *Social intelligence: The new science of human relationships.* New York: Bantam Books.

Goldman, A. I. (2012). *Theory of Mind.* The Oxford Handbook of Philosophy of Cognitive Science, 402-425. doi:10.1093/oxfordhb/9780195309799.003.0017

Goodall, J., & Berman, P. L. (1999). *Reason for hope: A spiritual journey.* New York, NY: Warner Books.

References

Gottman, J. M., & Silver, N. (1999). *The seven principles for making marriage work*. New York: Crown.

Gottschall, J. (2012). *The storytelling animal: How stories make us human*. Boston: Houghton Mifflin Harcourt.

Holy Bible: King James Version. (2010) Grand Rapids, MI: ZONDERVAN.

Hagerty, B. B. (2016). *Life reimagined: The science, art and opportunity of midlife*. Riverhead Books.

Haidt, J. (2006). *The happiness hypothesis: Finding modern truth in ancient wisdom*. New York: Basic Books.

Hanson, R. (2013). *Hardwiring happiness: The new brain science of contentment, calm and confidence*. Harmony.

Hergenhahn, B. R. (2005). *An introduction to the history of psychology*. Australia: Thomson/Wadsworth.

Holiday, R. (2014). *The obstacle is the way: The timeless art of turning trials into triumph*. Portfolio.

Jung, C.G. (1981). *Collected Works of C. G. Jung, Volume 9 (Part 1): Archetypes and the Collective Unconscious*. Princeton University Press.

Kornfield, J. (1993). *A path with heart: a guide through the perils and promises of spiritual life*. New York: Bantam Books

Levitt, S. D., & Dubner, S. J. (2005). *Freakonomics: A rogue economist explores the hidden side of everything*. New York: William Morrow.

Lipton, B. H. (2016). *Biology of belief: 10th anniversary edition*. Place of publication not identified: Hay House.

Maharshi, R. (1972). *The spiritual teaching of Ramana Maharshi*. by Sri Ramanasramam. Biographical sketch and glossary copyright 1998 Shambhala Publications, Inc. Boston: Shambhala.

McLaren, K. (2010). *The language of emotions: What your feelings are trying to tell you*. Boulder, CO: Sounds True.

McRaney, D. (2012). *You are now less dumb: How to conquer mob mentality, how to buy happiness and all the other ways to outsmart yourself*. Avery.

McRaney, D. (2014). *You are not so smart: Why you have too many friends on facebook, why your memory is mostly fiction and 46 other ways you're deluding yourself*. Avery.

Mehl-Madrona, L., & Mainguy, B. (n.d.). *Remapping your mind: The neuroscience of self-transformation through story*.

Mehl-Madrona, L. (2010). *Healing the mind through the power of story: The promise of narrative psychiatry*. Rochester, VT: Bear &.

Mendius, R., & Hanson, R. (2010). *Buddha's Brain: The Practical Neuroscience of Happiness, Love and Wisdom*. Paw Prints.

Miller, G. A. (1956). "The magical number seven, plus or minus two: Some limits on our capacity for processing information." *Psychological Review*. **63** (2): 81–97. doi:10.1037/h0043158. PMID 13310704.

Moyers, B. D. (1981). *Joseph Campbell: Myths to live by*. New York: Educational Broadcasting.

Nuland, S. B. (1995). *How we die: Reflections on life's final chapter*. New York: Vintage Books.

Pascual-Leone, A., Amedi, A., Fregni, F., & Merabet, L. B. (2005). The Plastic Human Brain Cortex. *Annu. Rev. Neurosci. Annual Review of Neuroscience, 28*(1), 377-401. doi:10.1146/annurev.neuro.27.070203.144216

Pearson, C. (1989). *The hero within: Six archetypes we live by*. San Francisco: Harper & Row.

Peirce, P. (2009). *Frequency: The power of personal vibration*. New York: Atria Books.

Peterson, C., & Seligman, M. E. (2004). *Character strengths and virtues: A handbook and classification*. Washington, DC: American Psychological Association.

Ponlop, D. (2011). *Rebel Buddha: A guide to a revolution of mind*. Boston: Shambhala.

Quenk, N. L. (2009). *Essentials of Myers-Briggs Type Indicator assessment*. Hoboken, NJ: John Wiley & Sons.

Rath, T. (2007). *Strengths finder 2.0*. New York: Gallup Press.

Ramana and Arthur Osborne. (2002) *The Teachings of Bhagavan Sri Ramana Maharshi in His Own Words*. Tiruvannamalai: Sri Ramanasramam. London, England: Rider & Company.

Riso, D. R., & Hudson, R. (1999). *The wisdom of the enneagram: The complete guide to psychological and spiritual growth for the nine personality types*. New York: Bantam Books.

Seligman, M. E. (2002). *Authentic happiness: Using the new positive psychology to realize your potential for lasting fulfillment*. New York: Free Press.

Shackell, E. M., & Standing, L. G. (2007). Mind Over Matter: Mental Training Increases Physical Strength. *North American Journal of Psychology, 9*(1), 189-200.

Shapiro, F. (2012). *Getting past your past: Take control of your life with self-help techniques from EMDR therapy*. Emmaus, PA: Rodale Books.

Shlain, L. (1998). *The alphabet versus the goddess: The conflict between word and image*. New York: Viking.

Silsbee, D. K. (2010). *The mindful coach: Seven roles for facilitating leader development*. San Francisco, CA: Jossey-Bass.

Stern, E. Mark. *Carl Jung and soul psychology*. New York: Haworth Press, 1987.

Trungpa, C., & Gimian, C. R. (2009). *Smile at fear: Awakening the true heart of bravery*. Boston: Shambhala.

Vedantam, S. (2010). *The hidden brain: How our unconscious minds elect presidents, control markets, wage wars and save our lives*. New York: Spiegel & Grau.

Wallace, D. F. (2009). *This is water: Some thoughts, delivered on a significant occasion about living a compassionate life*. New York: Little, Brown.

Walter, J. L., & Peller, J. E. (1992). *Becoming solution-focused in brief therapy*. New York: Brunner/Mazel.

Weiner-Davis, M. (1992). *Divorce busting: A revolutionary and rapid program for staying together*. New York: Summit Books.

White, M., & Epston, D. (1990). *Narrative means to therapeutic ends*. New York: Norton.

White, M. (2007). *Maps of narrative practice*. New York: W.W. Norton.

Williams, R. B., & Williams, V. P. (1993). *Anger kills: Seventeen strategies for controlling the hostility that can harm your health*. New York: Times Books.

Williamson, M. (1993). *A woman's worth*. New York: Random House.

Williamson, M. (2012). *The law of divine compensation: On work, money and miracles*. New York: HarperOne.

Zak, P. J. (2013). *The moral molecule: The source of love and prosperity*. New York: Dutton.

WEBSITE CITATIONS

International Coach Federation | Coachfederation.org

Project Implicit | Implicit Association Test (IAT). Implicit.harvard.edu

Authentic Happiness | University of Pennsylvania | VIA Character Strengths - Authentichappiness.sas.upenn.edu

Laughter Yoga | laughteryoga.org

Positive Neuroscience | Posneuroscience.org

Wikipedia | Wikipedia.org/wiki/List_of_cognitive_biases

LET'S BUILD A FIRE & YOU TELL ME A STORY

Are you interested in continuing your personal transformative process? Did you read this book and say, "Hey, I want to StoryJack my life, and I think I want some support in that"? Are you interested in one-on-one coaching, getting curious, developing your toolbox and then empowering yourself to live the life that resonates with your authentic self? Do you feel overwhelmed when you think about making the changes stick? Do you need someone to help you be accountable and hold the space so your insights and brilliance can shine?

Lyssa Danehy deHart has worked with thousands of people in her twenty-plus years of counseling and coaching, and she is always open to working with new individuals who are ready to StoryJack and need support in transforming themselves.

Lyssa works with people from all over the world. She is the Original Untethered Coach. Lyssa coaches her clients either by phone or on a virtual platform. You can live anywhere, and she can be anywhere, and if you have phone service or Internet access, you can have private one-on-one coaching sessions.

Lyssa is a certified mentor coach, regularly working with other coaches to gain their International Coach Federation credentials and she is an advocate for developing professional coaches to professional standards. She also coaches therapists looking to shift from counseling to coaching.

If you are interested in any of the exercises discussed in this book, they are available as a PDF at storyjacking.com. If you are interested in a discovery session to see whether you and Lyssa are a good fit for individual coaching, visit her website and sign up for a time to connect.

SPEAKER ENGAGEMENTS

When it comes to choosing a professional speaker for your next event, you will find no one more thought-provoking, humorous and inspiring than Lyssa Danehy deHart. Lyssa will leave your audience or colleagues with a renewed passion for their lives, careers and purposes. She shares stories and tools to help people transform their mindsets and change their stories. Since 1998, Lyssa has been speaking about everything from dealing with conflict and enriching relationships to how to find the love of your life, be a leader and embrace the entrepreneurial spirit in your career, either within an organization or in your own business.

Regardless of the size of the audience, 10 to 10,000, in the U.S. or abroad, Lyssa can deliver training or an inspirational message customized to your needs. Lyssa understands the need to offer insight and humor, keeping the audience engaged by combining stories, metaphors and learning all rolled into one so your audience members come away inspired to make the changes necessary for the success they crave.

To see a highlight video about StoryJacking and to contact Lyssa to see whether she is available for your next meeting or event, visit her website at the address below. Feel free to contact her by email to schedule a discovery conversation and find out how StoryJacking can benefit your event.

StoryJacking.com or email Lyssa: LyssadeHart@gmail.com

ABOUT THE AUTHOR

Lyssa Danehy deHart, MSW, LISCW, PCC is an author, professional speaker, podcast host and transformational coach.

Lyssa inspires her clients through stories and humor as she supports their personal and professional transformations. She has worked with the US Air Force, the State of New Mexico, as well as many small businesses, entrepreneurs and individuals to help them develop the awareness needed to become compassionate leaders within their families, communities and organizations. Self-mastery comes at the price of getting real with yourself, facing your fears, taking ownership and then changing the internal dialogue that keeps you stuck.

Working with clients from all over the world, Lyssa helps them to StoryJack and create the lives they want to live.

Please visit StoryJacking.com for the .PDF of the worksheets and questions in this book.

Thanks for reading! If you feel so moved, please add a short review on Amazon and let me know what you thought!

CPSIA information can be obtained
at www.ICGtesting.com
Printed in the USA
LVHW011618230620
658807LV00012B/1103